PRAISE FOR
IMPACT PLAYERS

"If you're trying to navigate the new world of work, this book is your GPS. With solid research and sparkling examples, Wiseman shows how to do the things they don't teach us in school—tackling ambiguous problems, surmounting unforeseen obstacles, hitting moving targets, and traveling beyond the boundaries of your job description to make a real contribution."

—Daniel H. Pink, number one *New York Times* bestselling author of
When, *Drive*, and *To Sell is Human*

"*Impact Players* is a gold mine! It is filled with powerful insights and actionable recommendations on how to move beyond being a competent employee to being a truly impactful team player. This should be required reading for individual contributors and leaders alike."

—Tina Seelig, professor and executive director,
Knight-Hennessy Scholars, Stanford University

"As we slowly get through the challenges of the global pandemic, we cannot declare victory and go back to normal. We must look further forward to face a future of unprecedented adversity and opportunity. We need more leaders with the right mindset and skills to tackle our biggest and most important challenges—like the climate crisis or technological disruption of jobs, work, industries, and institutions. The world needs fewer people accepting the status quo and more Impact Players who are actively working to create the future they see is possible. This book is a playbook that will help individuals work at a higher level, inspire teams to do great things, and enable organizations to create a culture that fosters growth and to become high-impact organizations."

—Rob Nail, associate founder and former CEO, Singularity University

"Every colleague, teammate, and contributor wants to be the 'go to,' high-performing, high-contributing player. Some might call them indispensable. Well, now you have the practical mindsets, strategies, and tools to achieve those goals. It doesn't take much, but it does take leaders and colleagues who are able to apply simple techniques to extract that extra engagement sitting just below the surface. Liz is a master, and every CHRO/CPO should read this book. If you're looking to take your organization and the amazing colleagues you have to another level of contribution, this is the guide to help you get them there!"

—Eric Hutcherson, chief people and inclusion officer,
Universal Music Group

"If you want to stand out early in your career, this book is required reading. Liz Wiseman highlights the practical, often surprising habits that will help you reach your potential and make your mark."

—Adam Grant, number one *New York Times* bestselling
author of *Think Again* and host of the TED podcast WorkLife

"Liz Wiseman has done it again. *Impact Players* is an engaging and practical guide to how anyone can be more effective at work. In a refreshing departure from the relentless emphasis on leadership that dominates the field, Wiseman digs into the important question of how people make themselves valuable and how they find ways to make an impact when and where it matters most."

—Amy C. Edmondson, professor, Harvard Business School,
and author of *The Fearless Organization*

"*Impact Players* will teach you how to have empathy for your boss without kissing up, how to step up and take charge even when you don't have formal authority, and when to step back and follow, so you can make big things happen for your team and your career."

—Kim Scott, author of *Radical Candor* and *Just Work*

"Being busy? Easy. Having an impact and making a difference? Well, that's hard, really hard. Liz Wiseman, in her typically brilliantly, generous, and rigorous way, shows how any of us can change what we do so we too can be an Impact Player. This book is every bit as important and as good as *Multipliers*. And that book changed the working world."

—Michael Bungay Stanier, author of *The Coaching Habit*

"In building innovative Silicon Valley companies and running US economic diplomacy, I've learned that Impact Players are the essential ingredient for growing transformative organizations. And Liz Wiseman's book gives you the recipe. *Impact Players* will help you develop the desperately needed next generation of bold, principled, transformational leaders to address our challenges and make sure the world of tomorrow is a better world for all."

—Keith Krach, former United States undersecretary of state,
chairman and CEO of DocuSign and Ariba

IMPACT PLAYERS

IMPACT PLAYERS

How to Take the Lead, Play Bigger, and Multiply Your Impact

LIZ WISEMAN

HARPER
BUSINESS
An Imprint of HarperCollinsPublishers

HarperCollins books may be purchased for educational, business, or sales promotional use. For information, please email the Special Markets Department at SPsales@harpercollins.com.

FIRST EDITION

Library of Congress Cataloging-in-Publication Data

Names: Wiseman, Liz, author.
Title: Impact players : how to take the lead, play bigger, and multiply
your impact / Liz Wiseman.
Identifiers: LCCN 2021033557 (print) | LCCN 2021033558 (ebook) | ISBN
9780063063327 (hardcover) | ISBN 9780063063334 (ebook)
Subjects: LCSH: Employee motivation. | Performance. | Value. |
Organizational effectiveness. | Organizational behavior.
Classification: LCC HF5549.5.M63 W59 2021 (print) | LCC HF5549.5.M63
(ebook) | DDC 658.3/14—dc23
LC record available at https://lccn.loc.gov/2021033557
LC ebook record available at https://lccn.loc.gov/2021033558

21 22 23 24 25 LSC 10 9 8 7 6 5 4 3 2 1

For the three Joshes who brought joy and
made work light during a tough year.

CONTENTS

INTRODUCTION

Some people are at their best in the most difficult circumstances; they make exactly the right move at the right moment and get results that land with impact. Those people are consistently tapped to lead, especially in critical moments.

You have probably seen this play out in sports: It's a crucial situation in a big game, and everything is on the line. The coach must decide whom to put into the game. There are a number of strong, capable athletes, but the coach taps one particular player—it may not be the strongest or the fastest player, but it's the one who comes through in the clutch. It's the one who understands the gravity of the moment and will step up and get the job done. It's the one who can be counted on.

This scene also plays out daily in the workplace. Take this example: Jamaal, a district manager for a large retail chain, learns that the CEO is coming for a store visit. Unfortunately, the store manager will be gone that day, off on a long-planned vacation. The manager needs someone to step in and host this high-profile visit. The challenge is to showcase the store's achievements but also address the store's problems with candor, someone who is personable and confident but who won't use this moment to self-promote. He taps Joya, who, as anticipated, performs brilliantly. It's a win for Jamaal and the entire team. For Joya, representing the entire team is second nature. She grew up without a lot of support and knows the value of community. She said, "My heart was pounding as I stood outside the store waiting to greet the CEO, but I stayed calm because this was about representing the store and my community to the best of my ability."

Some people seem to know how to make themselves valuable. They pay attention. They look for the most productive places to put their capability to use. They make things work, and they get the job done, even when the job gets difficult. They not only deliver results but send ripples of positive impact throughout their team and across the organization. Managers trust them when the stakes are high and turn to them in critical situations. They find a way to break through and make an impact while others are merely going through the motions.

For the first half of my career, I ran a corporate university and led talent development at Oracle. At that time, the corporate training world generally operated on the assumption that more is better, meaning when in doubt, train people and hope the situation improves. So we ran a lot of programs. We sent reports to various executives telling them how much training we'd conducted. These reports were largely ignored, and the training directors felt continually frustrated that the executives weren't more engaged. Training programs proliferated and everyone stayed busy, but not everyone or every program was impactful.

Ben Putterman, one of the training directors on my management team, took a different approach. The company was gearing up for a new product rollout, and he and several of his colleagues were preparing to brief the executive team on the status of product training for the field staff. Knowing that their past training reports hadn't provoked much of a reaction from the executives, they stepped back and asked: What do the executives really care about? When Ben put himself into the shoes of the divisional executives, he realized that he wouldn't really care about how much training people attended; he would care about who knew their stuff and how ready people were to work with customers to sell and support the new products.

He reoriented his entire approach around readiness instead of training. He and his staff introduced certification testing and actually encouraged people to self-study and test out of training if that allowed them to get up to speed faster. They reported on certification and readiness rather than training attendance. The executives started paying attention to the reports, pointing out where their data were incomplete and working with them to ensure accuracy. The senior executives were now actively engaged because Ben and his team were making it easier for them to do their jobs: to make the right investments, do the right thing for customers, and hold their organization and themselves accountable.

That approach, though perhaps commonplace today, was novel at the time, and it changed the business. While others stayed busy, Ben made an impact.

But this wasn't a onetime stroke of genius. Ben took setbacks in stride and treated problems as an opportunity to pivot and do something more valuable. It was easy to hand him the most challenging and vital work. Ben worked on my team for ten years and had a couple of nicknames for me: One was simply "Boss" and the other was "Busy Lizzy," an apt description. It often made me wonder: Was I just going through the motions of my job, or was I having a real impact? Perhaps you've wondered why sometimes you make an impact at work, while other times your efforts get lost in the shuffle. Maybe you've been passed over for a leadership position and wondered why your colleague was tapped instead.

While all people bring capability and intelligence to their jobs, much as in a card game, some seem to play their hand better than others. They develop a reputation as the impact players within an organization. Managers know who these top players are, and they understand their worth. Leaders come to depend on them and give them a steady stream of high-profile assignments and new opportunities. Their peers know who they are as well. Everyone seems to understand the value they contribute and can see the positive influence of their work, and these people seem to move through their careers with impact and purpose.

I have been privileged to work with many of these superstars in my years as a corporate executive, and I've witnessed their positive influence on teams and across entire organizations. I've also seen how the impact of their work creates a more meaningful and fulfilling work experience for them. Yet I've also noticed smart, talented people playing below their potential. It's hard to watch good people standing on the sidelines when you know they could be hitting home runs and winning championships.

Most people have seen this dynamic—two similarly capable individuals, both with talent and drive but whose work is having a markedly different level of impact—but not everyone understands what causes this difference. You might even have found yourself in one of these positions and wondered about the mindset and behaviors that set two equally capable people apart.

Corporate leaders sense the differences but often can't articulate them. They usually know who the superstars are and want more of them, but they struggle to explain what actually makes them different. Typically managers can articulate the more pronounced differences between their top and low performers; however, when it comes to their most influential, impactful players, the top of the top, there seems to be an ineffable quality about them. There is a certain *je ne sais quoi* in how they approach their jobs and an art form to the way they contribute.

Corporate HR and talent development professionals have tried to capture, understand, and communicate these differences using a variety of tools, for example, performance management systems meant to stratify employees into performance categories and provide feedback to help people improve, competency models to define critical skills for success, and statements of corporate values that prescribe the valued behavior. Yet most corporate values statements are too abstract to capture the nuance between behavior which is merely culturally acceptable versus truly impactful. On the other hand, the competency models tend to be too detailed; after all, few of us can remember dozens of critical skills and behaviors, let alone develop the skills before they become antiquated. These efforts dance around the right issues but miss the subtle distinction between a contribution that is good enough and one that is truly great. Further, these tools tend to overlook the powerful beliefs behind the behaviors.

Meanwhile, professionals are hungry to make an impact. Sure, most people want a good job, but they also want to make a meaningful contribution; they want their work to matter and to make a difference in the world. They want to be engaged and to be respected for their contribution. Lacking clear guidance, too many consume career advice dished out on social media and served up in sound bites in commencement speeches. These sources may sound enticing, but they tend to offer the junk-food versions of professional advice: prepackaged, overly processed, and lacking in nutritional value.

I too have sought answers to this question: Why do some people play at their full potential while others remain underutilized? For the last decade, I have looked to leaders as both the source of and solution to the problem. I am well aware of how a leader's behavior can either increase or diminish someone's ability to contribute—it's a thesis I explored in the book *Multipliers: How the Best Leaders Make Everyone Smarter*. Leaders too often overlook talent and intelligence sitting right in front of them. However, while leadership is an essential factor—and one that deserves further exploration—it isn't the only factor. Leaders certainly bear the responsibility for creating an inclusive environment and providing the right direction and coaching, but the way the contributor works matters as well. As one manager described it to me, "You can't multiply zero." He wasn't disparaging the individual's capability; he was suggesting that it's difficult to lead someone who doesn't bring the right mindsets and practices to the work. He's right, and so is the math: managers may be Multipliers, but the contributor is also a variable in the equation; the way they work determines their level of contribution, influence, and eventual impact.

As the workplace has become less hierarchical and more complex, numerous researchers, myself included, have articulated new models of leadership, but who has been studying the new model of contributorship? There are thousands of books about how to excel as a leader, but how does one become a top contributor? There is a host of unanswered questions: What makes someone influential inside an organization? What are the mindsets and practices that differentiate the most impactful players from others on a team? How do contributors influence their leaders and build organizational support for their ideas and initiatives without having positional authority? Are these skills learnable?

It is time to turn over the coin and examine what the best contributors do, how they create extraordinary value around them, and how that strengthens their voice and increases their influence in the world.

To find answers, we need to understand what causes individuals to wield influence and create value, particularly through the eyes of their stakeholders. When I wanted to study the best leaders, I didn't ask managers about their personal leadership philosophies; I asked the people who worked for them. They knew which leaders drew out their best work and what those leaders were doing differently. Likewise, to uncover the playbook of the most influential professionals, we need to start by hearing from the incumbent leaders—the managers who see the behavior and the stakeholders who benefit from the outcomes. We need to understand the subtle distinctions in contribution and uncover the invisible value systems to understand how small differences in behavior can generate an outsized impact.

I assembled a research team, anchored by two of my colleagues at The Wiseman Group: Karina Wilhelms, research director, and Lauren Hancock, behavioral economist and data scientist. Together, we talked to 170 leaders from some of the most admired companies, including Adobe, Google, LinkedIn, NASA, Salesforce, SAP, Splunk, Stanford Health, and Target. The managers worked in ten different countries. We asked each manager to identify someone on their team who was doing work of extraordinary value. We then asked the manager to describe that person's behavior and mindsets: How do they approach their work? How do they think about their role? What do they do? What do they not do? Why is their work so valuable?

We didn't stop with the top contributors; we also asked the manager to identify someone they had worked with who was contributing at a typical level as well as another person contributing below their capability level. We then asked the same questions. All three of the individuals identified by the manager were people the manager considered smart and capable. This enabled us to find the essential ingredients and deep practices that differentiate the most effective contributors from everyone else and the mindsets that prevent smart, capable people from contributing to their full potential.

We took the inquiry a step further by asking the managers to tell us, in general, what employees do that they most appreciate and what frustrates them most. Their reactions were remarkably similar and sometimes quite animated and emotional. Through this research, I came to understand what managers need most from the people they lead, why it's easier for them to entrust critical assignments to certain people, and why they hesitate to fully support the efforts of others.

During those interviews, I gained a deep appreciation of the challenge a manager faces when leading in an environment of uncertainty, whether they are a nursing supervisor or a sales executive. I saw how managers' team members either amplified or eased this burden. As I listened to hundreds of stories from appreciative managers, I came to see how deeply fulfilling it is to work with talented individuals who are playing at their fullest capability but also how frustrating it is to watch otherwise smart, capable people miss the mark and contribute far below their potential.

To complete the picture, I spoke with contributors. I began with twenty-five of the top contributors identified in our study to better understand how they thought and what they were doing that others deemed so valuable and impactful. I then added the perspective of hundreds of people who are working hard but not seeing the impact of their efforts as well as others who are trying to make a meaningful contribution but who feel unseen and unheard or sidelined, for any number of reasons. It became clear that the workplace is full of people who want to contribute at their fullest. This desire for high engagement and impact isn't just an ambition of corporate leaders; it's a deeply held need for all people. Everyone wants to contribute in meaningful ways and make an impact. Yet not everyone knows how.

Through the minds of both managers and aspiring leaders, I've come to understand what differentiates the most impactful players from everyone else and how small, seemingly insignificant differences in how we think and act can make an enormous impact. This book is about those differences. As you come to know this difference yourself, you can access this high-contribution, high-reward way of working, and you can join the ranks of the Impact Players and find deeper meaning and fulfillment in your work.

It's not necessarily easy to become an Impact Player. You don't need special talent or capability, but you do need to understand the mindsets and behaviors that differentiate Impact Players from other contributors. However, you can master these mindsets and practices. The book's pages will illustrate why, with a little coaching, this mindset is available to all those who want to step up and contribute at their highest level.

This book is written for aspiring leaders and striving professionals who want to be more successful at work, increase their influence, and multiply their impact. For some, leadership is about having a bigger voice and making a difference in the world. For others, leadership takes the form of a managerial role where you will be in a position to coach others. By working with the *Impact Player Mindset*, you will be a natural for these roles. You will already be seen as a leader, and you will be practiced in leading through influence and collaborating in a way that multiplies, not diminishes, the capability of those you work with.

This is also a book for today's leaders, those managers who want to cultivate more of this mindset on their teams. Managers, you will find a set of practices that will take your organization to the next level. You will also discover that these practices will help you increase your own impact. As such, I encourage team leaders and corporate managers at all levels to read this book in two distinct parts. Part one, chapters 2 to 6, will help you improve your personal effectiveness and bolster the contributor side of your role; after all, even CEOs and entrepreneurs still have a "boss": a board, a set of clients, or others whom they serve. As you read, you may find yourself reflecting on your days as a contributor. You may glean insights into why you were effective, why you moved up, and how you came to your role as a leader. Part two, chapters 7 to 8, will help you be a better leader and offers strategies to recruit more of this type of talent, develop the mindset across your team, and elevate the contribution level of an entire organization. In short, managers, use these practices yourself; however, don't lose sight of your primary job as a leader: maximize the contribution and impact of your entire team. Don't just aspire to be an Impact Player, aspire to lead a high-impact team.

The book is likewise a handbook for organization development professionals, the developers of internal talent and stewards of an organization's culture who must develop capability across the enterprise. The tools in this book will help you develop leadership at all levels, increase employee engagement, and inculcate the mindsets that support sought-after cultural values such as accountability, collaboration, inclusion, initiative, innovation, and learning. It is also a guide for mentors—parents, teachers, and workplace advisers—who want to help their mentees and loved ones develop valuable mindsets for career success in a changing world.

So let's get started. It's time to discover the secrets of the stellar professionals who play the game at a higher level and raise the level of play for everyone on the team.

PART I

THE
IMPACT PLAYERS

Chapter 1

THE IMPACT PLAYERS

Talent is everywhere, winning attitude is not.
—DAN GABLE

Monica Padman left college with two degrees in hand—one in theater and one in public relations, the latter acquired to appease her parents. She moved to Hollywood to follow her dream of becoming an actor and comedian—to make people laugh and feel. Like most striving actors, she worked a variety of part-time jobs in between auditions and small roles.

Padman scored a small part on Showtime's *House of Lies*, where she played the on-screen assistant to the actress Kristen Bell. They became friendly, and when Padman realized Bell had a young daughter, she mentioned that she did some babysitting. Bell and her husband, the actor Dax Shepard, took her up on the offer. As she became a trusted part of the household, she saw the challenges Bell faced juggling multiple acting and producing projects and offered to help her with scheduling. Though it might have been tempting for the aspiring actress to ask the Hollywood A-lister to help her get on-screen roles, Padman worked where she was needed—ironically, as Bell's off-screen assistant.

When Bell and Shepard asked her to work for them full-time, Padman was understandably reluctant—how would she find time to audition? The job could be a detour. But she decided to take it. Over time, she became more than just a trusted employee; she became a friend and creative partner to both Bell and Shepard. She worked energetically wherever she saw a need and was soon reviewing scripts and collaborating on projects. "Everything she does is at 110 percent," Bell said of Padman, "but she's so not a person who walks around showing you that she has 110 percent. [She has] no bravado." Before long, Padman had become so essential that Bell wondered aloud, "How did I do any of this without Monica?"[1]

While working for the family, she spent many hours sitting on the porch debating with Shepard, known for his contrarian ways. Their arguments were as fun as they were fierce, so when Shepard suggested they develop their banter into a podcast, she was up for that too. Thus was born *Armchair Expert*, a podcast where cohosts Shepard and Padman explore the messiness of being human with experts and celebrity guests. Smart, funny, playful, and thought provoking, the podcast became 2018's most downloaded new podcast and has continued to grow in popularity.

Two years and roughly two hundred episodes later, Padman reflected, "It's very, very easy, especially in pursuit of a career in the entertainment industry, to have tunnel vision. I think that's universal about any job. You have your sights set on something, and you have a tunnel to that goal. In my experience, it's better to have a looser grip on that."[2]

Padman could have pursued a direct path to her passion. Instead, she worked wholeheartedly where she could be most useful. By playing passionately where she was most needed, she found a bigger opportunity and, perhaps, her true purpose.

THE IMPACT PLAYERS

Professionals such as Monica Padman, and many more like her in other industries, are the all-stars of the workplace who bring their A-game everywhere they go and to everything they do. They are people who could be dropped into any of a dozen different roles and would find success. They are professionals who become instrumental to their organizations and thrive in times of economic hardship and change. They work with purpose and passion, but their passion is channeled, focused on what matters most to the organizations they work for and the issues of our time. These professionals often become influential voices in the world, known as much for their unique capabilities as for their broad impact.

They are *Impact Players*: players who make a significant contribution individually but who also have an enormously positive effect on the entire team. Like an Impact Player in sports, the superstars in the workplace all have "game." They are smart and talented and have an extraordinary work ethic; but as with Impact Players in athletics, there is something more than just talent and work ethic at play. There's also their mental game: how they view their role, work with their managers, and deal with adversity and ambiguity, and how willing they are to improve.

In this chapter, I'll share the insights gleaned from our study of Impact Players and introduce both the practices and the mindsets that differentiate these high-impact professionals from other contributors. However, a critical distinction is in order. In the research, my team and I studied these three different categories of contributors:

High-impact contributors: Those who are doing work of exceptional value and impact

Typical contributors: The vast majority of people, who are doing solid (if not great) work

Under-contributors: Smart, talented people who are playing below their capability level

This book will focus primarily on the distinction between the top two categories in order to explore the subtle, often counterintuitive differences in mindset that become big differentiators in impact. Throughout the book, I'll refer to the two groups as Impact Players and Contributors. Each has a distinct mindset and way of working; one leads to a job well done, while the other carves a path to leadership and generates outsized value and impact.

You can find a full account of the research process at ImpactPlayersBook.com, including our interviews with 170 managers from nine companies who worked in nine countries, surveys of 350 managers from broader industries, and in-depth interviews with 25 high-impact contributors.

UNDERSTANDING THE IMPACT PLAYER

So what did we find? For starters, we found Impact Players across a wide variety of job types, at all levels, and in every industry we encountered. Some of them serve in highly visible roles, such as Monica Padman, or receive public praise, such as Beth Ripley, a medical doctor and researcher who was honored with a 2020 Service to America Medal by the Partnership for Public Service for her pioneering work in 3D printing.[3]

Others, such as Arnold "Jojo" Mirador, a scrub tech at the Santa Clara Valley Medical Center, work in less visible roles. The surgeons he works with agree: when you step into Jojo's operating room, the procedure will go well. When Jojo prepares for surgery, he doesn't just lay out all the right instruments; he lays them out in the order in which they will be used. When a surgical resident asks for an instrument, Jojo doesn't just hand over the one the surgeons-in-training requested; he provides the instrument that they should have asked for, the one Jojo knows they actually need, and offers a gentle suggestion. Whether they perform behind the scenes or on center stage, the impact of these contributors is felt by their colleagues. In analyzing this cadre of high-impact players, I discovered four key differences in how they think and work. We'll begin with the fundamental difference in how they see everyday challenges.

Impact Players Wear Opportunity Goggles

Our data made it clear that the approach taken by Impact Players isn't just marginally different, it is radically different—and it's rooted in how these professionals deal with ambiguity and situations they cannot control. While others get frustrated and either check out or freak out, Impact Players tend to approach such situations directly yet sensibly. They dive into the chaos head-on, much as a savvy ocean swimmer dives into and through a massive oncoming wave rather than panicking and being tumbled in the surf.

Virtually all professionals deal with waves of ambiguity, regardless of where they work. These challenges are problems everyone can see but no one owns, meetings with many participants but no clear leaders, new terrain with never-before-seen obstacles, goals that morph as they get closer, and work demands that increase faster than one's capability grows. These are the everyday, perennial realities of the modern workplace that everyone deals with, and the way Impact Players view and respond to these external factors is at the heart of what makes them extraordinarily valuable inside organizations.

EVERYDAY CHALLENGES

Impact Players respond differently to these perennial forces and frustrations at work

1	MESSY PROBLEMS	Complex, interdisciplinary issues that don't fall within defined job boundaries
2	UNCLEAR ROLES	Lack of clarity surrounding who is in charge
3	UNFORESEEN OBSTACLES	Unprecedented challenges and unforeseeable problems
4	MOVING TARGETS	Changing needs or circumstances that render current practices ineffective or inadequate
5	UNRELENTING DEMANDS	Work demands that increase faster than capacity

A Problem to Avoid

If you work in a complex organization or a dynamic environment, you know that challenges are unavoidable. Still, many of us do our best to avoid them. But what happens when we try to sidestep these problems? Former NFL wide receiver Eric Boles recounted a moment of weakness in his rookie year with the New York Giants. As a wide receiver, his role was to run, catch passes, and keep running. So his mentality as a player was to avoid getting hit. But in addition to playing wide receiver, he played on special teams as a flyer. During the kickoff, his job was to sprint down the field toward the opposing players and break up their offensive formation called "the wedge"—a human wall of massive blockers who run in front of their kickoff returner to prevent the receiver from being tackled. In one of his first season games, as he came face-to-face with this enormous obstacle intent on destroying anything in its way, his instinct to avoid getting hit kicked into effect. Instead of hitting the wedge head-on, he cut to the left and ran around it. He then successfully made the tackle from behind, but on the 45-yard line rather than the 20. That 25-yard advancement ultimately cost the Giants the game and a chance to advance to the playoffs later in the season. As Boles put it, "Fear is expensive."[4]

Our study showed that typical professionals approach these difficult situations as if the challenge is a nuisance, lowering their productivity and making it difficult for them to do their job. They see them as problems to run around and avoid rather than tackle directly. What's more, under-contributors see them as not just threats to productivity but personal threats that could jeopardize their position or organizational status. Where others may spot a single bee but fear an entire swarm, the Impact Player is figuring out how to build a hive and harvest the honey.

An Opportunity to Add Value

The Impact Players in our study see everyday challenges as opportunities. To Impact Players, unclear direction and changing priorities are chances to add value. They are energized by the messy problems that would enervate or foil others. Lack of clarity doesn't paralyze them;

THREAT LENS VS. OPPORTUNITY LENS

Impact Players tend to see opportunity where others see threat

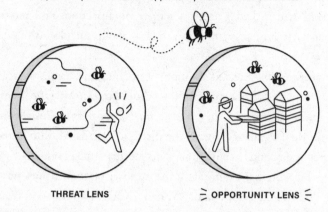

THREAT LENS   ⋛ OPPORTUNITY LENS ⋛

it provokes them. Invitations to make changes are intriguing, not intimidating. Perhaps most fundamentally, they don't see problems as distractions from their job; rather, they *are* the job—not just their job, but everyone's job.

For example, when Jethro Jones interviewed for the job of principal at Tanana Middle School in Fairbanks, Alaska, he learned that the school was being considered for closure due to declining enrollment. The school would continue operations for the next year or two, but without a major turnaround and increased enrollment, it would be shuttered. Unsurprisingly, the staff felt hopeless and were fairly pessimistic about the school's future.

But Jethro accepted the job, sensing an opportunity to innovate on behalf of the students. In his first staff meeting, he acknowledged the challenges, but told the staff, "We're in a great position. Everyone predicts that this school will be closed. We have nothing to lose, which gives us a unique opportunity to take risks and do things differently."[5] Willing to give the new principal a chance, the staff began thinking of ways they could personalize the learning experience for each student, which Jethro supported with staff training and other resources. Instead of feeling threatened by the possibility of the school's closing, the staff became energized and got students involved, too. In collaboration with the teachers, the students built hockey rinks, repaired furniture, and made escape rooms. They started programs and clubs; soon they had a dance team, a service organization, and programs to teach sign language, raise awareness about suicide, and prevent bullying.

By treating this threat as an opportunity for reinvention, the team at Tanana Middle School changed the school's trajectory. Unbeknownst to them, in the process they built a model for personalized learning that was then replicated across the district. Tanana Middle School is still open today and thriving under new leadership. Though the threat of school closure has evaporated, the mindset of opportunity has persisted. Jethro's successor said, "When COVID-19 hit, our teachers didn't skip a beat. The groundwork had already been laid, and they had developed new mindsets. COVID-19 and virtual learning were just the new obstacles for us to tackle."

In short, Impact Players see everyday challenges through an opportunity lens while others view the same challenges through a threat lens. This fundamental difference in outlook separates Impact Players from others.

Impact Players React Differently to Uncertainty

Because Impact Players see uncertainty and ambiguity as an opportunity to add value, they react fundamentally differently as well. While others are freezing, Impact Players are getting their arms around the chaos. Their outlook becomes a dividing line that functions much like the Americas' Continental Divide, the line of high mountain peaks along the main ranges of the Rocky Mountains and the Andes that separates the watershed systems of two continents. On the west of the divide, water flows to the Pacific Ocean; on the east, it flows to the Atlantic Ocean. Similarly, on one side of the outlook divide, behavior flows toward ordinary contribution; on the other side, it flows toward extraordinary contribution and high impact.

The following practices were the five key differentiators we found between Impact Players and their colleagues. Each is a set of behaviors that flow from the belief that opportunity can be found amid ambiguity and challenge.

1. **Do the Job That's Needed.** When dealing with messy problems, Impact Players address the needs of the organization; they venture beyond their assigned job to tackle the real job that needs to be done. Impact Players aim to serve; this orientation prompts them to empathize with their stakeholders, look for unmet needs, and focus where they are most useful. As they do, they increase organizational responsiveness, create a culture of agility and service, and build a reputation as flexible utility players who can be valuable in a variety of roles. In contrast, more typical players operate with a duty-oriented mindset, taking a narrow view of their role and playing their position. *While others do their job, Impact Players do the job that needs to be done.*

2. **Step Up, Step Back.** When it's clear that something needs to be done but it's unclear who's in charge, Impact Players step up and lead. They don't wait to be asked; they get things started and involve others, even when they're not officially in charge. They practice a fluid model of leadership—leading on demand rather than by command. They take their cues from the situation, stepping up when needed, but when their stewardship is fulfilled, they step back and follow others with equal ease. Their willingness to both lead and follow creates a culture of courage, initiative, and agility inside their organization. In contrast, when roles are unclear, most players act as bystanders. They assume that other people are in charge and will tell them when they are needed and what to do. *While others wait for direction, Impact Players step up and lead.*

3. **Finish Stronger.** Impact Players tend to be completion freaks; they stick with things and get the entire job done, even when the job becomes hard and plagued with unforeseen obstacles. They work with a heightened sense of agency and an assumption of personal strength, which prompts them to take ownership, solve problems, and finish jobs without constant supervision. But they don't just

push through roadblocks—they improvise and give themselves permission to do things differently and find better ways of working. And, as they deliver results despite setbacks, they reinforce a culture of accountability and build a reputation as clutch players capable of coming from behind. In contrast, more typical players operate with an avoidance mindset. They take responsible action, but when things get tough they escalate issues up the management chain rather than taking ownership; at worst, they get distracted or discouraged and stall out completely. *While others escalate problems, Impact Players move things across the finish line and build strength along the way.*

4. **Ask and Adjust.** Impact Players tend to adapt to changing conditions faster than their peers because they interpret new rules and new targets as opportunities for learning and growth. They certainly appreciate affirmation and positive feedback, yet they actively seek corrective feedback and contrary views and use this information to recalibrate and refocus their efforts. In the process, they strengthen a culture of learning and innovation, help the organization stay relevant, and build personal reputations as coachable players who up-level their own game and raise the bar for everyone on the team. In contrast, most professionals interpret change as annoying, unfair, or threatening to the stability of their work environment. In volatile conditions, they tend to stick to what they know best and keep playing the game by the rules that validate their current expertise. *While others attempt to manage and minimize change, Impact Players are learning and adapting to change.*

5. **Make Work Light.** When a team is weighed down by increased pressure and unrelenting demands, Impact Players make hard work easier. They provide lift, not by taking on other people's work but by being easy to work with. They bring a sense of buoyancy and equanimity that reduces drama, politics, and stress and increases the joy of work. By creating a positive and productive work environment for everyone, they reinforce a culture of collaboration and inclusion and develop a reputation as high-performing, low-

maintenance players—the type everyone wants to work with. In contrast, when the pressure is on and workloads are at a peak, more typical players tend to seek help rather than offer to help. As this becomes their default response, they add to the burden of already overtaxed teams during difficult times and can become a burden to their leaders and colleagues. *While others add to the load, Impact Players make heavy demands feel lighter.*

These five practices, along with the outlook that drives each, constitute the *Impact Player Mindset*, a framework for high-value contribution.

THE FIVE PRACTICES OF IMPACT PLAYERS

The beliefs and behavior that differentiate impact play from contributorship

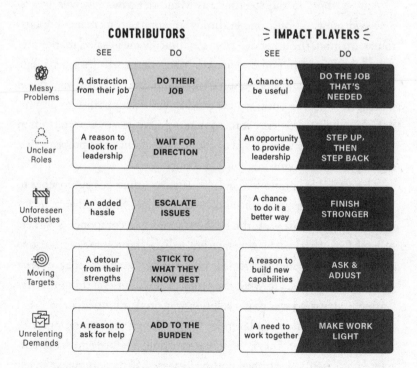

	CONTRIBUTORS		IMPACT PLAYERS	
	SEE	DO	SEE	DO
Messy Problems	A distraction from their job	DO THEIR JOB	A chance to be useful	DO THE JOB THAT'S NEEDED
Unclear Roles	A reason to look for leadership	WAIT FOR DIRECTION	An opportunity to provide leadership	STEP UP, THEN STEP BACK
Unforeseen Obstacles	An added hassle	ESCALATE ISSUES	A chance to do it a better way	FINISH STRONGER
Moving Targets	A detour from their strengths	STICK TO WHAT THEY KNOW BEST	A reason to build new capabilities	ASK & ADJUST
Unrelenting Demands	A reason to ask for help	ADD TO THE BURDEN	A need to work together	MAKE WORK LIGHT

Consider how Maninder Sawhney, the director of data analytics and insights at Adobe, dealt with several of the "everyday challenges" that differentiate the Impact Players.

It's a problem familiar to virtually every large organization: islands of data—independent information systems that don't talk to one another. Adobe was grappling with this problem, trying to build a comprehensive view of how customers engage with Adobe through various marketing and product experiences. There had been numerous efforts to solve the problem, but none of the measures was truly moving the company's goals forward. Meanwhile, Adobe's CEO, Shantanu Narayen, continued to stress the need for a streamlined way to get an accurate view of business performance across the end-to-end customer journey. Twenty-five people, mostly senior executives, gathered in the corporate boardroom for an all-day quarterly business review.

Among those in the meeting was Maninder Sawhney, who was to give two presentations: one outlining an approach to managing customer attrition, the other describing a unified view of sales, marketing, product, finance, and other data sets. Maninder, a self-described "data guy," was the most junior person in the room. But he had always taken a broad view of the business. He was known for his ability to decompose big, hairy problems into something easy to understand, often jumping up to the whiteboard to capture the essence of a problem that a group had been wrestling with for hours.

The assembled group had been discussing numerous approaches to improve customer retention and lifetime value. Some advocated for more dashboards to view the business's multiple components; others offered fixes that might generate immediate improvements. No one could agree on a solution to this opportunity; actually, they weren't even in agreement as to what the problem was. But one thing that everyone understood was that a solution was needed immediately.

It was now time for Maninder to give his first presentation. The topic was measurement of customer attrition. He presented the current data structures and then outlined a very different approach he felt the company should take to measure and analyze customer attrition.

The executives around the table dug deeper into his ideas, seeking to understand his rationale and strategy and the potential outcomes. It was a challenge Maninder met calmly as he explained that dashboards alone wouldn't solve the problem and why drawing conclusions from isolated data could lead to poor decisions. By the afternoon break, Maninder had a bigger job: at the behest of the CEO, he was now managing more than customer data—he was leading the customer retention strategy.

Following the break, Maninder began his second presentation to outline the full set of data structures for marketing and sales. Just a few minutes into his presentation, he realized the information he was providing was off target. Being invited to the meeting had given him a clearer view of the CEO's vision of an operating model. Maninder was giving the presentation he'd been asked to give—a technical briefing on a specific process—but it wasn't what the CEO needed in that moment. Maninder stopped presenting and asked if he could come back in two weeks with a plan that would address the problems the CEO wanted to solve.

It was a bold move—abandoning his presentation and stepping up to tackle a much bigger problem. The senior leaders in the room who were responsible for pieces of the solution could have challenged Maninder's boldness, but he had the trust of his colleagues and ultimately was the type of leader people like to get behind. According to his colleagues, he works without ego and never engages in politics or holds grudges. In fact, he has a T-shirt that sums up his mentality: LET SOMEONE ELSE CLIMB THE CORPORATE LADDER.

Two weeks later, Maninder presented a new framework that incorporated input from various stakeholders across the company. When one executive asked who should lead the massive endeavor, it was clear to Shantanu and the others. Maninder was commissioned to lead a cross-functional effort to build a data-driven operating model for the digital business.

Within six months, the system was operational and fundamentally changed the way Adobe ran its business. The new way of operating, which was made possible by the combined contributions of multiple groups across Adobe, is credited with adding hundreds of millions of dollars to the company's revenue. After leading the system's development, Maninder was put in charge of running the digital media business for the Americas (one of Adobe's largest businesses, which delivers billions of dollars of revenue each year) and is now responsible for driving long-term customer success.

What enabled Maninder to progress from running reports to running Adobe's biggest business?

He saw the real job that needed to be done, and he was willing to step forward and lead. He saw a complex problem as an opportunity. For Impact Players, problems become opportunities to serve, to find solutions, and make an impact.

Impact Players Tap into Unwritten Rules

One of the primary insights that emerged from the research was that Impact Players seem to understand the rules of the workplace better than others. They figure out the unwritten rule book—the standards of behavior that one should follow in a particular job or organization. They tune in to the needs of the organization and determine what's important to their immediate colleagues; they figure out what needs to get done and ascertain the *right* way to get it done.

This rule book is unwritten not because managers are secretive or no one has bothered to publish it but because the rules are also tacit for most managers, held at a level below conscious awareness. Many of the managers we interviewed commented on how much *they* had learned during our interview. Answering our questions helped them articulate for the first time the subtle differences between Impact Players and others on their team as well as behaviors that create value versus behaviors that create friction. Many managers realized they had never shared this vital information with their team, and many vowed to remedy that. The point is, the rules are tacit for everyone—except those who make an effort to discover them and share them.

So, what do organizational leaders value most? Managers want their staff to make their jobs easier—to help them lead their teams and be self-managing wherever possible. They need people who can think for themselves and step up to a challenge. They value compliance less than the success literature would have you believe and collaboration more than might be indicated in official corporate value statements. In reality, managers want people to help them find solutions and foster teamwork.

When Impact Players figure out these invisible rules and understand what their stakeholders value, they build credibility. Their leaders are delighted and eager to support them, and they expand their impact potential. Consider how each of these managers describes one of their Impact Players.

- LinkedIn sales leader Scott Faraci talked about account executive Amanda Rost, who had just handled an important sales meeting with ease and brilliance: "I was literally jumping around with excitement. I thought, 'This is crazy. Who is this superstar I just hired?' If I could have built a statue of her and put it in the center of our sales floor as a shining beacon of how to be a sales executive, I would have."
- Roberto Kuplich, a development manager at SAP Brazil, spoke about Paulo Büttenbender, a highly respected software architect on his team: "You can lay me off, but don't lay off Paulo."
- Julia Anas, a senior HR executive, described HR business partner Jonathon Modica as "the first person to raise his hand for the hard, hairy problems" and said, "I look forward to our one-on-ones because I get energy from him." This sentiment is a sharp contrast to how a manager at a different company reacts when he realizes he has a meeting with someone on his team who "just doesn't get it": "I feel like the gritting teeth emoji."

The insights we gained into what leaders value are peppered through the book (but you can also take a sneak peek at the full list in appendix A, "Building Upward Credibility"). Use these insights to help you build trust and alignment with your stakeholders—because once you know what's valued within your organization and what the leaders around you most appreciate, you have a playbook for success. Furthermore, when managers share their rule book, everyone on the team can play at a higher level.

Though it wasn't surprising that the most impactful professionals figured out the invisible rules, it was alarming to learn how many capable people were consistently missing the mark. These were smart, talented, and hardworking individuals, but they seemed to misunderstand what their leaders considered valuable and miss the subtext in the workplace norms. The typical contributors were often delivering a solid performance, but it would go unnoticed or fall flat as if they hadn't read the grading rubric before submitting an assignment or consulted the judging criteria before choreographing a routine.

There have been times I've missed the mark by merely doing what I was asked to do rather than thinking through what I should do. On one such occasion, a large company invited me to teach a leadership workshop to address a specific set of challenges its managers faced. My client outlined their challenges, and we held numerous discussions. I then prepared a plan that I felt would best address their issues, and we all agreed on the approach. A month later, I delivered the workshop as planned, ensuring that I hit each of the critical points in my remit. The session was solid, but I could tell it lacked impact. You see, in the month between the formulation of the plan and the delivery of the program, the COVID-19 pandemic had begun sweeping the world and disrupting nearly every aspect of work. Managers were now dealing with an entirely new set of challenges (managing uncertainty, suspending business operations, and staff working from home). I had done my job, but I failed to see that it was no longer the job that was needed.

Much like me, the professionals who miss the mark are well intentioned but misguided. They were doing what seemed valuable, either because it was important in the past or because it was widely touted as the way of the future. But many of their work practices were counterfeits—an illusion of value lacking real substance. I call these *value decoys*—professional habits or beliefs that seem useful and appear appreciated but erode more value than they create. They are shiny objects that distract us from contributing in valuable ways.

We saw some people tripped up because they were playing by an outdated rule book. Some were doing their job so diligently that they overlooked the real work to be done—the work no one was officially assigned to do but that the organization most needed. Workplace etiquette taught people to be diligent, vigilant, and unflappable. But as the environment changes, simply staying in our lane can sideline us. Whereas those professionals were trapped by playing by the old rules, others misconstrued the new rules of a modern work culture. They saw that the game was changing and that the workplace now valued innovation, agility, engagement, and inclusion. However, they missed the subtleties and subtext in the rules; they didn't realize, for example, that "Experiment and take risks" does not include crashing a production database or that "Be your authentic self" doesn't mean burdening your colleagues with everything happening in your world. They missed important signals because they were overanxious, overteaming, and deeply engaged to the point of obnoxiousness. Essentially, they were overplaying and overcontributing.

This brings us to a central insight: *we can under-contribute by overcontributing.* We can deliver too little value while working extremely hard. Whether we are tripped up by the ambiguity of new mores or the sacrosanctity of old rules, we can end up doing great but irrelevant work. We may be expending significant force, but the vector of our effort is off target.

Impact Players more easily spot counterfeits because they don't assume that what is valuable to them is valuable to others. They look beyond themselves and define value through their stakeholders' eyes. They learn what is important to their bosses, their clients, or their collaborators, and they make it important to them. By targeting their efforts where the greatest number of people benefit, they increase their impact and influence. While others are managing their brand, Impact Players are building a reputation as a player who is easy to work with and can be counted on to deliver when it matters most. While others may be trying to change the world, Impact Players are actually doing it. They start by changing themselves, continually seeking input and adapting to ensure they hit the mark. With the Impact Player Mindset, they escape the traps of old-school thinking and avoid new-age detours.

Impact Generates Investment

The way Impact Players think about and respond to uncertainty and ambiguity makes them especially fit for the challenges of the modern work world. They are flexible, quick, strong, agile, and collaborative—the type of people you want on your team when your world is rattled or something goes awry. Impact Players will help you find solutions while others point fingers at problems. As one manager put it, the Impact Player was "someone I would want to be trapped on a desert island with" compared to another employee, who is "someone I would have to help survive." While others might build a shelter and hunker down during a storm, the Impact Player is building a windmill to create power. In challenging environments, Impact Players are assets that appreciate over time.

When we asked managers to quantify the value of the Impact Player's contribution relative to their peers, they estimated, on average, that the Impact Players on their teams delivered more than three times the value delivered by a typical contributor. Further, they indicated that the value contributed by the Impact Player was almost ten times that of an under-contributor (a smart, talented colleague contributing below their capability). I was struck by one particular response from a senior engineering manager at NASA. When estimating the relative value of the contribution made by a former deputy division chief as compared with her peers, he said, "I would conservatively say twenty to thirty times greater."

The fact that Impact Players are perceived to be more than three times as valuable as typical contributors means everything in terms of access to rewards, both intrinsic (such as working on great projects) and extrinsic (such as promotions and compensation). And when it comes to the development of talent, these players receive an extra helping of mentoring and a double dose of challenging assignments. The tangible value they provide to others is like a deposit that prompts reciprocal investment and spawns a mutually beneficial cycle.

Value Building

Impact Players tend to be self-managing and offer their managers the assurance and peace of mind that they will complete the job, in full, without being told or reminded. They not only get the job done, they also do it the right way; they steer clear of politics and create a positive team environment. Leaders appreciate this compelling value proposition: the job is done well, and the experience is positive for the team and efficient for the team leader.

When managers realize that they can invest an ounce of leadership and receive a ton of value in return, they continue to invest—and reinvest—in these players. They typically entrust them with increased responsibilities and additional resources. Because they are efficient, managers give Impact Players their most precious resource: the manager's time and reputation. Impact Players tend to be the beneficiaries

VALUE BUILDING

The value created by Impact Players accrues and prompts reinvestment

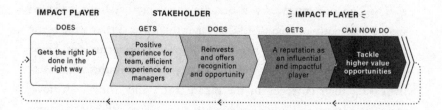

of extra mentoring and are called up often to represent the manager to the larger organization or external environment. However, the Impact Players in our study weren't blessed with trust and resources from the get-go; they earned it. The wisest of them proved early on that their colleagues could count on them 100 percent. By providing quick returns and operating with consistency and integrity, they catalyze the investment cycle.

In return, Impact Players develop a stellar reputation and earn the credibility that's needed to tackle the higher-value opportunities that begin flowing their way. They can now contribute at even higher and broader levels. Thus the cycle continues: they can do more, and their actions carry greater weight. They are seen as leaders who embody the organization's values and quickly become cultural paragons. Because they are influencers who affect prevailing attitudes and shape the workplace culture, their coworkers respect and seek to emulate them.

A Chain Reaction
As this cycle continues, the stakeholder investments increase, and the Impact Players' capability and cache grow exponentially, enabling them to contribute in increasingly extraordinary ways. But the cycle isn't an endless loop in which they repeat a winning formula; they are learning with each loop, adapting to changes in their environment, and becoming increasingly skilled at converting stakeholder resources into tangible value. This simple yet powerful cycle becomes accretive, like continuously compounding interest where small, continuous assessments and modifications result in significantly different outcomes over time.

Through our interviews, it became apparent that Impact Players were consistently progressing faster than their peers; they were being promoted more often and given more impactful opportunities. However, they weren't merely climbing a career ladder. Rather, they were increasing their currency in the organization and using it in novel ways. Some were ambitious and used their increased influence to move quickly up the organization chart. Others were content in their roles and used their political currency to pick their projects, direct their work schedule, or simply continue to work in a job they truly enjoyed. Either way, they were driven but not full of angst. What's more, the Impact Players we met reported high levels of job satisfaction and high levels of life satisfaction as well.

The Missing Player

It's worth noting that the high-impact contributors identified in our study were evenly split across gender, generations, and race/ethnicity. However, I'm also cognizant that this pool was filled with nominations from some of the best leaders in the best places to work. These organizations tend to be front-runners in recruiting for and valuing a diverse workforce. I realize that this may not be the case in the organization you work in, and it may not reflect the reality of your specific situation, which means that making your fullest and most fulfilling contribution may come with challenges.

In trying to understand why some professionals become extraordinarily impactful in a given organization or situation, one cannot ignore the effects of unconscious bias—our tendency to hold stereotypes about a certain group of people without our conscious knowledge. Because the potential for bias is hard-wired into human cognition, "sameness" tends to have a high default value. This can shape whose contribution is perceived as valuable and deemed influential and impactful. It also means that individuals who do not fit the dominant profile may be underrepresented or, even when well represented, underutilized and underappreciated.

Even in well-managed organizations, there are hidden pools of aspiring leaders and Impact Players who are not seen or getting their turn and who are not receiving the same levels of investment and reinvestment. The work world is missing out on the influence and full contribution of too many players. It is my hope that this book offers a framework to help level this playing field and strengthen the partnership between talent and management, giving contributors tools to help them increase their influence and providing managers with insights and practices to help them create more inclusive workplaces (see chapter 8 for specific practices for leading inclusively).

MULTIPLYING YOUR IMPACT

Studying leadership has taught me this truth about contributorship: people all around the world arrive at work wanting to contribute at their fullest. It's painful for them when they can't. They want to work in an organization where intelligence and talent are maximized and where people are deeply engaged, learning rapidly, and contributing in full measure. The underutilization of talent is avoidable—with leaders who bring out the best in others and players who bring an all-in mentality. Whereas my book *Multipliers* provides a leadership model for high engagement and utilization, this book will explore the talent side of the equation, what contributors can do to maximize their impact and what leaders can do to help all those on their team play at their full capability. The book serves as a companion to *Multipliers*, because when Contributors become Impact Players, the multiplier effect is exponential.

The Playbook

You, too, can be an Impact Player. This book will give you data-based insights and practical tools to help you take the lead, play bigger, and multiply your impact. In chapters 2 to 6 we will explore each of the five practices of Impact Players in detail. You'll learn the secrets of their success. Each chapter concludes with a playbook containing a set of Smart Plays for aspiring leaders to implement the practice wisely, create real value for others, and increase their impact. Chapter 7 provides a comprehensive training plan for those same aspiring leaders as well as for the managers who coach and mentor them. Chapter 8 is written expressly for managers and provides guidance for leaders and talent development professionals who want to build a high-impact team.

Throughout the book, we will address "the missing Impact Player" and how implicit bias and other systemic forms of discrimination create barriers that artificially limit certain people's contribution, visibility, and influence. Specifically, in chapter 7, we'll explore ways you can help others see the value of your unique contribution, and in chapter 8, we'll cover practices managers can use to ensure that all types of talent are seen and valued.

Finally, chapter 9 invites you to consider the possibility of playing "all in"—not a draining, all-out form of working in which people burn out but a form of working in which people do their best work *and* live their best life, in which all players are valued and can make a valuable contribution.

The Players

In the pages that follow, you'll meet a diverse mix of professionals who are delivering extraordinary value around the world. For clarity's sake, we will focus primarily on their individual contributions rather than showcase the efforts of all team members. Please know that virtually every one of the Impact Players profiled in these pages is uncomfortable with the praise they received and acknowledges colleagues who contributed to each win. They have graciously allowed me to shine the spotlight on them. They represent a variety of industries, experiences, and roles; some are individual contributors, others are executives. Most were discovered through our research. (Unless otherwise noted, all quotes are taken from our research interviews.) Some are well known: top athletes, an Oscar-winning actor, and a few Nobel laureates. A few of the examples are moments when I was at my best and several are my former and current colleagues (or their spouses). One gem is the mother of one of the Impact Players in our study. When this Google staffer told us about his "badass mom," I had to meet her. She is an extraordinary leader in her own right, and you'll want to meet her, too. Taken together, they form a pixelated portrait of excellence worthy of emulation. My hope is that you will see yourself in them, either in reality or in potential.

We'll go inside the minds of dozens of managers, from project leaders to CEOs—the quotes from leaders (both on the dedicated pages that precede each chapter as well as those interspersed throughout the book) are all from actual managers from our interviews.[6] In addition to reading about Impact Players, you'll find a number of examples of more typical contributors (referred to in the collective as "Contributors") and a few under-contributors, all of whose names have been changed. Through their stories, we will expose and explore the traps that hold us all back and the mindsets that steer us off our path of highest contribution. These are traps I have fallen into myself. I'll share a few of my own experiences—times when my overconfidence caused me to under-contribute or when my own views blocked me from seeing what mattered most. Perhaps you too will find yourself caught at times by the illusion of value. I hope these examples will help you break through.

Out of Bounds

Before we begin, let's clarify a few of the book's vital messages—not only what it is but what it isn't.

1. **The notion of Impact Players is not limited to sports.** Though the Impact Player idea is lifted from athletics, this is not a story about high-performing athletes or coaches. I've borrowed a few terms and metaphors and included several examples from the sports world because athletics provide vivid examples of excellence and clear outcomes. However, there are Impact Players in almost any organization or community.

2. **This is not a contrast between winners and losers.** Our focus will be far more nuanced. We will explore how the *Impact Player Mindset* differs from the *Contributor Mindset* and the subtle distinctions in thinking and action that make all the difference.

3. **The distinction between the Impact Player and the Contributor is not a classification of individuals but of practices.** This book will likely be of greatest value to you as you think of Impact Player

and Contributor Mindsets as modes of thinking—orientations that we all move into and out of—and periodically ask yourself: Which mindset am I using right now?

4. **Becoming an Impact Player isn't a winner-take-all competition.** The book's mentalities and practices are, by and large, learnable and coachable, hence available to all. Impact Players are stellar but not necessarily singular—much as a town may have multiple five-star hotels or restaurants. Likewise, a leader can develop an entire team with the Impact Player Mindset.

5. **This is not a rallying cry to work harder.** The Impact Player mentality isn't about pushing oneself and leaning in when you really want to lie down; the Impact Players we studied didn't necessarily work any harder or any longer than their peers, but they did tend to work with greater intentionality and focus while they were working. They created an energy and impact that prevented exhaustion.

6. **The book is not intended as a quick fix.** The Impact Players we studied evinced these practices authentically and consistently. When the Impact Player mentality is deeply held and authentically practiced, it can work for you, too. If you are looking for career practices that will help you cut the line and get ahead quickly, this is not the book for you.

Building a High-Impact Mindset

The astrophysicist Neil deGrasse Tyson asserts, "What you know is not as important as how you think."[7] If you aspire to have greater influence, start by thinking like an Impact Player. Don't just use the playbook; adopt the Impact Player mentality as your ethos. It is a powerful way of thinking about work that will enable you to make your most valued contribution, reap the subsequent rewards, and help others do the same. Some of the practices may not work well at your workplace or for you; others may become obsolete. However, the way of thinking—the mindset—will transcend and endure.

I encourage you not only to read the book as a guide for your current reality but also to see it as a harbinger of the future of work. The

Impact Player framework was developed through a study of top contributors in leading organizations, as seen through the eyes of some of the best managers. Hence, the framework has an inherently modern orientation. These ideals may not reflect your current reality, but they can become part of your future. For some, this may necessitate finding a new organization or cause worthy of your highest contribution. For others, you might find that as the most admired companies' best practices are studied and emulated, your organization evolves to keep pace. Either way, take a page from the playbook of the great Wayne Gretzky and "skate to where the puck is going to be."

There is a prize for those who do just that. By embracing the mindset and practices of the Impact Player, you will earn recognition as one of the all-stars in the new world of work. By recognizing the pitfalls, you can avoid the fate of the under-contributor. You can also help others break free and steer clear of the traps that hold back well-meaning professionals and build the type of team that everyone wants to work on. But above all, when you bring your A-game to everything you do, you will experience the thrill of contributing at your fullest and become the person everyone wants on their team.

CHAPTER 1 SUMMARY: THE IMPACT PLAYERS

This chapter introduces the differences between working with the mindset of an Impact Player and working with the mindset of a Contributor.

Impact Players. Individuals at any level of an organization who are doing work of exceptional value and having a extraordinarily high impact.

Impact Player Mindset. A mode of thinking that, when consistently adopted, leads to high-value contribution and high impact.

Contributor Mindset. A set of assumptions and practices that gets a job done and makes a contribution but falls short of full potential and high impact.

Findings

1. **Impact Players wear opportunity goggles.** Impact players see the following everyday challenges differently than others: messy problems, unclear roles, unforeseen obstacles, moving targets, and unrelenting burdens. Whereas others see these challenges as threats, Impact Players see them as opportunities to add value.

2. **Impact Players react differently to uncertainty.** They respond differently than their colleagues in these five ways:

CONTRIBUTORS	IMPACT PLAYERS
Do their job	Do the job that's needed
Wait for direction	Step up, then step back
Escalate issues	Finish stronger
Stick to what they know best	Ask and adjust
Add to the burden	Make work light

3. **Impact Players tap into the unwritten rules.** Impact Players figure out the standards of behavior that one should follow in a particular job or organization and adapt for maximum impact.

4. **Impact generates investment.** Impact Players tend to be entrusted with increased responsibilities and additional resources. Systemic bias can lead to hidden pools of talent going unnoticed or receiving lower levels of investment and reinvestment.

WHAT LEADERS SAY ABOUT . . .

CONTRIBUTORS	⋛ IMPACT PLAYERS ⋚
"She is a prolific doer and does more work than anyone else on the team."	"He saw people spending too much time on presentation slides, developed a tool to fix that, rolled it out globally. He saved us hundreds of hours of work."
"Focuses on pet projects that aren't necessarily a priority."	"It wasn't her job. She just did it."
"If this were Apollo 13 and there was a crisis and the engineering manager put the box of parts on the table and said, 'Let's figure it out" he would say, 'Okay, but I'm off work in fifteen minutes."	"Repeatedly pivots to become the expert in what is needed."
"He was shooting at a completely different goal."	"Looked at the whole picture, then fixed the problem for everyone."

Chapter 2

MAKE YOURSELF USEFUL

Opportunity is missed by most people because it is
dressed in overalls and looks like work.
—THOMAS A. EDISON

My career at Oracle Corporation began on a Sunday evening at a nondescript hotel in San Mateo, California. I was one of sixty new college recruits excitedly reporting for duty at the "Class of '88" boot camp—a three-week intensive program where we would learn Oracle's technology and the other basics we would need to be successful in the young, rapidly growing software company. Classroom instruction would begin the following morning; this evening was just for mingling and introductions. The participants had all recently graduated from an impressive array of universities, mostly from computer science and engineering programs. There were a few, like me, who had attended business school and others from the humanities.

The boot camp leaders briefed us on the rigorous training schedule, which would culminate in a highly competitive team project: each team would build and present a business application using Oracle software. The program leader stressed the importance of having a balance of skills on each team and then abruptly declared, "Okay, techies on this side of the room, fuzzies on the other." There were chuckles as the mass of programmers and engineers moved to the left side of the room, while the rest of us—the now self-conscious "fuzzies"—moved to the right side. The assumption was that we fuzzies would struggle with the technology on our own, so we were dispersed across the teams. The formal training hadn't even begun, but I had learned an important lesson: *there was a skill set that was highly valued at Oracle, and it wasn't mine.*

I tucked away that insight and after the boot camp began working as an education coordinator for the consulting division. But just one year later my department was disbanded in a reorganization, so I needed to find a new job inside the company. I set my sights on the new-hire training group that ran the boot camp. I was hoping the group's charter would expand to include leadership development, a field I was keenly interested in. I interviewed with the department manager and then her boss, Bob Shaver, the VP of administration. After answering his questions, I raised an issue. I'd seen young professionals thrown into management with little training, and I'd witnessed them wreak havoc on their teams. I confidently told him that Oracle needed a management boot camp, and that I'd love to help build it.

I will never forget Bob's reaction. He began, "Liz, this is compelling, but your boss has a different problem. She needs to get two thousand new hires up to speed on Oracle technology this year." His explanation was another indicator that at that point, technical skills were more important than management skills. He continued, "It would be great if you could help her figure out how to do this." His gentle guidance carried a loud message. What I heard was "Liz, make yourself useful."

I was disappointed. I knew the company needed people to teach programming, and I did want to teach, but I lacked passion for the nuances of correlated subqueries and the virtues of database-indexing techniques. To make matters worse, I was woefully underqualified, and the techies with their advanced degrees from MIT and Caltech would surely notice. I wanted to develop leaders, but now Bob wanted me to teach programming to a bunch of nerds. It was not the job I wanted to do, but it was the job that needed to be done.

Seeing the wisdom and promise in his invitation, I joined the training group and volunteered to be a product training instructor, channeling my ambition to where it could have the greatest impact. I dived in, ordering the full set of product documentation and quickly partnering with a coworker, Leslie Stern, who had real technical chops. (Leslie was one of the people who had stood on the techie side of the room on our first day at work.) She taught me how to think like a programmer, which didn't come naturally. But with her guidance and some very late nights, I figured it out. In turn, I shared a few ideas about teaching, and together we earned awards for outstanding technical instruction and taught many people who became pioneers in Silicon Valley, something I'm still proud of.

I never became a true techie. But by being willing to delve deep into the technology, I built a reputation as someone who understood the business and worked on what mattered most. That reputation would later unlock many opportunities for me. I received a promotion to department manager within a year, but strangely, at that time, I wasn't interested in a management role; I was enjoying my gig teaching programmers. Of course, when Bob explained why the company needed me to take the job, I once again gave up the job I loved to do the job that was needed.

Like many shortsighted professionals, I began my career seeking work that held interest for me. But when we look beyond our ideal job and do the job that needs to be done, we make ourselves useful—and much more valuable—and increase our influence. Are you bending your work to fit your personal interests, or are you flexing yourself to serve where you can be most useful?

In this chapter, you'll see that the most impactful players don't just do their jobs; they do the job that's needed. They venture out of the comfort of their role and work on the front lines of all types of problems. You'll find out why some people are always working where the action is while others are constantly wondering if they should be doing something to help. You will learn why job descriptions are irrelevant, why bosses hate being bossy, and how the simple act of fixing a broken copier can put you onto a path to leadership.

At the most fundamental level, this chapter is about how to make yourself useful—how to understand what is important and then do the things that are important in a way that is extremely beneficial to your career. But before we begin, a warning: be prepared to leave behind the comfort of a neatly defined job and work where things get messy.

THE CHOICE: DO YOUR JOB OR
DO THE JOB THAT NEEDS TO BE DONE?

The world of work is getting messier—more complex, more chaotic, and more interconnected—thanks in part to the combined effects of globalization and technology. Complex problems—those involving too many unknowns and interrelated factors to reduce to rules and processes—are on the rise.[1] These problems include challenges such as: standardizing customer experience worldwide, reacting to disruptive innovation, creating a personalized learning experience for all students, controlling health care costs, and transforming a culture. Organizations have tried to address this complexity by establishing interdisciplinary teams or matrix organizations; still, the most important work feels as though it is everyone's job yet no one's job. Too many professionals are stuck in organizational boxes that don't match the real work. The convoluted taxonomy of pay grades, job titles, and job descriptions meant to capture important initiatives and workflows typically reflects past priorities and rarely captures the real work to be done. This is one of the central problems of modern organizations: if you are doing today's job, you are probably handling yesterday's priorities.

As problems become messier and mutate faster than a formal organization can respond, agility must come from the culture—the daily decisions and actions of people—not the organization structure. This leaves professionals with a messy problem of their own: Should I stay in my lane, do my job, and attend to my duties? Or should I leave my post to pursue work in no-man's-land? If the latter, how can I make sure I still excel at what I've been assigned to do?

Consider how most professionals respond to these complex problems and nascent opportunities.

When James[2] was hired by a major video game studio, the bulk of the company's billion-dollar business consisted of games purchased and played offline, no internet connection required. James was the director of online gaming experience, and his team supported a limited number of games available to play online. He was smart, learned new technology quickly, and was an expert in internet gaming systems. He was also one of the professionals you could count on to always get the job done on time and on budget. His boss, Amika, who oversaw all gaming experience, relied on James to ensure that the studio's online offerings were consistently robust and functional.

Though James and his team were doing a great job providing a few games online, the world was changing. Internet gaming was the wave of the future, and the company began aggressively migrating content online. Amika was getting pressure from the CEO to make its entire inventory available on the Web.

That was no easy transformation. It involved coordination across many groups, each of which would need to reengineer its processes of promotion, delivery, and tech support. James understood the challenges better than anyone, yet he didn't see them as his problems to solve. He helped his team prepare for an incoming wave of games to add to the website and then waited for other teams to send over their products. What the other groups needed, though, was help shifting their business to the internet.

James was qualified to take on the challenge, but he was so focused on his defined role that he didn't see the bigger opportunity. Amika was puzzled by James's failure to act, so she stopped by his office to discuss the issue. James acknowledged the situation tepidly and assured Amika that his team could handle the higher volume of online games. Amika stopped by again the next day and the day after that. After a week of daily visits, James finally started to get the message: he'd been focused on doing his job, but he was missing the opportunity to make a bigger impact and really make a contribution to the company's growth.

Contributors see themselves as position holders. They do the work they're given and stay within the boundaries of their role but risk becoming so myopic that they lose sight of the overall strategy and veer off the agenda.

In contrast, Impact Players see themselves as problem solvers. They aren't trapped by antiquated organizational structures or overly enamored with their positions. They don't just do their job; they find ways to serve where they can be of greatest value. Consider the case of Scott O'Neil, a twenty-two-year-old college grad with a dream of working in sports management.

It was a Saturday morning in the summer of 1992, and Scott sat in the arena lobby waiting for a colleague to arrive with a key to the team business offices. He had recently landed an entry-level job as a marketing assistant working for the New Jersey Nets, a team in the National Basketball Association (NBA). It was a low-paying job, but it was a start. His daily responsibilities weren't inherently exciting—he took dictation, stuffed envelopes, made copies, and ran errands—but he was always excited about it. It had become his custom to arrive early and wait for someone to let him in so he could start his workday.

On that particular Saturday, he had come to the office and found the copier wasn't working. It was the era when a photocopier was an essential tool and a paper jam could bring an entire organization's productivity to a halt. When most professionals encountered cryptic error messages, they left in search of a working copy machine on another floor. But Scott had some experience repairing the copier in his parents' home office and figured he could make himself useful by fixing that one, too.

The office was empty except for a small group of top executives. Jon Spoelstra, the organization's president, spotted Scott on the floor, arms stained with printer toner up to his elbows, disassembling the massive machine. He recognized Scott as one of the new recruits and asked, "What's your name, kid?"

Scott looked up. "Scott O'Neil."

"What are you doing?"

"Fixing the copier."

"Why?"

"Because it's broken."

Spoelstra asked Scott to come into his office and peppered him with questions. "What do you do here? Do you think this department is efficient?" and so on. Eventually, he asked, "So what do you want to do here?" Scott told him that he wanted to sell sponsorships. Spoelstra responded, "Congratulations, you have just been promoted."

Scott was shocked. "When do I start?"

"How about today?" Spoelstra asked. "You can have that office," he added, pointing across the hall to an empty office.

"Wow, I get an office?" Scott was surprised and delighted.

Scott got his hands onto an SIC code book, which listed companies by industry, and "started calling every company in America," as he put it. He created games to track his work and pushed himself to master the perfect pitch. He made mistake after mistake but rarely made the same one twice. He learned fast and even tripped his way into a few sales.

However, his aim was to secure major sponsorships. Knowing that he wasn't going to hit the target with his current sales skills, he asked one of the senior sales executives if he could sit alongside him and listen to his sales calls for a week. His senior colleague dismissed the idea as ridiculous. Scott countered, "I don't know what I'm doing. If you don't let me sit in your office, I'm just going to sit outside your office, and that will be more awkward for everyone." Scott prevailed and spent the week listening and learning. He adjusted his approach and within a couple of months was closing major sponsorship deals.

Scott has brought this signature drive and attitude to every management and leadership position he's had since. He worked like this as the president of Madison Square Garden Sports, where he oversaw the New York Knicks and the New York Rangers. He helped transform the iconic arena, orchestrated some of the largest marketing deals in NBA history, and achieved record-setting ticket sales. He worked like this as the CEO of the Philadelphia 76ers. It was a turn-around effort that would take the struggling team from a win-lost record of 19–63 in the 2013–14 season to a competitive team that fin-ished the 2017–18 season with a win-loss record of 52–30 and placed third in the Eastern Conference. When he took charge of the team, the monetary value of its sponsorships ranked thirtieth in a league of thirty teams. The Sixers' brand was so weak that one sponsor—a small local restaurant—claimed that the team should pay *it* to hang up 76ers signage because the restaurant had the stronger brand. Six years later, the team led the NBA in attendance, season ticket memberships, and growth in TV broadcast viewership, and had achieved a sevenfold increase in the sponsorship base.

Scott has also led the renowned Team Marketing & Business Oper-ations department at the NBA and built an executive team of all-stars (many of whom have since become top leaders in the sports world), and later served as the CEO of Harris Blitzer Sports & Entertainment where he managed twelve teams and properties in the greater Phila-delphia region.

We can increase our impact when we find problems that need to be solved and make ourselves useful to our organization.

THE MENTAL GAME

Doesn't every manager want people who will do what they are asked to do? Aren't dream employees the ones who diligently do their jobs? That may have been true in the past, but today's leaders don't need more dependents, they need extensions—more eyes spotting oppor-tunities, more ears listening for unmet needs, more hands solving problems. When we polled managers about what reduces employees' credibility in their eyes, two of their top responses were "When they just do their job without considering the bigger picture" (the fourth-highest-ranked frustration) and "When they wait for the boss to tell them what to do" (the second-highest-ranked frustration).

Though we often think of bosses as power-hungry dictators, the truth is that most managers dislike having to tell people what to do. We asked the same group of managers what employee behaviors they most appreciate. Their number one response? "When people do things without being asked." See chart below for how to build (or kill) your credibility when dealing with messy problems. The most effective professionals look above their role and go beyond their job to get the real job done. In this section, we will explore how Impact Players do just that.

Building Credibility with Leaders and Stakeholders

CREDIBILITY KILLERS	Waiting for managers to tell you what to do
	Ignoring the bigger picture
	Telling your manager that it's not your job
CREDIBILITY BUILDERS	Doing things without being asked
	Anticipating problems and having a plan

See appendix A for the full ranking.

When we interviewed managers, they consistently described Impact Players as problem solvers. They told us about people who sought out hard problems and solved them all the way from strategy to detail. They said things like, *He solves gnarly problems. He can be pointed at anything. She's the one I turn to when work is difficult. She takes hard projects and crises and turns them around. In his free time, he'll just go out and solve problems.*

These contributors see messy problems as opportunities to serve where they are most needed. Unattended problems make them agitated, like unattended baggage in a crowded airport. They see themselves as first responders—empathetic and skillful heroes who are willing to inconvenience themselves to help others.

An overarching idea seems to govern their work: *I can be of service and solve problems.* This service mentality, which is the hallmark of the Impact Player, is captured delightfully by the slogan the Kaiser Sand & Gravel Company painted on its fleet of cement mixer trucks: FIND A NEED AND FILL IT.

A service mindset alone isn't enough to tackle the messiest problems; other underlying mindsets are also at play. Add to the service mindset a strong sense of agency (*I can act independently and make decisions*) and internal locus of control (*I, not external forces, control the outcome of events in my life*). Now we have a winning formula for dealing with complex, messy problems that require more than a perfunctory response.

People with this service mindset become problem solvers who can take action on their own, shape an outcome, and point themselves toward the problems where they can be of service. The Impact Player understands that *as I work on what's most important, I will be of greatest value.* They view themselves—and are viewed in turn by their peers and managers—not as silent support staff working in servitude but as key players and mutual beneficiaries of the work.

THE HIGH-IMPACT HABITS

Impact Players jump in because they believe they can make a difference. In this section, we'll review three of the habits that most differentiate Impact Players from their colleagues and discuss why these practices create value for their organizations while increasing the Impact Players' influence.

Habit 1: Learn the Game

To be of maximum value inside an organization—to be of service—we first need to know what is valued. We need to know the game being played. How clearly do you understand the skills and capabilities that are most prized in your organization? What are the top priorities?

What warrants attention and care? What's valued by your leaders, customers, and partners?

Understand the Goals

George Martin, the legendary record producer behind the Beatles, said, "Most artists, when they record something, don't listen to the whole thing. . . . When the music is played back, they listen to their part. The producer must sit back, view the whole thing in perspective, and make sense of it."[3] Impact Players think from the perspective of a music producer, not just a solitary musician. The most influential professionals are first thinkers and then doers.

A youth soccer coach once told me that the best players aren't looking at their feet—they have their eyes open, seeing what is happening on the field. If you work in a business, this might entail understanding the business model—what makes the cash register ring. For a nonprofit organization, it could involve knowing the outcomes that attract funding. Whether you work in a company or a public organization, in development or sales, you should have a broad view of what your organization does and a good grasp on how it succeeds. To help you see the big picture, use the questions in Smart Play 1 on page 59.

When you have identified the fundamental problems to solve, you will know how your work connects and see opportunities to help. You will know what to do—but to do it well, you need to know the values of the culture in which you are working.

Know the Rules

Every organization has a distinct culture, a set of values and norms that govern daily behavior and decision making. But as any careful observer of organizations also realizes, the stated culture is rarely the actual culture. Several studies have pointed out the incongruence between what companies state as the organization values and what employees perceive as the real values.[4] This incongruence suggests that employees need to decipher the real culture to be successful. Impact Players are active decoders of the culture; they read the posters on the wall *and* observe the behavior in the hall. They pay less attention to what people say and more attention to what people actually do—like the snickering at the term "fuzzy" I recall from my first day at Oracle. They are observing and asking questions: What types of accomplishments are celebrated? What groups have the most power and why? What's a fast way to get fired? By paying attention to what is valued, they learn how to add value. By adding value, they increase their impact.

The ability to decode and adapt to organizational culture is even more vital than you might think. New studies suggest that cultural adaptability might be the hallmark of the most successful employees. Researchers at Stanford University found that employees who could read and adapt to cultural changes over time were more successful than those who initially had high cultural fit.[5] Though many companies are searching for the right fit (and perhaps overlooking nontraditional candidates), it turns out that being able to decipher the cultural code and read the room may be more important than coming from the right background. In fast-moving environments, the most effective professionals are those who can be dropped into a new setting, decode the unspoken operating rules, and adapt as the game changes, which then can earn them the right to change the rules.

Empathize Upward

In addition to knowing what's important to their organizations, Impact Players know what's important to their leaders—and they make it important to themselves.

Evan Hong works at Target Corporation, the $92 billion US retailer, as a director on the enterprise risk team, the group that forecasts and helps mitigate business risk. What makes Evan so valuable is his ability to see things through other people's eyes. His manager, Aileen Guiney, says, "He pays attention to my learning style and preferences. He asks point-blank questions like 'Are you getting what you need?' It makes me reflect on what I really need and whether or not I am getting it."

Evan doesn't just learn what his boss needs from him; he sees everything on her radar. He asks Aileen about what matters to Matt, the senior vice president to whom she reports: How much time is she spending discussing each item with Matt? How can I help with those issues? "It's really nice to have someone else thinking about all the planes in the air," says Aileen.

When Aileen was preparing for the annual risk management presentation to Target's top executives, Evan helped her prep and gave her all the information she would need. Then he made a big request: Could he attend the meeting? He acknowledged that someone at his level typically wouldn't be included in a meeting with the top company leaders, but he suggested that if he and Aileen copresented, they could facilitate a more holistic discussion by having one of them focus primarily on the downside risks while the other addressed the upside. He didn't push the idea, but he suggested it early enough that she had time to consider it fully.

Aileen saw that copresenting could lead to a better outcome for the business, and she had complete trust in Evan's ability to represent both of them and their work well, so she invited him to join her. He executed his role perfectly; they walked the executive team through the various threats to the business, including the possibility of a recession. They presented various vulnerabilities and safeguards and facilitated a lively discussion. In what might be a first for any corporation, members of the executive team said they were actually looking forward to the next year's risk management meeting. The meeting wasn't just successful on the surface; it took place in 2019 and served as important preparation for the economic fallout triggered by the COVID-19 global pandemic.

Evan didn't just do his job; he made a point of understanding his boss's job, her boss's job, and the fundamental job to be done—all to ensure the corporation was risk ready.

Impact Players learn what their leaders need and are great practitioners of what I call *upward empathy*—the tendency to look up at managers and see not only a demanding boss but that boss's challenges, constraints, and best intentions. Upward empathy is looking beyond what frustrates you about your boss to appreciate what frustrates your boss, especially if the frustration is you. Upward empathy can be enhanced through *perspective taking*—the ability to take someone else's viewpoint into account.[6]

Perspective taking is much like its close cousin empathy but is practiced more from the head than the heart. It's the conceptual exercise of getting up from our seat at the table and seeing what the situation looks like from another vantage point. For example, as a junior consultant on a project team, we may see a string of last-minute requests from our boss. However, from the boss's perspective, we see a difficult client who abruptly changes the scope of the project. Through the eyes of that client, we can see the surprise internal reorganization that created a slew of new dependencies and users.

When we practice perspective taking and upward empathy, we develop a rich understanding of what our leaders and stakeholders see, think, and feel. This awareness can then guide our actions, as illustrated in the following chart.

UPWARD AWARENESS

Perspective taking and upward empathy enable a more focused, valuable contribution

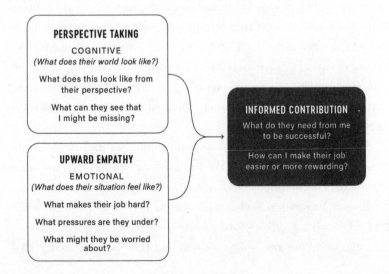

PERSPECTIVE TAKING
COGNITIVE
(What does their world look like?)

What does this look like from their perspective?

What can they see that I might be missing?

UPWARD EMPATHY
EMOTIONAL
(What does their situation feel like?)

What makes their job hard?

What pressures are they under?

What might they be worried about?

INFORMED CONTRIBUTION
What do they need from me to be successful?

How can I make their job easier or more rewarding?

Researchers have shown that perspective taking occurs naturally when we are at the low end of the power scale.[7] The less power and resources we have, the more attuned we become to people and events around us. However, increases in our power decrease our likelihood of trying to understand another's perspective. It's not like riding a bike; it is something we can forget how to do, which explains why senior executives and politicians can so often seem out of touch. It also suggests that as we advance our careers, we need to actively maintain our perspective-taking abilities. There's a reward for those who do; by practicing upward empathy, we open a channel through which senior leaders can better see our aspirations, and we develop a common language to discuss these aspirations in mutually beneficial terms.

See the Agenda

Perspective taking also helps us see the invisible agendas that guide action. Most leaders and organizations have an agenda, a collection of issues or objectives that they care about. Sometimes these agendas are tangible in the form of mission statements, strategic initiatives, or priorities for a particular period. However, in dynamic environments, tactical goals require adjustment as conditions change and new information emerges, which means that the stated agenda is rarely the real agenda. The real agenda is what's important right now, and it defines what is relevant and essential for success. But the real agenda is rarely written down.

In an ideal world, leaders make their agendas clear; they let you know what's important and why, then leave you to figure out how to get it done.[8] But often leaders are moving so fast they don't take time to slow down and brief their teams. Or because their agenda is so clear to them, they mistakenly assume it is clear to others. The corporate world has taught me not to wait for direction to be served to me on a platter. The reality is that contributors at all levels need to figure out the current organizational agenda on their own—a behavior pattern seen in high-impact contributors. The top contributors we studied intuit the real agenda the way a good defender reads the field and anticipates the imminent play; they know where the action will likely be, and they move into position. They figure out what I call the *W.I.N.—What's Important Now.*

Do you know what's important now? Do you understand your organization's top priorities? Would your leaders and colleagues say you "get it," meaning that you can converse easily about the strategy? Most important, do you know what is vital right now? If not, pay attention to what your leaders are spending their time on, what is being talked about, what has momentum, and what is celebrated. That's the agenda. That's the W.I.N.

Habit 2: Play Where They Are Needed

When you know the W.I.N., you can focus your energy on doing the job that needs to be done and playing where you can have the largest impact. When you understand your organization's real agenda, you aren't bound by the artificial constraints and org charts that limit most people. High-impact contributors work with greater fluidity than most, moving easily between strategy and tactical roles and working without borders. Specifically, the tendency to "work outside their official job scope to solve problems or realize opportunities" was one of the top three differences between high-impact and typical contributors. This practice was among the behaviors exhibited least often by both typical and under-contributors. In other words, it's a difference maker between Impact Players and their colleagues.

While Contributors play their position, Impact Players play where they are needed. They work in the interstitial space, where big, messy problems don't fall into any one person's job boundaries, strategic initiatives get stuck, and unmet needs go unanswered and eventually go elsewhere. For these top contributors, job descriptions are starting points—less like park boundaries that restrict their movement and more like base camps that enable them to respond quickly.

Chasing Down a Problem

In 2015, Unilever, the British-Dutch consumer package goods company, was preparing to release a new body wash in the Caress product line (known as Lux outside the United States). The marketing team had been eager to claim that the product provided twelve-hour fragrance, and the body wash contained an innovative new technology that made it possible: tiny beads that would release fragrance throughout the day.

Production had started at various locations throughout Asia, and the regional business units had raised their revenue forecast. The marketing team was preparing the product launch, targeting several important markets, including Indonesia, where the product would also be manufactured.

Nine months before launch date, the supply chain team raised a red flag: there would be significant delays due to unavailable parts and complex logistics. They warned that the product launch would be delayed by one or two quarters. Staffers did risk analyses, and the senior leaders met to discuss the sizable revenue impact. Even though the leadership team wanted to get the innovation to market, everyone assumed that the delay was unavoidable.

Sabine Khairallah, the brand manager for Caress/Lux, saw it differently. She said, "I was responsible for things like portfolio and brand strategy, PR, and lead management. I certainly wasn't expected to build the product, but I couldn't take a product to market if I didn't actually have a product." The five-foot-eleven Lebanese former collegiate basketball player had been raised in the United Arab Emirates by a mother who had taught her to be strong and a father who had instilled the idea that she should always be her own boss. Sabine carried that mentality into the workplace, working as if there wasn't anything she couldn't or shouldn't do. She understood the importance of this product innovation, so she chased down the problem.

Sabine phoned the supply chain manager, a quiet, behind-the-scenes player in Indonesia, jokingly introduced herself as his new best friend, and began asking questions. As he broke down the supply chain into pieces, the first problem became clear: the bottle caps were made in Thailand, but the bottles were made in Indonesia. And those caps were stuck in customs at the Indonesian border awaiting some missing details on the paperwork. Sabine and the supply chain manager worked through each item on the invoice, pulling in others who had the missing information, and within fourteen days, they got the bottle caps through customs and flowing from Thailand to Indonesia.

The manufacturing line resumed, but there were still more delays. At each step, Sabine asked, "What's the next thing holding up the supply chain?" The product required novel supplies, different packaging, and temperature-controlled transit, to name a few. One by one they worked through the list, resolving each of the issues.

Within three weeks, they had reduced the six-month delay to just one month, launching the product in time to realize almost all of the originally forecasted revenue (approximately $5 million in Indonesia alone) and establishing Unilever's market position as the leader in product innovation. Sabine could have easily left the supply chain problems to the supply chain team, but she went beyond her position.

When a pressing problem gets complicated, do you play your position, assuming that someone else will handle it? Or do you chase the problem down? Your impact increases as you shift your orientation from position holder to problem solver.

In the world of work, Contributors are like the plastic soccer players on a foosball table—well spaced but locked into position along the rod. They can spin but easily miss the action. In sharp contrast, Impact Players operate more like the best live-action midfielders, who watch for developing action and then shift up- or downfield to play where they are most needed. They don't leave their post; they play their position but expand their range.

Consider how Theo Ta, a presales consultant for SAP in Vancouver, Canada, provided extraordinary value to his team. An enterprise software company such as SAP has so many products that demos for prospective clients can sometimes require dozens of product specialists, which can overwhelm the client. Theo's manager, Mike Duddy, said, "Some presales consultants get comfortable in their particular product silo, but Theo learns enough about other areas that he can field the first conversation with the client and then bring in other consultants if the client wants to go deeper. He's like a good goalkeeper. He plays outside his box, just enough."

Get onto the Agenda

Working on the agenda should feel different than merely doing your job, much as driving on a freeway feels different than driving on rutted back roads. For starters, it's more intense; things move fast, and there's added pressure to perform. But with the added intensity comes greater efficiency; you can go farther and get there faster and with greater ease. When you are working on what's most important, stakeholders find time to meet with you and senior leaders provide needed resources, find funding, and clear obstacles from your path. The stakes are higher, but the barriers are lower. And perhaps the greatest reward for getting onto the agenda is that work is simply more joyful.

Impact Player Pro Tip

As a general rule, if you aren't working on your boss's top three priorities, you are not working on the agenda.

Consider the change for Josh,[9] a manager of music teams for a large multicampus church. After one of our webinars, he realized that despite his earnest work, he wasn't on his leader's agenda. He now understood why his weekly emails to the senior pastor weren't getting a response. He revamped his emails to the senior pastor, letting him know two things: (1) what he understood to be the most important work, and (2) how he was working in line with what was most important. He reported, "In the past, my emails seemed to disappear into a black hole. For the first time, I am actually getting email responses, encouragement, and gratitude. It's kind of a big deal!" Now imagine the pastor's reaction as he received confirmation that his vision for the church has been heard and internalized.

ARE YOU WORKING ON THE AGENDA?

Signs you are on the agenda:

People have time for you, calendars open up, and meetings get scheduled quickly.

Resources become available. Funds typically flow to the most important work.

Work gets easier. As support for the work increases, progress comes faster and more efficiently.

There's more pressure. Because the work matters, expect to feel more weight on your shoulders and greater pressure to perform.

There's more visibility. When your sights are set on what's important, all eyes are on you.

Signs you are off the agenda:

No time. Meetings are hard to schedule. You hurry up and then wait because people don't have time to meet with you. One-on-ones with your boss are often canceled.

No response. You send emails but don't receive replies.

No feedback. When you ask people to review your documents, you get little feedback or receive a cursory response such as "Looks good."

Stalls and delays. Initiatives get stalled and then scrapped. Or progress comes so slowly that the needs change before the work is complete.

Not on the boss's short list. Your boss isn't asking you about your work.

Habit 3: Play with Passion

Impact Players work with a sense of purpose and conviction, but they work in service of the organization's unmet needs rather than their personal interests. Managers rarely described them as being passionate about a topic (e.g., "He's passionate about artificial intelligence") but often described them as being passionate about the work itself (e.g., "He's passionate about solving problems"). Their energy is channeled into how they go about their work rather than into the type of work they do. Impact Players work *with* passion, not *on* their personal passion. Consider how working with this orientation helped Mike Maughan play bigger.

It was 2002 when Ryan Smith got the call: his father had throat cancer. Ryan was a college student and intern with Hewlett-Packard in California, and his father, Scott Smith, was a university professor in Utah. Ryan left his internship, went home, and dropped out of college to be with his dad. They needed a good father-son project as a way to spend their time together, but instead of working on a car, they started a software company. In between Scott's chemotherapy treatments, they built a software tool to power online research. As Scott's health improved, they vowed they would help others get better too: if the company ever made any money, defeating cancer would be their cause. That father-son project grew to become Qualtrics, the enterprise experience management company purchased by SAP in 2019 for $8 billion and taken independent in a public offering in 2021.

Mike Maughan joined the company in 2013 as a product marketing manager, and by 2016 he was the head of brand growth and global communications. By then Qualtrics had a strong relationship with the Huntsman Cancer Institute and was making annual donations in the hundreds of thousands of dollars. At the same time, the ice bucket challenge was sweeping the country, raising money for ALS research. Mike wondered: *Could Qualtrics do more than simply donate to cancer research? Could it become a catalyst to get thousands of people involved in the fight?* He saw it as a huge opportunity to help Qualtrics take their fight against cancer to a bigger arena.

For Mike, cancer wasn't personal and had never been his cause. A graduate of Harvard's Kennedy School of Government, he had been engaged in development initiatives in sub-Saharan Africa. Global development was his thing. But he had read an article in *Harvard Busi-*

ness Review several years earlier that suggested that to be happiest, don't follow your passion, go solve big problems.[10] He realized fighting cancer was an area where he could make a more significant contribution. He reflected on the decision point, "I could either do what I wanted on a small scale, or I could help steer an entire organization to do something really big. I realized my goal was less to follow my own passion and more to solve the biggest problem." He chose to lead a larger fight.

There was no budget and no staff, but Mike enlisted the help of the creative team and other colleagues to devise a campaign called "5 for the Fight," and garnered the support of Ryan Smith. Here's how it worked: People were invited to electronically donate five dollars to cancer research. They then wrote the name of a loved one affected by cancer on the palm of their hand and shared a photo on social media, tagging five friends and inviting them to do the same; five dollars, five fingers, and five more people for the fight. The campaign was launched in February 2016 at the X4 Experience Management Summit, and raised over $1 million in its first year.

A year later Qualtrics was approached by the state's NBA team, the Utah Jazz, to see if Qualtrics was interested in sponsoring a patch on the players' jerseys. Mike got another idea: Instead of putting "Qualtrics" on the patch, could the company sponsor a 5 for the Fight patch? The NBA was surprised, but not nearly as surprised as Ryan Smith, who knew Qualtrics was at a critical junction and the company needed brand recognition to achieve its growth goals. The sponsorship involved no small sum of money and was no easy decision to make. Ryan pressed Mike, repeatedly asking "Are you really sure?" Mike knew it not only would drive fundraising for cancer research but would be good for the Qualtrics brand and business. He also knew that the idea of being "all in" was a core value for the company and one that had deep meaning for Ryan personally. Mike pushed back, asking "Are you 'all in' on cancer research?" Ryan was, and on Monday, February 13, 2017, he stood with the then owner of the Utah Jazz, Gail Miller, as they announced the partnership and the patch, which, in the history of North American professional sports, was the first jersey sponsorship used for a cause instead of a corporation. The patch was so novel and inspiring that it received fourteen times more press coverage than any other NBA jersey patch.[11]

In the last three years, 5 for the Fight has raised more than $25 million. It now partners with leading cancer research centers across the United States, Europe, the Middle East, Asia, and Australia to fund some of the most groundbreaking cancer research being done today.

Mike laughed when I asked if that work had been outside of his job boundaries but quickly added, "I've never had job boundaries—at least not in my mind." But because he understood what was important, both to the business and to his boss, he could spot the high-impact play. Ryan Smith said, "It's one thing to be 'in the room where it happens,' but the thing about Mike is that he makes it happen no matter what room he's in." No one told Mike to venture into the world of social responsibility; it's just the way he works. As he put it, "I am always keeping my eyes open to things that no one has told me to do but that may need to be done."

Mike could have pursued a direct path to his passion. Instead, he worked wholeheartedly where he could be most useful. By playing with passion, he found a bigger opportunity and made a bigger impact.

Impact Players understand that their purpose is best discovered over time and with an outward orientation, not in endless self-reflection. The management theorist Tom Peters said, "Purpose rarely comes from sitting down and contemplating purpose. Mostly, surely in my case, one accidentally trips over purpose."[12] It's not built in a lab; it develops as a natural by-product of working with thoughtful observation: looking up, noticing what's happening around you, and identifying where you can be of greatest use. Purpose transpires as we follow the most important needs and serve them with full conviction.

The most influential professionals understand that allowing their circumstances to direct their work enables them to build credibility and deepen their impact. They also don't chase after any and every need; rather, they look for a match between a real need and their own deepest capabilities—a concept I call *native genius*, which we will explore further in chapter 6. When people use their greatest strengths in service to something larger than themselves, there's usually an extra spark of brilliance where everyone benefits. Are we working in service to something important, or are we simply doing our own thing?

In the next section, we will explore how well-intended career plans or professional interests prevent us from being truly impactful. We'll consider two decoys: the first is the downside of doing our duty, and the second is the shortsightedness of merely following our passion.

THE DECOYS AND DISTRACTIONS

Whereas Impact Players operate as problem solvers who serve where they are needed, the typical contributors we studied operated more like job holders, serving where they are appointed. They played their position, they performed well, and they stayed in their lanes. Like Impact Players, they saw themselves as part of a larger mission, but they tended to take a narrower view of their role, filtering out aspects that matter to others so that they see and act only on the parts that affect their own world. A manager at Adobe said of a typical contributor, "She's a prolific doer but a narrow thinker."

Managers frequently described their typical Contributors as diligent; they did the work they were given, much as a student works through a course syllabus, completing the assigned homework. They worked with a sense of duty; they had a job, that job had a purpose, and they worked to fulfill their purpose. The logic appears sound, even noble. But herein lies the problem. Meet our first decoy: Call to duty.

Call to Duty

In this mode, we are intent on doing our duty; we play by the rules and act with diligence. But we can be playing by the old hierarchical rules, where employees were given command of a post or assigned to positions on an org chart. The contributors I saw working in this mode may have been working with a sense of purpose and pride and doing a fine job, but their downfall was assuming their position—the job they held—was the source of their value.

When we overfixate on job descriptions, we see complicated problems as distractions. Unplanned projects and out-of-scope work are productivity threats and should be avoided. But for senior leaders, these "detours" actually are the job. Staying competitive in a constantly changing game requires agility and adaptation. While the Contributors saw themselves as doing their jobs, their leaders saw them overlooking problems and underreacting to opportunities.

Professionals operating with a Contributor Mindset risk missing the real agenda and straying off course—or worse, doing their own thing and dropping off the radar entirely. A NASA manager said of one engineer, "He did his job and delivered on his commitments, but his work needed so much more work to be mission ready. I really could only give him cookie-cutter projects." A VP at Target said about one of his smartest analysts, "He did the work that was in his wheelhouse. He did data pulls and ran reports but didn't think innovatively or engage with the problems that were important to Target. It was like he was shooting at the wrong goal."

When dealing with messy problems, call to duty isn't the only counterfeit at play. There's another decoy, a misinterpretation of one of the new rules of work.

Pursuit of Passion

Following your passion is another easy trap to fall into. Haven't we all heard the adage "Do what you love, and you'll never work a day in your life" or Steve Jobs's famous Stanford University commencement advice that "the only way to do great work is to love what you do"?[13] Furthermore, many newer members of the workforce have been raised on this advice.[14] The notion of following one's passion makes for compelling commencement speeches and is certainly a sound strategy in choosing a career, selecting the right company to work for, or starting one of your own. But once you're inside an organization, if left unchecked, following your passion can do more damage than good. What if your colleagues don't share or care about your passion? While you are playing your heart out, you may actually sound tone deaf. Consider the leader's perspective. While most leaders enjoy helping people pursue their passions, it's frustrating, if not painful, to watch someone cherry-pick interesting work and enthusiastically chase their pet projects rather than the priorities of the organization.

This pursuit of one's personal interests can actually come at a real cost to the contributor. Consider Andrew, who graduated from a top university and took his first job at a leadership development company to pursue his passion for leadership and learning. A philosophy major, he was a deep thinker and voraciously read everything he could about the company's programs. He could talk intelligently about the learning outcomes and design of each program, but when it came to making sales calls, well, that just wasn't his thing. His manager sat him down, re-explained his job responsibilities, and issued a warning: fill the seats or get fired. Though learning was his passion, he needed to become passionate about selling, or at least enthusiastic enough to keep his job. He wanted to get his career off to a good start, so he took out a stack of sticky notes, wrote "D.G.F." on a dozen of them, and then posted them throughout his cubicle. He didn't tell any of his colleagues what it meant, but Andrew knew that "D.G.F." stood for "Don't Get Fired!" He started making one hundred sales calls each day and became the top salesperson on his team. He learned to love what he needed to do rather than just do what he loved—and fortunately, he Didn't Get Fired. In fact, his stellar sales performance earned him a promotion into a role that better fit his interests and led him to a fulfilling career in leadership development. But Andrew's real fortune was having a manager early in his career who helped him see that he was following his passion straight down a dead end.

MULTIPLYING YOUR IMPACT

These decoys create a mirage of value much like an optical illusion, where the viewer is so focused on the image in black that they don't recognize the image in the negative space. We can become so fixated on doing our duty or following our passion that we miss the more valuable contribution that occurs in the white space of the organization and the cracks between jobs. Blinded by our diligence, we don't understand why we are passed over for opportunities or sidelined from the real action.

Meanwhile, Impact Players are taking a very different approach to their work, generating a chain reaction that creates value for their leaders, their organizations, and themselves, summarized below.

VALUE BUILDING: DO THE JOB THAT'S NEEDED

Impact Players work where they are most needed and get seen as utility players

Because Impact Players look for unmet needs and work where they are most useful, they are seen by their stakeholders as partners and across the organization as utility players, which explains why they are brought in on the biggest opportunities. They don't need to say, "Put me in, Coach." They are the first to be put into the game, especially when things get tough.

Let me return to my experience at Oracle. Roughly ten years had passed since I had taken Bob Shaver's advice and decided to make myself useful. I was now working as the global head of human resource development and leading sundry strategic initiatives for the company. It was exciting work, mostly acquired by saying yes to messy problems and working well with the senior executives.

One afternoon Jane, a colleague of mine from Human Resources, stopped by my office and told me she needed help securing executive buy-in for an initiative she was leading. She asked if she could buy me lunch sometime, preferably soon. Naturally, I agreed.

When we met for lunch, Jane explained the recruiting goals she had for the company and told me she needed the executives to make those goals a high priority for themselves and the company; basically, she wanted to get the goals onto the executive agenda. She then asked for my guidance.

I listened, thought for a moment, and then confessed, "I don't think I can be of much help. I don't actually know how to do this." Jane was confused. She responded, "Of course you do. You are a master at this. You know the executives well and have their ear." I explained that I had never really put anything important to me onto their agenda. What I had done was to find out what was important to them and then put that onto *my* agenda. By being the "how" to their "what," my work was valued. I further explained: if it looks like I was the one setting the agenda, it was only because I'd made a habit of working on what was important to my stakeholders; and over time, I had built influence and had probably earned the right to help shape the company agenda.

That wasn't what Jane wanted to hear, but it was the insight she needed to increase the visibility and impact of her work. We talked through the executives' priorities and problems, and as we finished lunch, we brainstormed how her work could be a solution to their problems.

There have been times when I've drifted off this strategy. There have been times when I didn't notice that the agenda had changed or I became consumed with a pet passion. But I've always had my greatest impact—and the most fun—when I was working on what was most important to the organization and making myself useful.

If you want your work to have impact, figure out the agenda and work on it. When you let go of your own agenda, you can be summoned to a higher agenda. There, you can create greater value and find greater joy.

THE PLAYBOOK

This playbook is for anyone who wants to increase the impact of their work and implement the mindsets and practices necessary to DO THE JOB THAT'S NEEDED. It contains Smart Plays—concrete practices and exercises to help you develop the habits of Impact Players. It also includes Safety Tips to help you experiment with new behavior without doing damage to your effectiveness, reputation, or relationships.

Smart Plays

1. **Find the double W.I.N.** A quick way to get onto the agenda is to look for a double W.I.N. (What's Important Now)—something important to the organization that's also important to your immediate boss (or stakeholder).

2. **Get in on the W.I.N.** Once you've established a double win, look for an opportunity to contribute where your capabilities overlap with the W.I.N. Maximize your impact by identifying a W.I.N. that is one of your stakeholder's top three priorities.

3. **Talk up the agenda.** Make the connection between your stakeholder's agenda and the work you are doing right now. Let them know that you are the *how* to their *what*. Craft a short statement that captures how your work will help them achieve the priorities on their

ORGANIZATION   LEADER

What's Important to the ORGANIZATION — Double W.I.N. — What's Important to Your LEADERSHIP

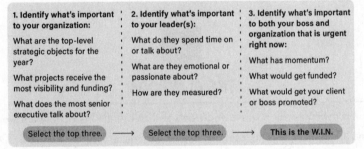

1. Identify what's important to your organization:

What are the top-level strategic objects for the year?

What projects receive the most visibility and funding?

What does the most senior executive talk about?

2. Identify what's important to your leader(s):

What do they spend time on or talk about?

What are they emotional or passionate about?

How are they measured?

3. Identify what's important to both your boss and organization that is urgent right now:

What has momentum?

What would get funded?

What would get your client or boss promoted?

Select the top three. ⟶ Select the top three. ⟶ This is the W.I.N.

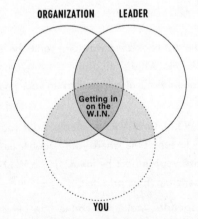

ORGANIZATION   LEADER

Getting in on the W.I.N.

YOU

What is one of your stakeholder's top 3 priorities to which you can make a material contribution?

How does your work help solve this problem or accomplish this objective?

agenda. For example, "I'm aware that increasing customer retention is our top priority, and I'm creating profiles of our various customer types so we can better understand their requirements." A great statement will communicate two messages: (1) "I get you," meaning "I understand what is important to you," and (2) "I've got you covered," meaning "I am making this happen." Begin your interactions, such as emails, presentations, and one-on-one meetings, with one of these statements so your stakeholders know that what is important to them is important to you.

4. **Practice "the naive yes."** Dealing with messy problems often requires working outside our comfort zone and beyond our current capabilities. Being underqualified can feel intimidating or overwhelming, and it is easy to say no to the added uncertainty and just do your current job. Try practicing "the naive yes" by agreeing to a new challenge before your brain kicks in and tells you it's not possible, or as Richard Branson said, "If somebody offers you an amazing opportunity but you are not sure you can do it, say yes—then learn how to do it later!" Once you've said yes, learn quickly by admitting what you don't know and asking intelligent, informed questions. Project the image of "intelligent learner"—someone with high self-confidence but low situational confidence. This lets your stakeholders know that you are in rookie mode but are capable of learning quickly.

Safety Tips

1. **Take out a permit.** While venturing out to address messy problems, you don't want to be forgotten by others. And if something goes awry, you want people to know where you are and why you left your post. Like a hiker who checks in with the authorities and indicates their destination before venturing into dangerous backcountry alone, you should obtain a permit. Agree with your manager about (1) where you are headed and why and (2) what parts of your core job you need to continue to do well.

2. **Stay connected and drop pins.** A leader's agenda can change as quickly as backcountry weather. When working in the white space be-

tween formal organizations, check in frequently with your team and your boss. Once you venture out, occasionally "drop a pin," much like a hiker using a satellite tracker to alert others to their current position. Don't just update others on your work; find out how their priorities are shifting so you can stay on the agenda.

3. **Maintain some distance.** Having empathy for one's leaders and staying aligned with the priorities of the organization are sound practices. However, taken to their extreme, such practices can lead to blind followership and become extremely dangerous. History is replete with examples of faithful followers who failed to question unethical orders and crimes committed by victims who sympathized with their captors.[15] As you serve, be mindful to maintain the psychological distance and independent thought needed to question the wisdom and ethics of any directive. In addition to the other ethics criteria, you might ask yourself: "Will I regret doing this when I'm no longer working for this person or organization?"

Coaching tips for managers: You can find coaching practices to help your team members do the job that's needed in "The Coach's Playbook" at the end of chapter 8.

CHAPTER 2 SUMMARY: MAKE YOURSELF USEFUL

This chapter describes how Impact Players deal with messy problems
and why they so readily venture out of their defined roles to address
real needs and strategic priorities.

	CONTRIBUTOR MINDSET	IMPACT PLAYER MINDSET
Practice	Do their job	Do the job that's needed
Assumptions	I'm here to do a specific job (*duty*)	I can be of service and solve problems (*service*)
		I can act independently and make decisions (*agency*)
		I can control the outcomes of events in my life (*internal locus of control*)
Habits	Take a narrow view	Learn the game
	Play their position	Play where they are needed
		Play with passion
Implications	Individuals get sidelined from the real action. Organizations are unable to solve the messy problems that lurk in the white space between departments or jobs.	Individuals build reputations as utility players who are flexible and can be utilized in a variety of roles. Increases organizational responsiveness and creates a culture of agility and service.

Decoys to avoid: (1) Call to duty, (2) Pursuit of passion

WHAT LEADERS SAY ABOUT . . .

CONTRIBUTORS	⋛ IMPACT PLAYERS ⋛
"He waits to be asked instead of knowing what to do and just doing it."	"You don't need to ask him to do something, he just starts it."
"If I ask him to do a project, he'll want to know what's in it for him."	"She gives credit to others and doesn't need to claim [all] the success."
"He's focused on not rocking the boat and keeping things going. He seemed to assume the most important thing was to not screw things up."	"She makes everything better."

Chapter 3

STEP UP, STEP BACK

I always wondered why somebody doesn't do something
about that. Then I realized I was somebody.
—LILY TOMLIN

To the world, it was the Northern Ireland Conflict; to the people of
Belfast, it was simply the Troubles. Centuries-old political tensions
exploded into a three-decades-long violent struggle between Protestant
unionists, who were loyal to the United Kingdom, and Catholic na-
tionalists, who sought to exit the United Kingdom and form a united
Ireland. The conflict was a low-grade street war of bullets and bombs
exchanged between paramilitaries and state security forces, with
civilians caught in the cross fire. Marches and demonstrations in
the late 1960s had led to riots and attacks in the early 1970s; the
violence peaked in 1972, after the events of Bloody Sunday, January
30, sparked approximately 1,300 bombings that killed nearly 500 people, many of them civilians.[1] By the late 1970s, both sides were war
weary, with no end in sight.

Like far too many Belfast residents, Betty Williams, a thirty-
three-year-old mother of two, had lost relatives to the conflict. Raised
by a Protestant father and a Catholic mother, she had grown up with
a strong sense of tolerance and years earlier had joined an antiviolence
campaign headed by a Protestant priest. She had spoken often of the
conflict at home, especially with other women, but didn't dare speak
out in public.[2] She was deeply concerned but a bystander in the conflict.

That changed on August 10, 1976, when Williams was drawn out of her private world and into the public fight for peace. She was driving home from her job as an office receptionist when she turned the corner to her home and witnessed a car careening out of control. The driver was a member of the Provisional Irish Republican Army who had been transporting weapons when he was shot and killed by a British soldier. The speeding car veered onto the sidewalk, crushing three children. Horrified, Williams stopped to help. Two of the children, an eight-year-old girl and an infant boy, were killed instantly. The next day the two-year-old died of his injuries in the hospital.[3] The mother, severely injured, eventually took her own life.[4]

There had been other tragic deaths, but that one enraged Williams. She had to speak out. She immediately began circulating petitions in Protestant neighborhoods calling for an end to sectarian violence. She then organized two hundred women to march through the neighborhood of the slain children, where she met Mairéad Corrigan, the children's aunt. They joined forces, and within days they had gathered six thousand signatures and led a march of some ten thousand women—both Catholic and Protestant—to the children's graves. They faced opposition but, as Williams said, "We just walked right through all the stones and all the bottles. We have won a major victory."[5] That march, along with their next march of twenty thousand people across Belfast, garnered widespread media attention. The two women established Women for Peace, a grassroots organization committed to a peaceful resolution of the Troubles in Northern Ireland, and then later changed the name to the Peace People after the Belfast journalist Ciaran Mc-Keown joined its leadership ranks. The movement they led is credited with having greatly reduced the violence in subsequent years.[6]

A year later, Williams, still working as an office receptionist, and Corrigan were awarded the 1976 Nobel Peace Prize. The *New York Times* reported, "In the space of four weeks, weeks that have stood their lives on edge, these two Belfast women have created more optimism and hope than anyone has seen in this dismal province in years."[7]

Williams stepped down from her leadership role in the Community of Peace People (passing the role to Corrigan) but continued her lifelong commitment to fighting for peace and the protection of children. The Troubles persisted for another twenty years, ending with the Good Friday Agreement of 1998.

Betty Williams was an ordinary citizen: an office worker, a wife, a mother. She alone had no power to end the violent conflict. But she could make the situation better, and she was willing to try. She didn't wait to be asked or appointed; she simply took the lead.

When you see a better way, do you step up or remain a spectator? People who make a big impact step up and lead.

In this chapter, you'll see that the most impactful professionals aren't just loyal followers; they are ready leaders—the adaptive breed who are willing to step up and lead but who can also step back and follow others. Their lissome approach to leadership helps organizations strengthen initiative taking in the culture. Whereas the last chapter was about stepping out of the comfort of one's job, this chapter is about stepping up.

We will explore the "art of the start": how to initiate change and break free from the ever-present pull of the status quo. We will talk about how you can increase your influence and power, not to control but to spark good outcomes. You'll learn how to lead like a boss when you aren't actually the boss, how to cede leadership to others, and how to get invited to the best parties (okay, meetings).

You'll learn how to recognize a leadership vacuum and provide valuable leadership when the next steps are unclear. You'll be prepared for situations that require volunteers rather than bystanders and stewards rather than permanent owners.

THE CHOICE:
LET IT BE OR STEP UP AND TAKE THE LEAD?

In the last chapter, we explored how Impact Players deal with big, messy problems—challenging situations that attract attention, such as a grocery store loudspeaker announcing "Cleanup needed on aisle eight!" There's another type of problem that might be more vexing. I call them ambient problems. They're the nonglaring, low-grade issues where the status quo is suboptimal but tolerable, such as a clunky business process that everyone complains about but isn't broken enough to fix. Some of these perpetual problems manifest themselves as organizational drag, a collection of institutional factors that interfere with productivity yet somehow go unaddressed, costing the US economy more than $3 trillion each year[8] and reducing productivity by 25 percent.[9]

Most people learn to live with these problems, but ambient problems erode performance over time. They are particularly damaging because they are easy to ignore. It's the leaky faucet that you know is wasting water but you stop seeing because you've walked past the problem so many times, or the creaking door, a mild frustration that you eventually stop hearing. These problems become white noise in the organization. Left unattended, they become institutionalized, as people begin to accept them as inevitable or intractable, like low-grade sectarian unrest in a community or something as mundane as a slow response time on customer service requests.

That is, until someone takes notice and decides that the organization can, and should, do better.

But even when everyone agrees that something should be done, it's hard to know where to start. When everyone's aware of the problem but no one's in charge, there is a leadership vacuum—a space devoid of direction or control that sucks up time and productivity. Solutions to ambient problems tend to involve many players, but getting the necessary collaborations started can be as awkward as preteens at a middle school dance. Someone is needed to step up and get things going, but who? If you look high enough in the organization, you'll likely find a leader who could take charge, but senior leaders can't be everywhere.

Solving ambient problems requires leaders at all levels. But taking charge without being appointed has consequences. When you step up to lead, you can step on toes; your well-meaning initiative can look like a nefarious land grab to someone else; advocating for change can ruffle feathers. Recognizing that something must be done creates a choice point: Do you settle for good enough or step up and make it better? Do you let it be or step up and lead?

SIGNS OF AMBIENT PROBLEMS

How to identify the low-grade problems that erode productivity:

1. **No owner.** Like a stray dog, everyone knows it but no one knows who owns it.

2. **Recreational complaining.** People vent but don't expect a resolution.

3. **Hacks and workarounds.** It's easier to work around the problem than to fix it permanently.

4. **No documentation.** Workarounds get shared but aren't written in any training manual.

5. **Hidden costs.** The problem doesn't seem expensive until the costs of the individual workarounds are aggregated.

6. **Selectively seen.** Problems are visible to those who are most affected but unseen by those who have the power to address the issue.

The way managers described what typical team members do in these circumstances illustrated how easy it is to wait for direction when we encounter performance gaps and leadership vacuums. For example:

> "He doesn't proactively look for problems. He only fixes problems given to him."
>
> "She does her job well, but when I ask her if she has any suggestions or ideas, there's no creative thinking or identification of things that could be improved. There's no initiative."
>
> "She does what I want rather than what she thinks we should

do. She'll tell our vendors, 'Here's what my boss wants.' It's like she is carrying out my wishes."

When roles are unclear, people operating with a Contributor Mindset look to their leaders for direction. They are loyal followers and supporters who carry out requests from their managers and collaborate with colleagues. Though they provide a certain degree of comfort to their bosses, they don't make waves and don't bring about needed change. When they spot problems, they are concerned, but without a clear remit from above, they don't act.

In contrast, Impact Players take charge of situations that lack leadership. When they see an opportunity for improvement, they don't wait for permission to act. They step up, volunteering to lead long before higher-ups in the organization ask them to do so. They are disruptors of the status quo who choose to lead rather than let things be. They offer a higher value proposition; instead of just carrying out the boss's direction, they can also rally others.

As we searched for examples of this type of leadership—collaborative leaders who arise from the middle—we found numerous examples at Target, the US retail giant that, in 2015, embarked on a massive transformation. Its goal: to create a seamless shopping experience for guests across all channels—in stores, online, and via mobile. Successful execution of the transformation would require radical changes to the company's business practices, and teams were established in each organization to effect those changes. By 2019, Target's stock price had increased by 75 percent,[10] and the company was ranked eleventh on *Fast Company* magazine's annual list of the world's fifty most innovative companies.[11] In this chapter, we'll take a deep dive into the emergent, collaborative leadership style we saw at Target. We'll begin with Paul Forgey, a former military intelligence officer turned supply chain director.

Paul was the leader of one of the transformation teams inside the supply chain organization. He is the senior director responsible for the

Reverse Logistics Operations, a process by which Target moves products out of the company, for example back to suppliers or off to liquidators or recyclers. Paul is a nineteen-year veteran of Target who has held numerous operational and logistics roles across the company. He's also a veteran of the US Army—he graduated from the US Military Academy at West Point and served as an intelligence officer. He has a mind for operational detail, is driven to make things better, and likes to win. His manager, Irene Quarshie, vice president, Global Supply Chain & Logistics, describes him as a difference maker, saying "He doesn't ask for permission. He just takes initiative and knows how to navigate the organization."

Paul and his team were given a mission to examine the customer return process, identify and document problems, and recommend solutions. With his signature attention to detail, he and his team identified a number of friction points for their guests, including the amount of time it took to make a return. Returning an item in a store was easy, but the process for returning an online purchase via mail was clunky and time consuming, with customers waiting up to ten days for their money to be refunded. To make matters worse, the responsibility for the returns process was split across five different functional groups: supply chain, store operations, digital products, digital operations, and guest services. Per its remit, Paul's team outlined the problems and proposed a solution.

Paul's team was not in charge of implementation. It would have been easy to submit its report and call it done, yet Paul felt an obligation to do more. Improving the process wouldn't be easy; he would need to get five separate organizations aligned on the problem and working together on a solution. Complicating this further, each was already working on its own solution, and getting them to abandon their current efforts in favor of a collective approach would be tough. To top it off, Paul had no formal authority.

Paul decided to call a meeting of fifteen managers from a variety of levels across the five departments. That took a month just to schedule. The makeshift crew assembled in one of Target's office towers in downtown Minneapolis, and Paul kicked off the meeting with a vision exercise used by a number of innovative organizations: he handed out a mock press release and asked each person to read it. It began "Today, Target announces sweeping changes to guest returns, focusing on providing a simple, flexible, and interactive experience that allows guests to choose how, where, and when to return or exchange goods." The statement described the problem in detail and outlined the new, transformative solution offering guests more choices and effortless exchanges, whether or not they were in a store. It concluded with quotes from delighted customers and proud Target executives.

At that point, the press release was only fiction, but the vision was bold and attractive and got peoples' attention. It also cast light on the ugly realities of the current situation. Initially, there was some hesitation; some attendees weren't sure why supply chain was leading the effort, and others probably felt they had just been told their babies were ugly. One participant asked, "Why does the supply chain organization care about this?" Paul understood that the guest experience wasn't really the jurisdiction of the supply chain staff, but he calmly responded, "Why shouldn't I? I work for Target, you work for Target, and this is a friction point for our guests." Discussion ensued and concluded with an agreement to work together, forming a cross-functional team of directors to fully define the problem and propose an integrated solution.

The group worked together and emerged two months later with a single view of the problem. With the problem fully illuminated, the solutions became clearer and felt within reach. Within six months and before the next peak retail season, the team had developed a technology solution that reduced processing time from ten days down to just one. For 98.5 percent of mail-in returns, customers were now getting cash back within twenty-four hours—a win for all five organizations and every person on that cross-functional team. Proud but not yet satisfied, the team continued working to reach 99.5 percent. At that point, their faux press release was an unnecessary aspiration—actual customers were saying, "The whole process took less than a minute and is by far the best returns experience I've had, period" and "I was originally scared of mailing returns but Target just made it so easy. Mind blown!" Target COO John Mulligan highlighted the new process in the next earnings call and told Wall Street analysts that they have seen a meaningful improvement in guest satisfaction levels compared with the previous year.

Paul reflected, "When there are unclear roles, you have a choice to make. My choice is to lead." It's certainly not a surprising orientation for someone with a West Point military background. But Paul didn't just take charge and lead with the loudest voice. He convened the right minds, concerted their voices, and created many heroes.

The most impactful players take charge even when they aren't in charge. They show initiative and take responsibility. And when they lead, they lead collaboratively, so others want to play on their team.

THE MENTAL GAME

Managers love a good handoff—that feeling of passing a piece of work to someone who will move it forward and get the job done. Ammar Maraqa, the chief strategy officer at Splunk, described one Impact Player this way: "He's a no-look pass kind of person. I can always throw the ball to him and know he'll not only catch it but run with it and score for the team." Players who are trusted with the ball are those who not only are in position but know what to do next—how to move forward and make a play. They are professionals who step up and do things without being asked. Ammar then described another staff member, who was operationally strong but waited to be asked before taking action: "He couldn't work independently, so I couldn't count on him to catch a ball and drive it."

When managers see one person in need of hand-holding and another ready to take the handoff, whom do they choose? Who gets passed the high-profile assignment? Managers generally don't choose the one waiting to be told what to do (a frustration that ranks second highest among the managers we surveyed and include in the chart below). In many ways, managers dole out the most important work not simply to the most capable but rather to the most willing. Much like in a classroom, the person who is called on is usually the one who raises their hand.

Building Credibility with Leaders and Stakeholders

CREDIBILITY KILLERS	Waiting for managers to tell you what to do
CREDIBILITY BUILDERS	Doing things without being asked
	Figuring it out yourself
	Making your leaders and the team look good

See appendix A for the full ranking.

Joya Lewis grew up in Muncie, Indiana, in a tough neighborhood, in a poor family, and without a lot of support. As a young girl she made her own breakfast, got herself ready for school, and did her homework by herself. At fifteen she had her first job, washing dishes in a sandwich shop. It was hard work, and she had to move fast. But there were times when she wasn't busy and would notice coworkers doing other jobs who were struggling to keep up. So she started clearing tables and sweeping floors until the dishes piled up again. The manager noticed her initiative and gave her a raise. She was delighted but shocked, saying, "Oh, I'm just doing what is right and helping out." At fifteen, the first of several important connections was made: when you take on more responsibility, you make more money.

Joya wanted a better life, so she kept volunteering for the hard jobs and taking care of the responsibilities she was entrusted with. In college, she worked multiple jobs simultaneously but still offered to take the extra shifts no one else wanted. While working at Target in overnight stocking, her colleagues would show relief when the night's shipment was small, saying, "It's a small truck. It can be an easy night." Joya would unload the truck and then offer to do more. Her initiative led to promotions and quickly became a mindset: "If I raise my hand, I will be rewarded."

Joya still works for Target, currently as a store director of a high-revenue store in St. Louis, Missouri. She's now financially secure but is still taking responsibility for the hard jobs and using her influence to give back to her community.

The Impact Players we studied had a stewardship mentality. They had a heartfelt desire to make things better—both for themselves and for others—and a willingness to take responsibility for making things happen. They were people like Betty Williams and Paul Forgey, who were committed to making things in their part of the world better and who took action without being directed. Many people want change; what distinguished these people was that they believed they had the personal power to initiate change. Their fundamental guiding belief is *I can improve this situation*. Once again we see a strong sense of personal agency and the presence of an internal locus of control as drivers. This inclination to fix what is perceived as wrong, change the status quo, and take initiative to solve problems rather than passively accept one's environment is what psychologists refer to as a proactive personality.[12] Impact Players are, as Stephen Covey put it, products of their decisions, not products of their circumstances.

They don't just believe things could or should be better; they take action to make them better. They take charge of teams, lead others, and instigate collective action. As Tony Robbins bluntly said, "Any idiot can point out a problem. . . . A leader is willing to do something about it!"[13] From our interviews with managers, it was clear that Impact Players see themselves as capable of leading, making an impact, and contributing to larger goals. Our survey confirmed these findings. Specifically, 96 percent of high-impact contributors always or often take charge without waiting to be directed, compared to 20 percent of typical contributors. Ninety-one percent of the Impact Players were always or often seen as good leaders; by comparison, 14 percent of typical contributors were seen the same way.

This brings us to another core assumption of the Impact Player

Mindset: *I don't need formal authority to take charge.* While others are stuck in hierarchical, by-command forms of leadership, Impact Players are practicing on-demand leadership. By-command leaders wait to be appointed from above and typically find it difficult to relinquish control when the job is done. On-demand leaders rise up when the situation summons them. They take ownership, but they think and act more like temporary caretakers than permanent owners. They are willing to take the lead, but they don't hold on to power longer than is needed to solve a problem.

In order to understand the role and impact these stellar professionals have on their teammates, we can look to playmakers in association football (soccer in the United States). Playmakers make important passes and put themselves and others into position to score and win. They control the flow of the team's offensive play and use their vision, creativity, and ball handling to orchestrate critical passing moves.[14] These instrumental athletes can operate from a variety of positions on the field. Marta Vieira da Silva, the prolific Brazilian scorer known for her quick feet and ability to play off of her teammates, plays in a forward attacking position. Midfield winger David Beckham would find teammates making runs and deliver the ball with his signature long, curved, killer passes. Like da Silva and Beckham, playmakers often serve as team captains. But from any position, they make plays happen and are a thrill to watch and a joy to play with.

Both on the field and in the workplace, playmakers lead in bursts. Sparked by an opportunity for improvement and fueled by a belief that they can make a difference, they take charge of the field and make critical plays.

It's a belief system that propels them to take responsibility. The Impact Player Mindset is the pathway to leadership because, after all, isn't the very essence of leadership the desire to make something better and a willingness to do something about it?

THE HIGH-IMPACT HABITS

The Impact Players we studied step up when it's unclear who's in charge. Some, such as Betty Williams, witness a need and are moved to make a difference; they volunteer to lead, prompted by circumstance. Some are volun-told, called upon by managers who identify a leadership vacuum and turn it over to them, trusting their ability and proclivity to fill it. Some rise up from that middle ground; a senior leader points out a problem, and the individual offers their leadership before being asked. Regardless of the impetus that propels them forward, Impact Players follow a distinct pattern as they step up and lead, bring others along, and, at the right time, step back.

Impact Player Pro Tip

Your peers will be more likely to get behind your efforts to lead if they know it's temporary. Show them that you will step back once the work is done and are willing to follow them when they are leading.

Habit 1: Step Up

That was the case for Joya Lewis, then in her seventh year at Target. She was working as a human resource business partner covering a thirteen-store district in the greater St. Louis area. One of the high-traffic stores in St. Louis was operating without a store manager (because its manager had been transferred) and was now struggling to keep the shelves stocked. Products were arriving nightly, but the team wasn't getting the boxes unpacked and onto shelves, which meant that customers were arriving to empty shelves while the products sat in the store's backroom. Jamaal Edwards, the district team leader at the time, was understandably concerned.

Joya was in regular contact with Jamaal and was aware of the situation. She knew that getting inventory from truck to shelf was the foundation of every store's operation and that the team needed to find a way to finish unloading the trucks each night. She had also built solid relationships with the department managers and had their trust. Jamaal never asked Joya to step in, but she knew that the issue needed to be resolved, so she offered, "Let me go see how I can help."

Joya arrived early the next day, gathered the department managers, and explained, "The store is not running well. We're in a tough spot, and we need to figure this out. This isn't just about sales, it's about safety, too." She asked them to step out of their departmental roles and look at the store as a holistic operation. She explained, "We need to finish these trucks and I need your help to get this back on track." She divided the managers into groups, asking them to cover new areas. When it became clear that there wasn't enough personnel to finish the trucks each night, she pulled in team members and leaders from nearby stores to help. She showed up each day, met with the team and reviewed progress, and then did her HR job at home in the evenings.

Within two weeks, the backlog was clear, goods were moving from trucks to shelves, and guests were arriving to fully stocked shelves once again. When the new store leader arrived and settled in, Joya briefed her on the situation, spotlighted the team's stellar work, and then stepped back.

Joya didn't wait for a formal invitation to contribute. She knew she could make a valuable impact—one that would be appreciated by her boss and the store employees. So she stepped in and put herself into the room where things needed to happen. It then came as no surprise that when Jamaal needed someone to host Target's CEO for a store visit, he tapped Joya.

Invite Yourself

When you see an opportunity to step up, the first step is getting into the room. And often, you won't receive an invitation. There are times when it's appropriate to invite yourself.

Years ago, when I was at Oracle, I ran a program called the Oracle Leaders' Forum, which assembled the company's senior leaders from around the world to ensure that they understood and could implement the corporate strategy in in their countries. It was a high-visibility program, so three of the company's top executives (the president, the CFO, and the CTO) were actively involved in developing and teaching the program. I was clearly the junior member of the four-person leadership team and felt lucky to be able to work alongside those executives.

In the course of running the program, it became clear that the strategy was too complex to be shared worldwide; what we thought was a training problem turned out to be a strategy problem. The president, CFO, CTO, and I met, concluded that the company's strategy would need a major decluttering, and decided to suspend the Leaders Forum program until they could rearchitect the strategic message and create a new presentation. A meeting was scheduled to assemble the heads of each of the product divisions to revise our product strategy and simplify the message. I wasn't included in the meeting, but as the manager of the training program in which the strategy would be debuted, I was relieved to know the executives were working on it.

The meeting was to be held the following week. I marked it on my calendar, not as an FYI but because I was planning to attend. To be clear, I had not been invited. It wasn't my role, and it was above my management level. Plus, there was bound to be heated debate during the meeting, so the executives would not necessarily appreciate having an audience. But I had a good understanding of the problem, I knew what needed to be done, and I figured that I could help. I was confident the top executives (and project sponsors) would appreciate having me there, so I didn't ask for permission; I just arrived early and took a seat. As the product division executives arrived one by one, several greeted me warmly. But when Jerry, who ran the largest and most important product division, walked in and saw me, he said more dismissively than curiously, "What are you doing here? You're in charge of training, not product strategy." Jerry was a strong personality and one of the influential executives in the company, so his less-than-warm welcome was noticed by others in the room.

"Right now the strategy isn't clear enough for us to communicate to our leaders," I explained. "This group needs to sort through a lot of ideas and PowerPoint slides to distill this strategy down to its essence." I squared my shoulders and spoke directly to Jerry. "I'm pretty good at this type of work, and I think I can help."

He didn't seem particularly sold on the idea, but he didn't push back, either. The president retorted, "Hey, Liz knows what she's talking about, and we could use her help," and the meeting moved forward. I listened intently, made note of key issues and themes, and then played back what I'd heard. The others nodded. After a while, some executives began to seek my observations. Soon I was leading the process, calling the meetings and organizing the work, including hiring C. K. Prahalad, the renowned strategy professor, to advise us.

After reviewing the existing material, we decided to wipe the slate and rewrite the strategy with a new framework. C.K. asserted that a good strategy has many thinkers but only one author. Given our recent experience, we could see the wisdom. But before we could discuss which of the top executives would author the final document, C.K. suggested that I be the lead author. I was shocked. I wasn't the most experienced, and certainly, I would not have been cast in the role had anyone conducted a real talent search. But I was willing to take the lead, and the executives supported the notion. Together we crafted a strategy that was both compelling and straightforward.

At the next Leaders' Forum, the participants received a clear strategy, articulated brilliantly by three top executives. That piece of work is one of the highlights of my career and one I'll return to in subsequent chapters, drilling down into the actions that enabled me to make a meaningful contribution.

Through that work, I learned that you don't need to be the boss to be the leader and you don't always need an invitation to play big. Sometimes you have to invite yourself to the table (but if so, do it wisely to ensure your presence will add value and be welcomed).

What opportunities are you missing because you are waiting for someone to discover you or invite you in? If you have value to bring, you may need to invite yourself to the party. This is a tendency we saw repeatedly in the Impact Players we studied: They didn't wait to be asked. They knew when it was appropriate to invite themselves, asserting their ability to contribute and lead despite their lack of seniority and securing permission to contribute where they thought they could be most useful.

Take Charge

Once in the right room, the Impact Players we studied weren't satisfied with passive participation. When an opportunity for them to contribute surfaced, they presented themselves as capable leaders and took charge. Here are a few of the descriptions managers used: *unapologetically proactive; takes charge; picks it up and runs with it; assertive and takes control of the room.* Furthermore, 74 percent of managers surveyed said that high-impact contributors always or often act boldly and make tough decisions, making it one of the top ten behaviors consistently found across our sample. They actively assume a leadership role, flexing their managerial muscle and presenting themselves with confidence. It's a strong but fluid form of leadership, one we saw again at Target, this time in a young, bright project manager in the technology organization.

Ellie Vondenkamp's job is to ensure the technology needed to get new stores up and running is operational before that store opens. This includes systems such as internet access, backroom servers, security and safety, telephony, and of course cash register operations and electronic payment systems for Target's recent rate of roughly thirty store openings a year. These are major construction projects with strict timelines and little room for failure.

Ellie is in her late twenties, sunny and joyful, a real people person who leads mission trips for her church in her spare time. But Ellie is also tough as nails, which comes in handy leading technology projects in new builds where she needs to take charge and is typically outnumbered by men.

A significant portion of her time is spent on-site, inspecting progress and guiding the work of technology vendors and some of the construction crew. Ellie arrives wearing her hard hat and asks for the construction manager. She introduces herself and then quickly finds an opportunity to establish that she's no pushover. When she gathers the various construction teams together, she takes complete control of the room (in this case a massive shell of a building). Although she has never worked as a construction foreman, she lets the crew know that she's done her homework and understands their world. She directs the team, "I understand why you think we'd drop cable using the gridiron over there, but we need lines dropped here to support the store plan for servicing guests in this area." She uses all the right construction terms, acknowledging the builders' constraints but letting them know what needs to be done differently.

In one such conversation she was leading with two of her Target colleagues and six construction staff, one of the construction managers turned away to resume his work before she finished speaking. Ellie called to him, "Come back, I'm not finished. Hear me out." She then laid the construction plans on the ground, explained her rationale, speaking the language of construction and talking directly to the general contractor. She was heard, and the job was done right.

Ellie doesn't leave anything to chance; she takes charge, and under her leadership, there's never been a store opening delayed by technology. Ellie's manager, Mary Ball, said, "The one skill I value most in any team member is initiative; Ellie models this continuously. She doesn't need to wait for direction from me to go after something—she sees an issue and jumps on it, while keeping me informed or escalating if she needs support."

Not a single one of the Impact Players we learned about was a bully or even a bull in a china shop leaving messes for their bosses to clean up; rather, they were described as collaborators who were easy to work with, an idea we'll explore further in chapter 6. They offer leadership that is confident and compelling but not overly aggressive. It's a light but strong form of leadership, which former Supreme Court justice Sandra Day O'Connor captured well when she said, "The really expert riders of horses let the horse know immediately who is in control, but then they guide the horse with loose reins and seldom use the spurs."

They take charge by listening and responding, inviting others to come along.

Secure Permission

US Vice President Kamala Harris wrote, "Never ask anyone's permission to lead. Just lead." [15] The individuals we studied did just that. They had the mettle to step forward and offer a better way. However, just because someone steps forward doesn't mean anyone will follow. Those who take charge without a formal commission need tacit approval from their would-be supporters. Essentially, their peers and colleagues need to vote them into office.

A typical political campaign speech provides a good illustration. In such a speech, the candidate makes a case for a better world and their particular ability to lead to this promised land. The speech intensifies, building to the crescendo—the big ask—in which the candidate, having made their case, asks for the audience to vote for them. The presidential speechwriters Barton Swaim and Jeff Nussbaum created a standard template that flows like this: "We know we can make progress. But for us to do something, I need you to do something. I need you to vote. . . . I ask you to stand with me. Join me. And together we'll build the country we know we can be." [16] In asking for constituents' votes, the candidate has asked for permission to be their leader.

When leaders wield influence, not formal power, others follow by choice rather than obligation. Leaders need people to opt in. Think of this as a contracting process in which the emergent leader offers leadership and improvement and in exchange their colleagues provide permission and support. This permission-seeking might involve explicitly seeking a manager's approval to activate a new project, but it might be subtler, more like raising one's hand in a classroom, getting a nod of approval before speaking out. The would-be leader raises their hand to let the group know: I see a better way, I'm willing to lead, will you support me?

A common mistake informal leaders make is asking for a colleague's support before building relationships or earning trust. When Paul

Forgey reflected on his experience leading the team that transformed Target's guest returns, he realized that he should have invested more time with the fifteen key people, building relationships and trust before he needed it. He had come across initially as the new guy from supply chain coming in to tell them that their business was broken. Paul said, "You need a lot of relationship to do big things together." Keith Ferrazzi wrote in *Leading Without Authority*, "It is through real human connections that we earn permission to lead our teams, achieve our goals, and elevate our teammates—and ourselves—in the process."[17]

Voluntary leaders need the initiative to step up and take charge, but they must also demonstrate the humility to seek permission and garner support. When they can do both, other people chose to follow of their own volition.

Habit 2: Enroll Others

Ellie Vondenkamp is not only adept at taking charge, she also leads a team from problem to solution with remarkable ease. For her, it's a standard play that she runs over and over, surprising no one but consistently achieving wins for all.

It starts with frustration as she discovers a lingering problem and then wonders: *Why hasn't anyone done anything about this?* She usually concludes: *Well, if not me, then who?* She disassembles the problem, identifies the responsible parties, calls a meeting, lays bare the issues, gets to the root, and then asks individuals to own the solution. She takes notes and follows up, escalating for additional support when necessary. It's a formula that generates action and ownership. Here's how that played out when Ellie discovered that wires were getting crossed when ordering new phone systems.

For years, Target's alarm system, which alerted authorities in the event of a fire, had run through land-based phone lines. But with the availability of high-speed fiber-optic cables, the old phone lines weren't needed—at least not in most stores. Determining if the old-fashioned phones were still needed required a decision tree. But the complexity of this new process meant that old phones were being ordered by default and new stores continued to receive both types of phone lines. That duplication of spending was not an enormous expense for a \$92 billion company, but it wasn't trivial, either. Plenty of others knew and spoke about the problem, but it wasn't yet an issue with finance, so it was pushed aside. With so many groups involved in the process, it wasn't clear who was supposed to solve it. Ellie wasn't responsible for any of the telco technology herself, but she thought something should be done about the avoidable waste.

Ellie gathered information and then organized a conference call, providing the critical information in advance. With everyone gathered on the call, she stated the problem, explained—without judgment—how it transpired, and then walked the others through the decision tree that determined whether or not telco lines were actually needed in the stores. After a few comments and clarifications, she asked for owners who could implement solutions. There were some awkward pauses. But with the problem now visible, eventually the right people stepped up. The call took just half an hour. With transparency, a problem that had persisted for months was resolved in thirty minutes. After the call progress stalled briefly, but with calm persistence, the process was fixed.

Ellie led by illuminating the problem. She pulled people in and gave them an opportunity to take ownership. Her manager described this superstar as a sun that shines daily and remarked, "People are drawn to her." Are you creating the visibility people need to see the real problems and take action? Are you bringing the right issues into the light? If you want to find a solution, invite people in and illuminate the problem.

Impact Players can lead without authority because they've acquired the power of assembly. By using their colleagues' time in efficient, productive, positive ways, they earn a reputation as someone who not only makes things happen but also respects others in the process. When they call a meeting, people come ready and willing to contribute.

As Ellie Vondenkamp explained her approach to group problem

solving, I was struck by how quickly these short and simple meetings led to solutions. Cross-functional problems were solved in minutes, not months. The secret was not just identifying a genuine problem but addressing the problem with total transparency, putting her effort into revealing the problem rather than prescribing the solution. She clarified the problem, not by overexplaining it but by making it fully transparent the way a chef might clarify butter by applying heat, skimming off the less valuable substance, and leaving only pure liquid. With full visibility into the essence of the problem, the group could easily form a common view of both the problem and potential solutions. As part of the process, complex problems were broken into pieces, a skill that Impact Players demonstrate nearly twice as often as their counterparts do.[18]

With a common view of the problem, the group can now establish a collective intent and a game plan. The leader continues to guide the nascent effort, ensuring the team takes action, achieves interim wins, and builds the momentum needed to sustain the effort. But once others have stepped up themselves, the emergent leader has played their most valuable role and is free to step back and let others lead.

Habit 3: Step Back

The Impact Players we studied were able to step away with the same grace as they had stepped in and taken charge. They are versatile players who can both lead and follow, who pass the ball and share the glory. This flexible approach to leadership is again similar to the role of playmakers on a sports team, whose ability and willingness to move the ball to another player so he or she can make an attack is as important as their ability to take possession of a ball.[19] This willingness to share and rotate the lead role creates a fluid, on-demand leadership model that enables organizations to respond quickly, adapt, and sustain commitment for the long haul.

Consider two vastly different leadership models from the animal world: a flock of geese and a pride of lions. A flock of migrating geese flies in a distinctive *V* formation, which scientists estimate enables a flock to travel 71 percent farther in a given period than solo flight.[20] In this formation, the bird in the front of the flock breaks the air, reducing drag for the birds flying behind. Eventually the lead bird tires, falls back into the formation, and another bird rotates to take its turn in the lead. But the benefit of the *V* formation works in both directions: the birds in the rear fly behind and to the side, creating a force from the upward pull of the follower birds' wings that helps propel the lead bird. Contrast this energy-efficient approach with the leadership model in a pride of lions: the king of the pride reigns for life; however, the alpha leader's life is typically cut short by the hostile takeover of a contending leader. It's a model of leadership that may be fit for the savanna but is a dying breed in a work environment where agility and endurance rule.

Create Heroes

Though Paul Forgey was instrumental in radically improving the returns process at Target, he wasn't the only star of the show. When the initial group of fifteen commissioned a cross-functional team of senior managers, Paul handed the baton to Dave, one of his direct reports who would serve on this team. He briefed Dave, "In absence of leadership, I want you to take the lead. But if someone else comes in ready to take charge, support them." Dave got things going initially, but three other senior managers—Kelli, Caitlin, and Melissa—also played key roles during the initiative. They became role models of people who were willing to work differently and make things happen, and their work together became an early testament to the power of cross-functional teaming within the company.

Paul acknowledged, "The cross-functional team deserved the credit. They did the creative thinking and ultimately came up with the solutions." His manager, Irene, said, "He pulls the best out of people and leverages the expertise of everyone on the team." She said people love working with him because he is "Mr. No Drama"—no politics, no games. He doesn't blame others when things go wrong, and he doesn't seek a lot of praise. People know that when they work with him they will be given a chance to contribute and will get their share of the credit.

Impact Players are not just heroes; they are hero makers. They pull others into the spotlight and lead the team so that there are multiple winners and potential leaders. And when the entire team looks good, so does the boss.

Transfer Leadership

Mary Parker Follett, a management philosopher in the early twentieth century, said, "Leadership is not defined by the exercise of power but by the capacity to increase the sense of power among those led. The most essential work of the leader is to create more leaders."[21] When you've used your influence to launch an initiative and the effort has reached escape velocity, it's time to let someone else command. But how do you let go with the same confidence with which you took charge? Paul Forgey of Target admitted that after getting the guest returns process under way and caring so much about it, it was hard to give the baby back. It helped knowing that the initiative was in good hands and that he had never intended to keep it. He said wryly, "I have plenty to do and enough to own."

My research over the last decade has shown that people do their best work when they have ownership, when they are given real responsibility and the accountability that goes with it. A good leader puts others in charge, transferring ownership to them. This transfer requires an explicit handoff of responsibility, similar to the way a property title is transferred from one owner to another when a house is sold. The new owner cannot take charge of the property until the previous owner releases all claims on the title. Imagine trying to move into a new house with the old owners telling you where to put your furniture.

Perhaps there is something you are holding on to that you need to transfer to a new leader. Where might you have already contributed your value as a leader? Where would you do well to step back and let someone else lead?

Follow Others

The best leaders are willing to lead, but they are fluid leaders, rising up and falling back as the situation commands. It's a radically different mindset than that of the perpetual leader—the career-minded manager acts like once they are cast into a leadership role and become a boss, it's their role for life. It's no surprise that people resist working with these managers and that organizations replete with this mindset become sluggish, ineffectual hierarchies.

However, beware the other extreme; getting stuck as a perpetual follower leads down the same path. In the next section, we'll consider two decoys that can keep us from contributing to our potential.

THE DECOYS AND DISTRACTIONS

Whereas the Impact Player initiated action and directed the contribution of others, those working with a Contributor Mindset waited for direction. Managers most often described such team members as smart and capable but passive, like spectators watching for clarity to emerge or waiting for someone else to take charge. *Just tell me what to do and I'll do it* is how many managers described their style. It's an approach to work driven by respect for authority and an assumption that *other people are in charge*—a bystander mentality. This mindset is captured in the southern US saying "I'm not in charge," which is a euphemism for "They're doing it wrong." It provides a convenient outlook, because if you aren't in charge, the problem isn't yours to solve.

At its most innocuous, the Contributor Mindset keeps professionals on the sidelines, as they watch and wait for someone else to invite them to get involved or take charge of a situation. This bystander mentality generally creates passivity, and over time it can wear down initiative and create a culture of mediocrity. The inclination to wait and deference to authority bring us to another decoy that misleads many aspiring leaders.

By Invitation Only

Too often capable people miss opportunities to act nobly because they are waiting to be knighted. Perhaps they've been taught to respect authority or that it's impolite to arrive at a party uninvited. Or maybe they don't want to appear bossy. But while we timidly wait for an invitation, we can miss the party and the opportunity to contribute and lead. We also keep our organizations stuck in rank-based systems. Though we may still be perceived as good followers, we will likely be overlooked for leadership roles.

Consider Donna,[22] a low-maintenance project manager who's a solid performer, cares about her job, and has built solid relationships. She has told her manager on several occasions that she wants to be assigned more responsibility and be recognized and promoted. But she's waiting for her manager to issue an assignment. Her manager said, "I plant the seeds and let her know that we could really use a process improvement here, but she doesn't go for it." It's as if Donna is waiting for her boss to update her quarterly objectives or make an announcement to the team. The frustrated manager continued, "I'm opening the door for her, but she needs to go in." Even if her boss has time to coax her, Donna would face the same situation at the next job level. Though a higher level might carry a weightier title, to effect change, she would still need to negotiate her way into places where she wasn't invited.

Team of Equals

Whereas some professionals become stuck in the paradigm of old-school leadership, others too quickly adopt an experimental new curriculum, one that assumes that innovation and agility are by-products of free-flowing collaboration—an alluring half-truth. Insisting on a team of equals is another decoy and involves overplaying the collaboration card.

Cross-functional, autonomous teams, which operate on partnership and agreement, have become increasingly popular methods of fostering agility and innovation. Though this form of teaming can undoubtedly increase creativity and communication, what happens when peer collaboration becomes a de facto way of working, especially when it's used informally without clear rules of engagement? What might go wrong when the whole group is in charge? Egalitarian teaming can work well when meeting at the roundtable, but it can easily fall apart between gatherings when it's unclear who is supposed to schedule the next meeting or connect with another department.

Diffused leadership can dilute the power of collaboration. When ownership is jointly held, confusion can ensue, much like doubles players on a tennis court who both call "Mine!" to an oncoming ball but fail to swing, assuming that their partner is returning the shot. Though we often think that a leaderless situation creates anarchy (something akin to a scene from *The Lord of the Flies*), it is more likely to cause inaction. The truth is that when everyone's in charge, no one is really in charge. Or, as I say at my house, when everyone is in charge of feeding the cats, the cats go hungry.

Collaboration and clear leadership are not incompatible. It's not only realistic to have both; it's advisable. Beware of teams in which everyone's in charge. Instead, structure a collaboration in which everyone contributes and has an opportunity to lead some portion of the effort or at some point in time but in which there's only one leader at a time.

MULTIPLYING YOUR IMPACT

When roles are unclear, people get stuck. The organization becomes mired in the status quo as people wait for the clouds to part and reveal the will of the higher-ups. However, if just one person is willing to step up and lead, roles don't seem to matter; in fact, they then look altogether unnecessary. When individuals volunteer to step in and lead, progress is made, even when it's unclear who's in charge and what needs to be done. With each win, the culture becomes more courageous and people learn to take initiative and be unafraid to lead. When an organization has playmakers, it needs fewer formal managers.

VALUE BUILDING: STEP UP, THEN STEP BACK

Impact Players lead and follow with equal ease and get seen
as influential leaders and trusted team players

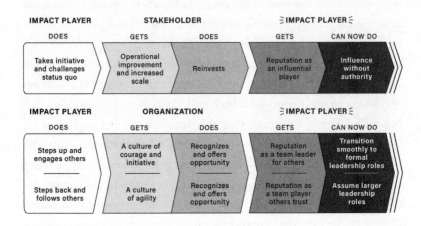

IMPACT PLAYER	STAKEHOLDER		⋛IMPACT PLAYER⋛	
DOES	GETS	DOES	GETS	CAN NOW DO
Takes initiative and challenges status quo	Operational improvement and increased scale	Reinvests	Reputation as an influential player	Influence without authority

IMPACT PLAYER	ORGANIZATION		⋛IMPACT PLAYER⋛	
DOES	GETS	DOES	GETS	CAN NOW DO
Steps up and engages others	A culture of courage and initiative	Recognizes and offers opportunity	Reputation as a team leader for others	Transition smoothly to formal leadership roles
Steps back and follows others	A culture of agility	Recognizes and offers opportunity	Reputation as a team player others trust	Assume larger leadership roles

The decision Betty Williams made on August 10, 1976, changed the course of history and helped end violence in a region. Her willingness to take the lead put her on a path of leadership and advocacy for the next three decades. In June 2008, Williams reflected, "Thirty years in the field has convinced me of one thing, the obvious fact that there are no answers from the top down. Governments do not have the answers. Indeed quite the reversal. A lot of times they not only do not have the answers, they themselves are the problem. If we are committed to helping our world's children, then we must begin to create solutions from the bottom up." [23] She decided to work for the world as it should be rather than settle for the world as it is.

Williams's contribution was indeed extraordinary, but don't we all encounter problems that someone needs to fix, small injustices that should be remedied, inertia that must be countered? In these situations, do we settle for the status quo or work to find a better way?

Impact Players don't settle, and they don't wait. They don't necessarily right every wrong they encounter, but they look for ways to leave things better than they found them, without compulsion or even invitation.

While others are making excuses, Impact Players are making things happen and making a difference. Those who embody this mindset don't need to wait until they are in a leadership role to lead. The American military general George Patton once said, "Lead me, follow me, or get out of my way." When roles are unclear, do you lead or do you follow? Those who can do both are likely to become the leaders of the future; those who do neither may get pushed out of the way.

Every great leader can recall a defining moment when they decided that "good enough" simply wasn't good enough and made the choice to lead. The same holds true for top contributors at all levels. If you want to maximize your value, look for the quietly persistent problems and take initiative to solve them. Look for leadership vacuums and fill them. As you step up, you will earn respect, influence, and greater opportunities to lead. So start something.

THE PLAYBOOK

This playbook contains tips for aspiring leaders to exercise and strengthen the assumptions and habits necessary to STEP UP, THEN STEP BACK.

Smart Plays

1. **Listen for white noise.** Listen for ambient problems—low-grade, persistent problems where the organization can make marked improvements with a little bit of leadership and focus. What is everyone complaining about but not doing anything about? Where are there seemingly small inefficiencies that are repeated and add up to a large waste over time? What problems have staff members become numb to that might be shockingly obvious to a new customer or a newcomer on staff? Do the calculations, create transparency, and build a makeshift team that can fix it once and enjoy the benefits over time.

2. **Fill a vacuum.** Look for situations that lack clear leadership. Don't wait for a transformational moment or a chance to change the course of history; provide leadership in everyday moments, including these two all-too-common leadership vacuums:

   - **Unclear meetings.** It is estimated that 63 percent of meetings have no planned agenda.[24] You can provide much-needed clarity by suggesting the group agree on intended outcomes for the meeting. This can be done by asking, "What is the most important thing for us to accomplish during this meeting?"

   - **Unsung heroes.** Most employees express a need to be recognized by their boss, peers, and clients; however, according to a Glassdoor survey, only two-thirds of employees said that their bosses showed them enough appreciation.[25] You can fill this leadership void by speaking up up to recognize the contributions of your peers or collaborators, especially those who work behind the scenes. Elevating the contributions of others gets them the credit they deserve and engenders the trust you need to lead without authority.

3. **Invite yourself to the party.** To step up and take the lead, sometimes you'll have to invite yourself into the room where things are happening. But don't be a creepy interloper who appears without warning, takes up a seat without contributing, or hijacks the agenda. Rather, let the meeting organizer know why you'd like to be included and what value you offer. Once there, make a meaningful contribution to the agenda at hand and conduct yourself so you are sure to get an invite next time. Last, if you plan to arrive uninvited, be sure you have at least one strong, credible supporter in the room.

4. **Act the part.** An easy step to becoming a leader is to start acting like one right now. As Amy Gallo of *Harvard Business Review* wrote, "If you want to become a leader, don't wait for the fancy title or the corner office. You can begin to act, think, and communicate like a leader long before that promotion."[26] When you act the part, demonstrating the characteristics and attitudes needed to lead, you increase your chances of being cast into the role later. Emulate the positive leadership qualities you see demonstrated by the leaders one and two levels above you. Get started by picking a leadership trait from any of these

sources and start practicing it: (1) one of your boss's best leadership qualities (e.g., asking good questions), (2) a positive characteristic of someone who was recently promoted into a managerial role (e.g., innovative thinking), (3) one of your organization's stated leadership or cultural values (e.g., collaboration).

5. **Pass the baton.** To build leadership credibility, show your colleagues that you can follow as well as you lead. Perhaps you've been holding onto a leadership role too long and should pass the baton to a new leader. Is there a project or initiative that you've successfully led that would benefit from "fresh legs" or "new eyes?" Is there a colleague or team member who is capable of stepping up and leading the work during the next phase? As you make the handoff, don't just transfer the work, transfer authority. Go further by letting the rest of the team know that this person, rather than you, is now in charge. Lastly, quickly find an opportunity to visibly support their leadership.

Safety Tips

1. **Share three things.** To avoid stepping on toes, let your peers and colleagues know that although you are stepping up to lead, you come in peace. Build trust by sharing three essentials: (1) *share your intent*: let people know what you are trying to accomplish and how it will benefit others; (2) *share power*: create opportunities for others to lead pieces of the work, or let them know the leadership role will rotate; (3) *share the spotlight*: make heroes of the people you are leading. When others win, too, people will follow.

2. **Cover your bases.** Though you may not wait for management approval before taking charge of a situation, you do want to keep your management informed. Before chasing after a discretionary project, ensure your boss knows you've got the bases covered on your core job. Check in regularly to let them know what you are working on and how it's going. Additionally, "inviting yourself in" doesn't mean you should surprise a meeting leader with your presence; rather, check with them first and suggest how your attendance can benefit the outcome.

3. **Pick your battles.** In stepping up to lead, avoid overcommitting. As with community volunteerism, overzealousness can dilute one's impact and lead to burnout and disillusionment. Take charge selectively, saving your strength for battles in which momentum and organizational support are on your side. When you choose your causes wisely, you will be viewed as a leader, not a rabble-rouser.

Coaching tips for managers: You can find coaching practices to help your team members *Step Up and Step Back* in "The Coach's Playbook" at the end of chapter 8.

CHAPTER 3 SUMMARY: STEP UP, STEP BACK

This chapter describes how Impact Players deal with unclear roles and why they so easily move in and out of leadership roles, sharing power and creating an on-demand leadership model.

	CONTRIBUTOR MINDSET	IMPACT PLAYER MINDSET
Practice	Wait for Direction	Step Up, then Step Back
Assumptions	Other people are in charge *(bystander)*	I don't need formal authority to take charge *(stewardship)*
		I can improve this situation *(proactivity)*
		I don't have to be in charge to take charge *(informality)*
Habits	Defer to leaders	Step up
	Follow direction	Enroll others
	Collaborate as needed	Step back
Implications	Individuals miss opportunities to solve critical problems because they are waiting for direction from above. The organization gets trapped in the status quo.	Individuals become playmakers because they spot opportunities and put themselves and others in position to score. Willingness to lead without formal power creates a culture of courage, initiative, and agility.

Decoys to avoid: (1) By invitation only, (2) A team of equals

Unforeseen Obstacles

WHAT LEADERS SAY ABOUT . . .

CONTRIBUTORS	⋛ IMPACT PLAYERS ⋛
"He will put reasonable effort in, but the work may not get done if I don't push."	"It is more often that he'll remind me of a deadline than I have to remind him."
"If there is debate or challenge, she cannot move something through. It ends up getting escalated to me, and I have to come in and get it across the finish line."	"She recognizes problems and issues before they become big problems and solves them. She doesn't rely on anyone else to solve her problems."
"He wants things to run smoothly and is frustrated that they don't."	"He can hit a roadblock, figure out a way around it, and keep on moving rather than getting disheartened and slowing down."
"She says the right thing in meetings, but it falls short on execution."	"She sees things to the end even if she gets no credit."

Chapter 4

FINISH STRONGER

I was taught that the way of
progress was neither swift nor easy.
—MARIE CURIE

In my town it's known as the Big Game—the annual football matchup between Stanford University and the University of California, Berkeley, rival schools on opposite sides of San Francisco Bay. It's a 129-year rivalry, with the winning school taking possession of the coveted Stanford Axe trophy. The stakes and emotions run high.

The eighty-fifth Big Game was played on November 20, 1982, at California Memorial Stadium in the Berkeley Hills. The California Golden Bears were winning 19–17 late in the fourth quarter. With eight seconds left in the game, Stanford scored a three-point field goal, taking a one-point lead over Cal.

Now just four seconds remained on the clock. Stanford kicked off with a short, low kick recovered by Cal's Kevin Moen near the 45-yard line. To win, he would need to run the ball fifty-five yards on a single play. Moen began running forward and scrambling but was impeded by the Stanford defense. Moen tossed the ball backward to a teammate, Richard Rodgers, who advanced a yard, was blocked, and passed back to a third player, Dwight Garner. Garner was able to advance a few yards but was quickly tackled by a mass of Stanford defenders.

The Stanford fans erupted in celebration. The notoriously raucous Stanford band rushed onto the field and into the end zone to celebrate the Big Game victory. The game was surely over; at least it appeared that way from the stands. But Garner hadn't yet hit the ground when he passed the football laterally to Rodgers, who caught it midstride, ran twenty yards, was tackled but while falling pitched the ball to Moen on the 30-yard line. Moen kept running. Their five wild lateral passes had eluded the Stanford defense, but now Moen faced an unforeseen opponent—throngs of band members, cheerleaders, and the Stanford Axe Committee who had rushed onto the playing field to celebrate their victory. Moen darted around oblivious band members, crossed the goal line, and collided with a stunned trombone player standing in the end zone as he scored the winning touchdown.[1] The game ended 25–20, and Cal took possession of the Stanford Axe.

The game's final moments became legendary, known as "The Play," one of the great finishes in sports history. Stanford still contends that a Cal player was down before the final touchdown was scored. Of course, Cal sees it differently. The game film is inconclusive. But one thing is certain: when the band rushed the field in those final seconds, the game was not yet over. Cal kept playing and won.

A lot of professionals play a good game. They take action and work hard but too often stop before the job is finished. What happens when we stop just short of the goal line or celebrate early only to find that something we thought was done became undone? The most influential professionals—and entire teams—make a greater impact because they finish the job and finish stronger than others.

This chapter is about how the highest-impact players deal with adversity and unforeseen obstacles and get work done once things become difficult. In the last chapter, we explored how to take charge and get things started; this chapter will explore how to take ownership and move work across the finish line. We will examine the first element of the Impact Player performance guarantee: how top contributors deliver both predictability and upside surprise and why they are entrusted with the high-visibility, high-stakes projects.

This chapter isn't about overcommitting or working to a point of exhaustion; it's about working in a way that you can finish a job well, with your well-being intact. As you dig in, you will learn how to bring in reinforcements without relinquishing accountability, how to pivot instead of panic, and how to negotiate instead of just persist. Whether you're crossing the goal line or merely crossing something off your to-do list, you'll learn to finish stronger—not worn down but built up by the unexpected challenges along the way.

THE CHOICE:
SOUND THE ALARM OR SORT IT OUT?

Every business faces obstacles, and every organization deals with setbacks; they're part of work and life. There are the known challenges, such as earthquakes in California and tornados in the Midwest, that you can prepare for and deal with. Then there are the problems that are nearly impossible to foresee, the ones you didn't see coming, the ones that don't show up on radar or that drop in unannounced. These are unprecedented challenges such as the COVID-19 global pandemic of 2020–2021 and the shuttering of businesses and schools around the world. These are the "unknown unknowns," as former US secretary of defense Donald Rumsfeld put it. They are, of course, the most difficult to manage, because they can't be easily predicted.

Unknown obstacles of every kind were omnipresent in NASA's Apollo program. The NASA engineers didn't know the condition of the soil on the moon, but they knew they didn't know it—making it a known unknown. Because they recognized what they didn't know, they could build a lander that would accommodate all the possibilities.[2] But there were unknown unknowns as well, such as when the *Apollo 12* spacecraft was struck by lightning—an event never previously considered.[3] As a NASA official explained, "It would be hard to expect a program manager to project that his spacecraft was going to be struck by lightning. On the other hand, I think it is not unreasonable to expect of program managers that they should realize that somewhere in any major development program you will figuratively be struck by lightning."[4]

Though unknown unknowns can't be predicted in any specific or reliable way, they can be broadly anticipated and responsibly dealt with. Though all people deal with issues out of their control, some assume responsibility to resolve the problems while others choose to escalate to a higher-up, someone seemingly more powerful. Here's an example from the perspective of a NASA manager.

An engineering manager for NASA described "Ed," an apt pseudonym for an engineer on his team he considered a Steady Eddie type. The manager said that Ed came in, did his job, did what was asked of him, and when asked for updates, gladly gave them.

Ed generally submitted his work on time and did it well, but when his colleagues reviewed the work, it was clear that more work was needed. As with any complex project, there were almost always unanticipated integration issues or bugs to be fixed. When asked to do more, Ed would let his colleagues know that he was already working on another project. The message was essentially "Gotta go. Got another job to do. Good luck to you. See you later." The team was left to fix the problem and complete his work so the overall mission wouldn't be compromised.

Ed worked hard and seemed engaged, but when the mission became complicated, he bumped the issues up for his boss to resolve, often saying, "This one is above my pay grade." He was like a tennis partner who takes the easy shots but with harder incoming shots calls, "Yours!"

When Ed collaborated with other engineers on team projects, he would say things such as "You are doing too much. It doesn't need to be perfect. Just get it done and move on," as if the old saying "good enough for government work" somehow applied to manned space travel. To be clear, in the end Ed's work always got done and was mission fit. But it wasn't Ed who got it across the finish line.

We heard similar stories of other contributors: "She got derailed far easier than others on the team," or "He tends to get stuck and isn't sure how to progress without redirection." These descriptions reminded me of several of my children when they were first learning how to do housework: they took action and made an effort, but as soon as something went wrong, they told me they couldn't finish the job. Or they wandered off and did something easier.

Professionals operating with a Contributor Mindset take action, but when things get tough, they escalate issues rather than taking ownership, or worse, they get distracted and discouraged and stall out completely. They learn to avoid the hard projects and leave them to higher-ups.

In contrast, the Impact Players ensure the job gets done in full, despite unforeseen obstacles and hardships.

As an undergraduate student at Cornell University, Steve Squyres walked into a room full of pictures of Mars. It was 1977, and the pictures were fresh from NASA's new *Viking* orbiters. Few people had seen the pictures, and even fewer understood them; Squyres certainly didn't. Still, they took his breath away. He wrote, "I left that room knowing exactly what I wanted to do for the rest of my life."[5]

Twenty years later, Squyres was an astronomy professor at Cornell, NASA's Mars exploration program had progressed from basic photography to in-depth geologic exploration, and NASA was soliciting proposals for mission plans from the scientific community. Squyres assembled a team of top scientists and engineers to design a rover. After a decade of unsuccessful proposal writing, their project was finally approved. They were elated, but the excitement soon gave way to panic as they began to tackle a daunting set of challenges.

It was a project born into hardship. For starters, they would need to build two rovers in the hope that at least one would survive the journey to Mars and function there. The rovers would need to remain operational for ninety sols (ninety-three Earth days). Their plan was based on having at least forty-eight months to build the two rovers, but because of the delays in proposal acceptance, they would have only thirty-four. More important, there were time constraints placed on them by the universe: they had to launch during a specific window in which the alignment of Earth and Mars was favorable. And those were just the challenges they knew about.

The life span of each rover would depend on how many solar panels it had. The solar panels were wired together into groups called strings, which had to fit onto the rover, which had to fit inside an existing lander.

The first unpleasant discovery came when Squyres received an email from the project scientist with the subject line "Bad news." Mass limitations meant they could fit only twenty-seven strings onto the rover, and at least thirty were needed to ensure a ninety-sol life span. "I had a moment of despair," Squyres wrote, "but then it dawned on me that this 'bad news' might actually be the best news I'd gotten in months."[6] Unable to use thirty strings, they were forced to redesign the lander. Redesigning the lander was a lot more work in the already limited timeline, but it meant they no longer had to sacrifice functionality and explorative power to keep the old lander design. Rather, it let them build the right lander for their rover—which allowed them to build a better rover. The team worked quickly to design the new lander while the leaders scrambled to secure the budget.

The team solved puzzle after puzzle to complete the twin rovers, eventually named *Opportunity* and *Spirit*. Deputy project manager Jennifer Trosper, brought on to lead the systems engineering, recalls the effort as an all-hands-on-deck experience: "Hardware and software were being tested in three eight-hour shifts, 24 hours a day, seven days a week."[7]

The *Spirit* rover launched successfully, but with the launch of *Opportunity*, "Everything that could go wrong, did go wrong," joked NASA launch manager Omar Baez. The launch date had already been delayed twice, and their window would soon close for four years. At seven seconds left in the countdown, the launch team called a hold. Those monitoring the spacecraft detected an issue with a valve. The launch team could have thrown their hands up and said that the spacecraft wasn't ready. Instead, they rapidly fixed the valve and reset the clock to launch in four minutes. The launch was a success.[8]

From the day *Opportunity* landed, a team of mission engineers, rover drivers, and scientists on Earth collaborated to overcome challenges and get the rover from one geologic site on Mars to the next.[9] Over the next few years, *Opportunity* nearly lost power due to a stuck heater, survived a two-month dust storm, and lost the use of its 256-megabyte flash memory, among other issues. With each obstacle, *Opportunity*'s team found and implemented a solution that enabled the rover to recover.[10]

For the next fourteen years, both rovers sent hundreds of thousands of spectacular high-resolution full-color images of Martian terrain as well as detailed microscopic images of rocks and soil to Earth.[11] Eventually a massive dust storm brought the steadfast rovers to a halt. Designed to last just ninety Martian days and travel one thousand meters, *Spirit* and *Opportunity* vastly surpassed all expectations for their endurance, scientific value, and longevity. *National Geographic* called it "hitting the scientific jackpot."[12] In addition to exceeding its life expectancy by sixty times, the *Opportunity* rover traveled more than twenty-eight miles by the time it reached its final resting spot on Mars, apropos in name: Perseverance Valley.

The rovers endured on Mars because Squyers and team were doing the same on Earth: adapting to unfamiliar terrain and moving beyond each new obstacle. Trosper reflected, "We worked hard, we designed it right, we did the due diligence and the engineering, and those things just lasted forever."[13]

THE MENTAL GAME

An agent on a mission: it's the theme of many a crime thriller action movie. Whether it is James Bond (007) or Black Widow (of *The Avengers*), the agent overcomes dangerous obstacles and menacing villains with ingenuity and equanimity. These agents are mission-minded, mentally tough, and resilient, and in the end, they always get the job done.

The Impact Players we studied had a touch of special agent in their blood—like Mary at NASA, dubbed "Mary the Mission Slayer" by her colleagues for her relentless drive to resolve problems that jeopardized her team's mission. They are ordinary people who have developed an extraordinary mental ability to withstand opposition and survive the gauntlet of everyday problems and ordinary challenges. They get the job done—hardships, villains, and all. As in the movies, they complete the mission without constant direction but summoning support from headquarters as needed.

This propensity to see things through and finish what they start is what I call *the completion gene*. It's a single-minded tenacity, a get-it-done ethos found in people who take ownership and finish without reminder. Unresolved issues and unmet objectives make them uncomfortable. Though overcoming obstacles might feel difficult for others, to people with the completion gene, it's painful not to finish. So they always finish the job.

This penchant for completion requires both resilience (the capacity to recover quickly from difficulties) and grit (sustained persistence in pursuit of achievement).

Resilient people are not easily stymied; they bounce back from setbacks. With their fundamental belief that *I can overcome adversity*, challenges are interpreted as resistance necessary to build strength and opportunities to prove oneself. In this mental model, losses are viewed as temporary setbacks, not final outcomes. In a 2013 article in *Harvard Business Review*, Rosabeth Moss Kanter wrote, "The difference between winners and losers is how they handle losing . . . no one can completely avoid troubles and potential pitfalls are everywhere, so the real skill is the resilience to climb out of the hole and bounce back." She concluded, "When surprises are the new normal, resilience is the new skill."[14]

Resilience is what keeps us bouncing back, restored to whole and strengthened through growth after overcoming hardships. Grit is what keeps us moving forward, despite setbacks and without artificial rewards along the way. It stems from the simple but powerful belief that *I can get this done*. The leading authority on grit, University of Pennsylvania professor Angela Duckworth, reported, "Grittier students are more likely to earn their diplomas; grittier teachers are more effective in the classroom. Grittier soldiers are more likely to complete their training, and grittier salespeople are more likely to keep their jobs. The more challenging the domain, the more grit seems to matter." [15]

Fiona Su, a planning manager at Google's Media Lab, personifies this plucky tenacity. She's the type who takes ownership, knows how to make things happen, and produces the output of at least two people, according to her manager, John Tuchtenhagen, head of media for North America. John explained why Fiona secures buy-in and keeps projects moving when others stall: "Fiona works from an assumption that all problems can be solved; you just have to keep poking at it, keep trying." For Fiona, "no" is a squishy word, one that has a lot of wiggle room. She explained, "When I'm told no, my reaction isn't to fight back. I ask why they said no. I then start from no and find a path forward."

As we combine the capacity to bounce back with the courage to persevere, we develop the belief that *I can handle this*. This belief prompts them to take personal responsibility rather than escalate emergent problems, which means that others give them greater latitude to handle these problems in unorthodox ways.

THE HIGH-IMPACT HABITS

Why do these resilient, gritty contributors become so valuable on teams? For starters, when we asked the 170 managers what most frustrates them, three of the top ten responses involved failure to finish. The most frequent frustration managers expressed was people bringing them problems without having first tried to find solutions, such a the employee who "instead of taking a stab at something would, like a cat, drop a dead rat at your front door." The number three frustration was having to chase after employees to remind them to do the things that they had committed to do, which relegates managers to professional nag or micromanager. Then there are the dreaded surprises, employees springing bad news on them at the last minute when little can be done. These are the surprise parties that are bound to make the manager look bad, like when your cat drops a rat on the porch right as guests arrive at your party

In sharp contrast, Impact Players offer a low-maintenance, high-accountability proposition: they take ownership, anticipate and wrestle down problems, and do what it takes to complete the whole job. They can finish strong because they anticipate problems and develop a plan (which ranks second overall in credibility builders, as shown in the following chart).

Building Credibility with Leaders and Stakeholders

CREDIBILITY KILLERS	Escalating problems without offering solutions
	Making your manager chase you down and remind you
	Surprising managers with bad news
CREDIBILITY BUILDERS	Anticipating problems and having a plan
	Doing a little extra
	Figuring it out yourself
	Finishing the job without being reminded
	Getting to the point and telling it straight

See appendix A for the full ranking.

Habit 1: Finish the Whole Job

Parth Vaishnav is a principal software engineer at Salesforce, the customer relationship management giant with a reputation for devotion to customer success. Parth is known as a brilliant programmer with a natural curiosity for how things work and fearlessness when tackling technical challenges—someone who will jump into the fray and climb out with a solution.

It was the end of a four-month release cycle. Teams all across the company had developed the latest versions of their products, complete with new features and performance improvements. The upgrades were packaged together and pushed all at once to 150,000 Salesforce customers globally. But something wasn't right. Parth got an urgent call from a colleague: the release was up and running, but strangely, the new product features weren't visible to customers. The team was stumped and asked if Parth could help. Parth replied, "I'm on it."

He began investigating and discovered the problem: one of the product customizations in the new release had broken a piece of the release framework (a bit of old procedural code that no one owned but was used by all product groups) upon which the entire suite of products depended. That meant that every new feature and improvement across all products—the result of over a hundred thousand person-days of engineering—was now on hold. You can imagine the frustration building internally.

Parth dug in further, identified the root cause, and formulated a fix—but he wasn't done yet. Years earlier, Parth had received some stinging feedback after his isolated actions nearly broke a system, and now he knew better than to implement the fix on his own. He needed to ensure he understood the big picture and had support from the various product groups that would be affected by his fix. He quickly assembled a meeting of software architects, explained the problem, and built consensus for the solution.

The blocked features were released, but Parth still wasn't done. He worked for another week, checking all possible dependencies to ensure there were no adverse side effects and collaborating with the other product groups to define an improved work process. Finally, he found a group to take ongoing ownership of the framework. Problem solved, permanently.

Once again, we see an Impact Player who didn't just do his job but did the job that needed to be done, working in the cracks and interstitial spaces of a complex organization. Further, we see someone who did more than just a good job; he did the whole job, crossing the finish line and running another hundred yards just to be sure the race was won and the mission was complete. All the way done, and then some.

I'm on It

The most impactful players tend to stick with problems longer. An Adobe manager described one such member of her team: "She's highly persistent. The harder the problem, the more she'll persist. The intellectual challenge drives her." Another manager said, "He doesn't take the easy way or no for an answer. He figures out how to navigate hurdles and solve problems creatively." Because these players persist longer, they make progress in the face of ambiguity (the eighth highest differentiating behavior between Impact Players and Contributors). They don't take shortcuts, even when no one else is watching.

Sandra Deane, a speech language pathologist and swallowing specialist formerly at Stanford Health Care, knew patient outcomes could be improved if an instrumental swallow study (Flexible Endoscopic Evaluation of Swallow, or FEES) was administered before certain patients were discharged or put on a diet. That created a significant change in practice for the speech pathologists, nurses, and physicians. Sandra ensured every speech language pathologist on staff was trained to administer the test. She co-organized a two-day course on FEES that included using the simulation lab at the Stanford School of Medicine so they could practice in a "real life" setting. To ensure patients were being referred appropriately, she offered to coach the nurses. There was some initial resistance, but her offer to attend nursing huddles, present at nursing conferences, and work with nurses on a one-to-one basis got them on board. When the physicians initially showed reluctance to order the tests, she explained the improved outcomes and convinced them as well. As a result of her vision and tenacity, Stanford continued the program and is now involved in clinical trials related to the FEES procedure. Her manager said, "She sticks with it, wins people over. People really admire her."

Consider It Done

Top contributors are known for sticking the landing. But what really sets them apart is that they don't require reminders; they manage and monitor themselves. As a LinkedIn manager said, "With Tara, I've never checked in on status." At NASA, some managers call this "fire and forget": the manager can fire off a request and then forget about it; once in the person's hands, it's as good as done. The managers we surveyed indicated that 98 percent of the time, high-value contributors always or often get the job done without being reminded—compared to 48 percent for typical contributors and 12 percent for under-contributors.[16]

Count on It

The predictability with which Impact Players get the job done, without reminders, becomes something that managers come to depend on. This completion guarantee is part of a larger performance guarantee that these individuals provide their stakeholders. As we analyzed the frequency of behaviors across professionals, we noticed that there were certain things that high-value contributors always (or nearly always) did. There were five in particular: (1) take ownership and get a job done without being reminded, (2) act with integrity and do the right thing, (3) be easy to work with, likable, approachable, and positive, (4) learn quickly, and (5) apply their strengths to the work at hand. Typical contributors often did these things, too, but not always.

Here's the key point: these behaviors are important, but the real value comes from the *always* factor. If someone always performs well, their leader can fully unload responsibilities and not worry. If someone delivers only most of the time, the manager still has to worry all the time. Impact Players deliver with such consistency that it creates a veritable guarantee that their colleagues count on, which is why they are handed the most visible opportunities with a no-look pass. We call this the *performance guarantee* of Impact Players.

THE PERFORMANCE GUARANTEE

Others can count on Impact Players to:

1. Take ownership and get the job done without being reminded
2. Act with integrity and do the right thing
3. Be easy to work with, likable, approachable, and positive
4. Learn quickly
5. Apply their strengths to the work at hand

100 Percent Done and Then Some

There is more to the story; Impact Players are known for doing just a little bit more. In our survey data, the second highest differentiator between Impact Players and Contributors is that Impact Players "exceed expectations in delightful and surprising ways." In addition to preparing a detailed report, they might add an executive summary and highlight key points; on top of closing a big deal, they may secure a client testimonial for the company website. While their under-contributing colleagues surprise with bad news, Impact Players deliver a complete job with a surprise bonus. They offer both predictability and upside, making them dependable and delightful to work with.

Habit 2: Maintain Ownership

It's not surprising that Impact Players take full responsibility. What is remarkable is that they retain it, even during setbacks and obstacles beyond their control. They don't hand it back when things get tough.

Most of us have felt the urge to hand a challenge back. Most honest parents will tell you that the thought has crossed their minds a time or two—likely with an inconsolable newborn or a moody teenager. Though they may not actually want a refund, they probably wouldn't mind handing the responsibility to someone else during the most trying times. When people escalate problems to their management, it often comes with an implied transfer of ownership. A Stanford Health Care manager described one such employee: "She sends emails that essentially say, 'Hi, this is a problem. Goodbye.' She doesn't seem to investigate problems, just escalates them for someone else to fix them."

Call in Reinforcements

Though the Impact Players we studied were persistent finishers, they didn't forge ahead alone or suffer in silence. They did their part, but they knew when to call in reinforcements from their leaders and their colleagues.

Most of us know when we need help, but few of us enjoy asking for it. In fact, for most it's a painful experience. Heidi Grant wrote in *Harvard Business Review,* "As research in neuroscience and psychology shows, the social threats involved—the uncertainty, risk of rejection, potential for diminished status, and inherent relinquishing of autonomy—activate the same brain regions that physical pain does. And in the workplace, where we're typically keen to demonstrate as much expertise, competence, and confidence as possible, it can feel particularly uncomfortable to make such requests."[17] But as Grant pointed out, humans are neurologically wired to want to help and support one another. When we make a responsible request for help, it brings out the best in both parties.

The most influential professionals can escalate an issue and ask for help while maintaining ownership of the solution. Google's Fiona Su manages to do both. She's known for her tenacity, independence, and ability to manage various internal stakeholders, but when she runs into trouble, she has no qualms letting her manager, John, know that this one is over her head and she needs help. She'll get him involved, but more as a consultant than as a new owner. John says, "She knows how to bring me in and bring me along." Not only is he willing to help, but he's eager to, because he gets to contribute without taking back responsibility.

There are legitimate reasons to escalate issues. As illustrated above, you may want to engage a senior leader in problem solving. You may want to simply keep people informed. As John also pointed out, "Fiona never blindsides me." It can also dissipate the inevitable frustrations of unexpected obstacles and help us get unstuck or, as an engineering director for Salesforce put it, "He just doesn't get stuck on things. He can get frustrated, but he vents and moves on."

When Impact Players called for reinforcements, it wasn't lazy avoidance; they didn't dump problems on their colleagues or appear helpless to their leaders. The message was clear: "I need your guidance or action so I can move this forward." Like Fiona, they sought help but never relinquished accountability, which assured their colleagues and stakeholders that an ounce of help would go a long way.

Negotiate the Necessities

I'd like to return to my previously mentioned experience with the Leaders Forum at Oracle. After running the first program, we could see that it was a success (other than the feedback that the strategy was unclear). The following week we met to review the feedback in more detail and determine the next steps. It was a feel-good session as we celebrated the early win.

As the junior player, I felt fortunate to have a seat at the table with these executives, whom I admired greatly. They did their part, showed up to meetings, and worked well together. But I also knew that it's easy to start an initiative and a lot harder to finish it. Aside from Larry Ellison, our brilliant and mercurial CEO, they were the three most important and busiest executives in the company. I worried that they might get pulled in other directions, particularly the president, Ray Lane, who was responsible for $25 billion in revenue annually.

As our meeting closed and the three executives were about to stand up, I decided to speak up. I knew if I didn't say something now, it would only get harder later. I said, "Ray, you know how hard my team and I have worked on this. And you know me; I'll break down brick walls to make sure this program is a success." He nodded. He had seen my level of commitment and obsession. I continued, "I will work my tail off, but the day you no longer have time for this is the day I stop working on it." I restated for clarity, "So if you stop, I stop."

I wasn't sure how I'd mustered the courage to say it. I suspect it arose more from necessity than bravado. I knew the program would fail if the executives didn't remain personally involved. And I wasn't willing to fail. I was, however, willing to negotiate for what was needed. I will never forget the look on Ray Lane's face. He stopped and looked at me for a second as he processed my firm but gentle stipulation. I like to think he was contemplating his willingness, not my audacity. He then resolutely said, "You have a deal."

He immediately stood up, walked over to his executive assistant's office, and said, "Terry, for the next year, Liz has whatever time she needs on my calendar." The look of astonishment on Terry's face was also memorable. As the program continued to roll out over the next year, never once did Ray back off his commitment. He was at every session and every meeting I called. He never stopped, so neither did I. There were, of course, bumps in the road, but we had the support needed to resolve them.

Not only was it a time when I did my best work, those three executives were at their best too. But their commitment wasn't a matter of good fortune or a result of charm. I got the support I needed because I negotiated the necessities.

Are you clear about what you need from others to be successful? If so, have you asked for it? If you want to make it across the finish line, be sure to negotiate the necessities.

When you take the lead on an important piece of work, make sure you've set yourself and others up for success by negotiating for what you need. We often assume what we need is additional budget or head count; however, in reality, our most vital resources are less tangible. The Wiseman Group surveyed 120 professionals from various industries about the resources they most need to be successful in their work. These six factors were rated of similarly high importance (with variations based on job, industry, or personal preference): (1) access to information, (2) action from leaders, (3) feedback or coaching, (4) access to key meetings and people, (5) time, and (6) help establishing credibility. However, across all industries, countries, and demographics, one thing was consistent: budget and head count were rated in seventh and eighth place—the least important factors by a significant margin. We may not agree on what we need most, however, by and large, people agree that it's not more money or additional people. We don't need resources as much as we need to be set up for success and know our leaders will finish strong alongside us. In fact, when we negotiate the necessities, we are better able to navigate uncertainty and thrive amid ambiguity.

Remember: timing is everything. Don't wait until a problem arises; negotiate for what you need at the outset—before you've committed to the work and while your clout is high. When we fail to arrange for the help we'll need later, we must address problems alone or relinquish responsibility to higher-ups when we run out of personal power. Negotiating for what we need not only helps ensure a positive outcome, it increases our influence.

A determination to negotiate the necessities at the outset flows out of a deeper understanding shared by so many of the highest impact players: the assumption that problems are inevitable. While many of the more typical professionals try to avoid the gnarly problems, the most impactful players plan for them.

Habit 3: Anticipate Challenges

It's a scene so distressing, so grisly, that it's hard to imagine it happened. On October 1, 2017, a gunman opened fire on a crowd attending an open-air country music festival on the Strip in Las Vegas, Nevada. Fifty-nine lives were lost, including that of the gunman, whose motives still elude investigators. In all, 851 people were wounded, 422 by gunfire. It was the largest mass shooting incident in US history.[18]

Imagine the scene at the nearest emergency room, Sunrise Hospital, where most of the gunshot wound victims were taken. Further, picture being the senior physician on duty that night. How could you possibly treat 250 critically wounded patients at once? It was an unprecedented, almost unimaginable challenge for the medical and administrative staff. Fortunately, Dr. Kevin Menes, the attending physician in charge of the Emergency Department (ED) that night, had imagined such a scene, many times in fact. Menes had not only trained in emergency medicine but had also worked as a tactical physician with the Las Vegas Police SWAT team.[19] Aware that Vegas was an easy target, he had contemplated the possibility of a mass casualty incident, wondering how he and his team would respond and mentally preparing for a day (or night) that he hoped would never come.

It was 10:00 p.m. when Dr. Menes first heard the alert come through. He knew the number of incoming patients with gunshot wounds would be unprecedented, but he had a plan worked out. He described the events of that night in an article for Emergency Physicians Monthly written with Dr. Judith Tintinalli and Logan Plaster.[20] He wrote:

> It might sound odd, but I had thought about these problems well ahead of time because of the way I always approached resuscitations: 1. Preplan ahead, 2. Ask hard questions, 3. Figure out solutions, 4. Mentally rehearse plans so that when the problem arrives, you don't have to jump over a mental hurdle since the solution is already worked out.[21]

Invoking his speculative plan, Menes directed the administrative staff to summon the medical teams from home; clear every operating room, treatment room, and hallway; and gather all available beds and wheelchairs. Anyone capable of pushing a gurney should report to the ambulance bay to receive incoming patients.

While resources were mobilized, Menes rapidly reconfigured the workflow of the ED. There would be no time to tag each patient with the severity of their condition (from code red to green), so he tagged rooms instead. The first 150 victims arrived within the first forty minutes.[22] As the patients arrived, Menes called out their condition by color, and staff rushed them into the designated room. That allowed patients to be immediately placed with the right medical staff, equipment, and medicine and enabled the medical staff to monitor and rapidly move each class of patients through the process. As Menes did triage, the three other ED doctors resuscitated the red-coded patients while surgeons and anesthesiologists arrived.

Meanwhile, nurses were to watch for patients rapidly declining in the orange and yellow rooms and to insert an IV catheter into each patient while it was still possible to locate a vein. As the reds moved into surgery, the ED team treated the orange-coded patients who were reaching the end of the "golden hour" when intervention could prevent death. When the flow got backed up, Menes turned triage over to a senior nurse, so he could stabilize patients and get them into the operating room. As additional physicians arrived in the ED, he briefed them on the new layout and directed, "Find dying patients and save them."

With each new obstacle, Menes invoked a workaround or had the presence of mind to ensure each patient got treatment. Here are a few examples of his quick-witted problem solving: When he wasn't able to move fast enough between destabilized patients, he moved to the middle of the room and had the patients' beds brought to him. He recalled, "I was at the head of multiple beds, spiraling out like flower petals around its center. We pushed drugs on all of them, and they all got intubated, transfused, chest tubed, and then shuffled to Station 1."[23] When the staff ran out of ventilators, they used a last-resort solution and put two patients of the same size onto a single ventilator by using a Y-shaped hose and doubling the ventilator output. When the demand for X-rays spiked, Menes brought the radiologist down to the X-ray room to immediately read results from the X-ray machine's monitor.

By sunrise, just seven hours later, all 215 patients had moved out of emergency care and into outpatient care, and 137 patients had been discharged. It was an unprecedented feat. The ED treated an average of thirty gunshot wound patients each hour. The surgery team performed sixty-seven surgeries within twenty-four hours, twenty-eight of them within the first six hours. None of them was a minor emergency; those had flowed to other hospitals. This heroic response wasn't merely a function of ingenuity in the moment but of forethought, proactive visualization, and mental rehearsal for a worst-case scenario.

Could you better plan for unforeseen obstacles simply by expecting them and mentally preparing for them? The surest way to overcome obstacles is to expect them from the start. By anticipating problems, we can finish strong, even in the worst of circumstances.

Seeing Around Corners

When we anticipate and even normalize the possibility of problems, we don't lose time lamenting an unexpected problem but instead channel 100 percent of our faculties into finding a quick, effective solution. A Stanford Health Care manager described a highly influential player on her team this way: "She is constantly looking for potential pitfalls and takes steps to head them off at the pass. Problems get handled before they arrive." Impact Players don't have a superpower to see through walls or into the future; their strength lies in understanding that problems are constantly lurking around corners. They expect unpleasant surprises and normalize the challenges. The psychoanalyst Theodore Rubin captured this orientation when he said, "The problem is not that there are problems. The problem is expecting otherwise and thinking that having problems is a problem." With this mindset, obstacles aren't destabilizing or even distracting. Roadblocks become building blocks for growth, providing the resistance needed to become stronger and smarter and prove one's mettle.

Thinking on Your Feet

Unflustered by emergent challenges, Impact Players become masters of improvisation and redirection. They find unconventional ways to get the job done or bring a project home, much like Norwegian musher Thomas Waerner, the winner of the 2020 Iditarod, who upon finishing the race discovered he had just begun another endurance challenge, this one much longer.

Impact Player Pro Tip

Increase your range of vision by enlisting a colleague to be your wingman. Ask them to monitor your weak spots and help you see problems on the horizon. Do the same for them.

The Iditarod is a 1,100-mile sled dog race from Anchorage to Nome, Alaska, where mushers and their teams of dogs race through blizzards, whiteouts, and subzero temperatures for nine or more days. The athletes are the sled dogs. These dogs, typically a husky-malamute mix, have unique endurance capabilities that enable them to run at high speeds over long distances without tiring.[24] Remarkably, most dogs finish the race with the same baseline vitals they started the race with.[25] In fact, the dog teams that do best in one ultramarathon are the ones that recently finished another race.[26]

As Waerner crossed the finish line in March 2020 behind his ten-dog team, he noticed the crowd was unusually scant. During the race, the COVID-19 pandemic had escalated and air travel had come to a halt. Most of the spectators had already left Alaska, including his wife, Guro, who was home alone with their five children, working as a veterinarian and caring for thirty-five dogs in their kennel (making everyone else's work-from-home challenges pale by comparison).[27] Waerner would need to get creative; getting himself home wouldn't be hard, but his sixteen canine companions couldn't fly commercially.

After three months, Waerner found his ride: a 1960s-era DC-6B airplane that had not been used since the 1970s. It was unconventional, to be sure. The decommissioned plane was being readied for flight, bound for a museum in Norway, and it looked as though Waerner and his team could hitch a ride. But when the virus began destabilizing the economy and the Norwegian currency, the deal became complicated. After negotiations with the museum, help from sponsors, and a thirty-hour journey with multiple stops for fuel and unplanned mechanical work, Waerner and his champion sled team crossed the real finish line, home at last. Waerner told the *New York Times*, "It's a great ending to the race."[28]

In the workplace, the finish line can also move. Just when we think we're done, something comes undone, such as getting the green light from an important stakeholder only to discover that more documentation and additional approvals are needed. When things get difficult, too many professionals stop short of the finish line. But the most impactful professionals get creative, improvise, and go the extra, unexpected mile.

Finishing Well

In a strong finish, the job not only is done well, the people involved feel well when they finish—physically, mentally, emotionally. Unlike procrastinating students who finish their final exams and are totally spent, crash, and sleep for a week, Impact Players may give it all they have, but after a brief rest, they can start the next game as strongly as they did the last. Why? Because they've anticipated and prepared for unforeseen problems, they aren't thrown off their game when problems arise. Because they know how to call for reinforcements, they can maintain ownership without crumbling. Because they negotiate for the resources and support they need, they can cross the finish line without suffering exhaustion.

When all is said and done, the true Impact Players are neither worn out nor depleted. Like the husky-malamutes, they finish with the same vitals with which they began the race. It's more than a completion gene; it's an endurance gene. And you need both to finish strong. When you add smart pacing to this mix, you have the energy and presence of mind to learn from setbacks along the way, enabling you to not just finish strong but stronger.

THE DECOYS AND DISTRACTIONS

Whereas Impact Players work from an assumption of strength, which causes them to stick with challenges, the typical professionals we studied had an avoidance orientation, meaning that when things get tough, they escalate issues rather than taking ownership. They take responsible action but not accountability for the success of the mission. In an action thriller, they are the ones who put up a good fight but, when the enemy eventually eludes them, phone headquarters to report that the threat is still present.

The tendency to avoid the difficult problems is based on the belief that adversity hurts and should be avoided. In this worldview, unexpected challenges are seen as inconvenient and threats to the plan. To be successful, these professionals need a stable environment—something not often seen in spy thrillers or most places of work. They might make a valiant effort, but they finish before the job is done.

Whereas some make the mistake of finishing too early, others foolishly persist. Finish at All Costs is the first of two decoys that keep us from finishing strong.

Finish at All Costs

When encountering a setback, it's tempting (if not noble) to power through and persist. Like the great Stoic philosophers, we embrace the obstacle and patiently endure; we assume suffering in silence builds character. This fallacy is not only a misguided adherence to the old rules of work but a misuse of ancient wisdom as well. Finishing for the sake of finishing can result in a Pyrrhic victory, named for the Greek king who sustained heavy losses as he won battles against early Rome only to be quickly driven out afterward. In these costly victories, success inflicts such heavy tolls on the winners (and their teams) that the victory is indistinguishable from defeat. The job may get done, but there is blood on the floor. In the wake of these battles lie exhausted, alienated colleagues who become reluctant to join the next campaign. Likewise, we're also exhausted and fall victim to burnout.

A dogged determination to finish everything we start can lead to misplaced energy and wasted resources. A friend of mine once half-jokingly remarked that he finally stopped dating a woman when he realized he was spending all his time with someone else's future wife. Similarly, when we can't let go of unproductive projects before they finish, we can rob our organization of the time and resources needed to pursue higher-value opportunities. Furthermore, we risk becoming exhausted and burnt-out ourselves. Instead of finishing at all costs, you might need to cut your losses and let some projects go. We can avoid Pyrrhic victories by engaging in calculated, inclusive decision making that disregards the sunk costs of previous action and considers the collateral damage and opportunity costs of persisting.

False Alarms

When we see problems as threats, we are quick to sound the alarm. But when we sound the alarm too early and too often, we dilute our influence and credibility. We might develop a reputation as someone who overcommunicates problems but underdelivers solutions. A manager at Adobe described one such staffer: "She laments about everything that isn't working." When we see threats more often than we see opportunities, we can get into the habit of recreational complaining, grousing at each hardship that might interfere with our comfortable work existence or damage our careers. Eventually others will tune us out, like the proverbial boy who cried wolf.

But even helpful alarmists can wreak havoc. They alert their superiors to potential dangers but do so far too often. When individuals sound the alarm without offering corresponding solutions, managers respond too quickly and micromanage where their help is not needed. When I was a relatively new manager, I had one such contributor working on my team. In one particular one-on-one meeting, she spent at least twenty minutes explaining to me the myriad technical difficulties jeopardizing a mission-critical training program to be conducted the following week. Concerned, I picked up the phone seeking help from the company's data center, but she seemed surprised by my action. She clarified that she didn't need me to intervene. She said she would resolve the problems; she just wanted me to understand the challenges she was dealing with. I was stunned because her venting sounded remarkably like a cry for help.

MULTIPLYING YOUR IMPACT

When the job gets particularly challenging, it's tempting to escalate upward. When leaders take the bait and let their staff off the hook too soon, they deny their staff the learning that comes from struggle. Grit and resilience are then strengthened in the leadership ranks rather than in the lower layers that form team culture.

In contrast, Impact Players are entrusted with the most important projects. As a technical director at Splunk said, "I give him the hardest projects because I know he will succeed and do it in the most efficient way." Furthermore, because Impact Players get the job done in full, they provide the assurance that allows their collaborators and

VALUE BUILDING: FINISH STRONGER

Impact Players take ownership, finish the whole job, and get seen as clutch players

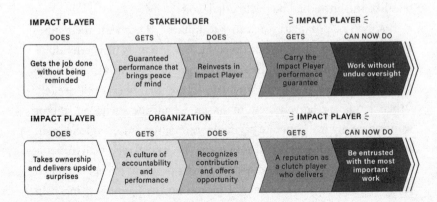

IMPACT PLAYER	STAKEHOLDER		≷ IMPACT PLAYER ≷	
DOES	GETS	DOES	GETS	CAN NOW DO
Gets the job done without being reminded	Guaranteed performance that brings peace of mind	Reinvests in Impact Player	Carry the Impact Player performance guarantee	Work without undue oversight

IMPACT PLAYER	ORGANIZATION		≷ IMPACT PLAYER ≷	
DOES	GETS	DOES	GETS	CAN NOW DO
Takes ownership and delivers upside surprises	A culture of accountability and performance	Recognizes contribution and offers opportunity	A reputation as a clutch player who delivers	Be entrusted with the most important work

leadership to sleep easy during a storm, which means they can work independently without undue supervision or micromanagement. They can then use 100 percent of their energy where it's most needed: anticipating and resolving the unknown unknowns.

The most influential professionals take an idea from conception to completion, realizing its full promise and impact. Like the best runners, they start fast and finish strong. As we saw in chapter 3, they take charge and are quick to initiate, but they finish what they start. They possess the completion gene, the inner drive to keep going and get the job done—all the way done, without constant supervision and without reminders. It's the performance guarantee that comes with these players and the reason why they are repeatedly entrusted with the missions that matter.

They are players who, in the words of the legendary basketball player Kobe Bryant, "rest at the end, not in the middle." [29]

When obstacles arise and problems persist, what will you do? Will you sound the alarm and hand the problem off to another? Or will you finish strong? The reward for those who finish well is not merely a job well done; it's also the pride in the crossing. It is the assurance expressed by Paul of Tarsus at the completion of his apostolic mission, recorded in the book of Timothy: "I have fought the good fight, I have finished my course, I have kept the faith." [30] The real reward is not what we have accomplished by finishing but what we have become by persisting and what is now possible because we are stronger.

NASA reported that when the Mars rover *Opportunity* completed its mission, it had surpassed all expectations, serving fifty times longer than originally planned, delivering groundbreaking science, and inspiring a generation. [31] Its success paved the way for future Mars exploration, including later rovers such as *Curiosity* and *Perseverance*. NASA administrator Jim Bridenstine reflected, "It is because of trailblazing missions such as *Opportunity* that there will come a day when our brave astronauts walk on the surface of Mars." He continued, "And when that day arrives, some portion of that first footprint will be owned by the men and women of *Opportunity*, and a little rover that defied the odds and did so much in the name of exploration."[32] As one mission ends, another begins.

THE PLAYBOOK

This playbook contains tips for aspiring leaders to exercise and strengthen the assumptions and habits necessary to FINISH STRONGER.

Smart Plays

1. **Draft a Statement of Work (SOW).** It's easier to finish a job well and completely when you've started with a clear remit. But you don't need to wait for your boss or client to provide clear direction; you can define the Statement of Work yourself. Create a shared vision of the work by documenting: (1) *the performance standard:* what a great job looks like; (2) *the finish line:* what a complete job looks like; (3) *the boundaries:* what's not part of the job. Start by capturing what you've already heard, then use your judgment to fill in what's missing. Lastly, review this with stakeholders to add anything they think is missing and to confirm mutual expectations. You might say, "Here is what I think success looks like. Where am I off?" Once you have agreement, you have a clear Statement of Work and can take ownership for its successful completion.

2. **Negotiate the necessities.** Be clear about what you need to be successful, such as information, time, access, guidance, and resources. Be sure to negotiate this support at the outset of the work, before you'll need it. You don't need a formal negotiation, just a mutual understanding. Try a simple "if/then" statement, such as: "If I am to be able to do [this thing you need from me] then I will need you to do [this thing I'll need to be successful]." By using if/then logic, you accomplish two important objectives: (1) reminding your stakeholder

what you stand ready to deliver and (2) making them aware of what you need to deliver successfully.

3. **Reframe obstacles as challenges.** The way we characterize a situation changes how we respond. When we view unexpected obstacles as problems, solutions elude us. After all, problems, by definition, lack solutions. When we reframe obstacles as challenges, we engage our mental faculties and become energized for the contest. To reframe obstacles as challenges, start by assuming every workday or project (or boss!) will be full of obstacles, so you aren't surprised when they surface. And when they do, reframe them as (1) an intellectual puzzle begging for a solution, (2) a character test requiring patience or humility, or (3) a physical challenge requiring pacing and endurance.

4. **Add a surprise.** When you complete a project or another piece of work, do something a little extra, above and beyond the original request or remit. Doing something extra doesn't need to involve a Herculean effort. It could be as simple as highlighting the key points when you forward a report to your manager. The best surprises will be (1) something unexpected, (2) something that supports their agenda (see chapter 2), and (3) something that doesn't distract you from other mission-critical work. Ask yourself: What's a small extra they aren't expecting but would be delighted by?

Safety Tips

1. **Know when to let go.** If you suspect you are working on yesterday's priorities, engaged in an unwinnable battle, or headed for a Pyrrhic victory, ask yourself: (1) Is this still relevant, given changes in the larger environment or market? (2) Is this still important to the organization and my leadership? Is this on the agenda (see chapter 2)? (3) Is this something we can still be successful at, even if we finish strong? If the answers are no, it might be time to let it go. But don't abandon the work without getting clearance from your leader(s) or stakeholders, and be sure to let them know what you will do instead to stay on the agenda—or let them direct you as you pivot to a higher-priority project.

2. **Vent with intent.** It's perfectly reasonable to want to share your frustrations with your manager. And it's healthy for managers to acknowledge the challenges their team members face. But there's a proper way to whinge and moan: keep it infrequent, brief, and focused. If you need to let off some steam, vent a little, but don't release ownership. Let your leaders know what actions you are already taking and be clear whether you are looking for sympathy or solutions.

Coaching tips for managers: You can find coaching practices to help your team members finish stronger in "The Coach's Playbook" at the end of chapter 8.

CHAPTER 4 SUMMARY: FINISH STRONGER

This chapter describes how Impact Players deal with unforeseen obstacles and how they complete work amid adversity, delivering both predictability and upside surprise.

	CONTRIBUTOR MINDSET	IMPACT PLAYER MINDSET
Practice	Escalate Issues	Finish Stronger
Assumptions	Adversity hurts and should be avoided (*avoidance*)	I can handle this (*strength*) I can overcome adversity (*resilience*) I can persevere and get this done (*grit*)
Habits	Take action Escalate issues Avoid the most difficult problems	Finish the whole job Maintain ownership Anticipate challenges
Implications	Individuals miss out on the learning that comes from struggle. This shifts ownership up to senior leaders.	Individuals build reputations as clutch players who perform well in critical situations. This reinforces a culture of accountability.

Decoys to avoid: (1) Finishing at all costs, (2) False alarms

WHAT LEADERS SAY ABOUT . . .

CONTRIBUTORS	⋛ IMPACT PLAYERS ⋚
"He assumes that he is generally correct most of the time, he just needs to convince the organization."	"He seeks out new information without being prompted."
"She has a tendency to overreact, is negative and emotional."	"She takes feedback as a positive."
"He is generally willing to take feedback, but it takes a long time to see any improvement."	"She learns quickly from errors."
"He doesn't respond to feedback. He was a nice guy, but it didn't look like he was strong enough to make a change."	"When I have feedback, she takes it and does something with it. She doesn't get down, she sees it as a chance to improve."

Chapter 5

ASK AND ADJUST

Intelligence is the ability to adapt to change.
—STEPHEN HAWKING

The movie director trains the camera on Jason Robards, Jr., the legendary stage actor. It's a tight shot intended to expose the character's inner conflict and the details of his emotions. After several takes, the director knows that the shot isn't right, so he calls, "Cut!" Later the director recalled, "I didn't think he was registering enough. I didn't feel that pain." Now the thirty-four-year-old director has to find a way to correct the work of a renowned performer nearly twice his age with multiple Tony and Oscar awards.[1]

The director is Ron Howard, the former child actor and prolific director known for such films as *Apollo 13*, *The Da Vinci Code*, and *A Beautiful Mind*. The movie is the poignantly funny 1989 film *Parenthood*. In the scene, Robards's character, a crotchety grandfather, is grappling with one of the many dilemmas of parenthood and confronting his shortcomings as a father. It's one of those quiet moments in which a mere facial expression from a master actor can replace pages of written exposition or convey a lifetime of pain or disappointment.

Howard approaches Robards and begins rambling as he tries not to offend but to provoke a different performance. Robards reaches over, touches Howard's hand, and simply asks, "Ron, do you want a sadder face?" Howard feels relief. But he's also convinced that the veteran actor's question is sarcastic and that Robards might deliver a ridiculously despondent face on the next take just to mess with him. Howard figures they'll just do the next take and calibrate from there.

But when the cameras roll again, Robards redelivers his performance, making the slightest, most nuanced adjustments and nailing the scene. Howard later said, "It was the most honest, organic, truthful depiction of that moment I could have dreamed of." It's the take that is in the movie. Howard reflected, "That is the lesson learned. Actors can keep getting better."[2]

The most valuable players are never finished. They are continually adapting, adjusting to hit the mark. How might the smallest adjustment to your approach lead to greater performance?

Moments like these are delightful not just for film directors but for leaders everywhere who must provide guidance to help others recalibrate their performance or simply improve with time. Though Impact Players finish strong, great work is never finished, and the best contributors are never complete—they are works in process.

Throughout this chapter, we'll focus on the idea of correction—not the slew of red marks one might receive from a pedantic teacher but rather the vital information that allows someone to correct course when they've veered off target. We'll examine why top contributors and aspiring leaders seek correction and how they respond to invitations to change in a way that helps them adapt quickly and learn faster than their peers do.

Though this chapter is about change, it isn't about making radical, disruptive change; it is about the power and importance of making micro-changes, the small adjustments needed to stay on track. It's about tune-ups, not transformation. In this chapter, you will learn how to stay in tune with the needs of your stakeholders, specifically how to ask for corrective guidance that enables you to receive more than your fair share of it and respond so people are willing to further invest in you. And because we all fail to see warning signs, we'll explore ways to recover quickly when you've messed up big time.

We'll begin by examining why everyone needs corrective guidance, particularly now when so many of our performance objectives are dynamic.

THE CHOICE: PLAY TO YOUR STRENGTHS OR LEARN A NEW GAME?

For many professionals, work used to be like a game of darts: a game of skill with a clear target and a scoring system that makes it obvious how well you are doing. One can practice the game, master the techniques, and hit a bull's-eye, perhaps even blindfolded with enough repetition. But as business needs continually shift, business targets are set into motion as well. The shot you once perfected no longer guarantees you'll hit the target. It now requires continual recalibration.

The New Game of Work

This constant shuffle creates so-called wicked problems—problems that change faster than we can solve them. Just when you figure out the game, the game changes. You'll need to learn new rules, work with new players, and develop new skills and strategies. To avid, confident learners, this continual adaptation and revision sound like fun; to perfectionists or star performers accustomed to always getting things right, it can feel like a toothache. What do you do when what you've been doing all along isn't working anymore? Relying on feedback gathered in an annual performance review won't suffice. When targets are continually moving, you need continual feedback, guidance, and correction so you can adjust your aim.

Rigging the Game

Continually adjusting our aim is demanding; wouldn't it be nice if we could adjust the target instead? That's exactly what Mark Rober, a former NASA Jet Propulsion Laboratory engineer and inventor, did. Mark, now a YouTube personality, uses his engineering skills to build highly sophisticated and outrageously fun devices. This brilliant engineer is mediocre at darts, so he teamed up with a former NASA JPL coworker and built a dartboard to solve this problem. After working for three years, they created the "AutoBullseye Dart Board." This dartboard calculates the trajectory of the dart using infrared directional detection cameras and adjusts the board's position using multidirectional motors, all within a half a second, to score a bull's-eye every time![3] Assuming a directionally accurate throw, an off-target shot is autocorrected, literally on the fly.

This one-of-a-kind dartboard is an impressive engineering feat, but too many professionals take the same approach at work: they may sense change on the horizon, but instead of preparing for it, they hope the new work world will value their old skills. They treat shifting winds like a storm they can ride out, hunkering down and waiting for life to return to normal, when in reality shifting winds are the new normal.

Sticking to What You Know Best

One technology marketing manager was described by her boss as smart, capable, and fairly confident. But her confidence was based on the notion that she was doing a great job—not on her ability to adapt or learn (what the psychologist Carol Dweck refers to as a growth mindset). Her boss explained, "She's constantly seeking validation and confirmation. She shows no interest in feedback. Actually, anytime she gets challenged, it's viewed as a direct personal threat, as if her capability and success are being called into question." As her self-perception veered farther and farther from reality, her career growth stagnated. Her manager lamented, "I wish I knew a way to help her receive feedback and get to the next level."

Other managers expressed similar concerns as they described how typical staff members responded to feedback or course correction:

> "When a patient complained, she would get defensive and explain why things had to be done that way."

"She would portray that she was coachable and open to feedback, but ultimately, nothing moved the needle with her."
"He's good at what he does, but I'm not sure he wants to get
better."

Learning a New Game

Impact Players view changing conditions and moving targets as opportunities to learn, adapt, and grow. Though they may appreciate affirmation and positive feedback, they more actively seek out corrective
feedback and contrary views and use them to recalibrate and refocus
their efforts. In the process, they build new capabilities for themselves
and their organizations.

When Zack Kaplan started at Google as a brand marketing manager in the consumer products division, he had six years of experience at the Wieden+Kennedy advertising agency but was new to the
tech industry. Just two weeks into his job, his manager, Tyler Bahl,
then head of brand marketing for Google's consumer applications,
assigned him to a visible advertising project. The division's approach
to advertising to that point had been a mixed bag with mixed results,
with each product group developing its own ad campaigns. The leadership team set a new aim: replace the disparate advertisements with
a single unified umbrella ad campaign that would give consumers a
consistent message. Internally, the project was called "the multiapp
campaign."

It had the usual challenges: a short timeline, a team that spanned
multiple organizations (both inside and outside Google), and a litany
of approvers to satisfy. Zack's role on the team was also unclear—as a
brand marketing manager, was he supposed to just architect the brand
message or oversee the development of the ads as well? Tyler briefed
Zack on the project, then gave him room to run. Zack was about to
learn why the ability to thrive amid ambiguity was one of the key hiring criteria at Google.

Midway through the project, the team learned that marketing management needed a new, different message featured in its ad campaign. Zack began asking questions—not questioning the new direction but rather trying to understand how to best adapt. He met with Tyler to ask: What does this mean for our overall message? How should the story change? What content tweaks need to be made? Once they developed a new approach, Zack connected with each of the stakeholders and the advertising agency to loop them in.

Just as Zack and the creative teams had found their footing, another critical target shifted under them: their audience needed to change. They revised their launch date and made additional edits. Zack and Tyler found ways to adjust to the new targets, but the real challenge was that even after making the adjustments, their approach still wasn't hitting the mark. The plan called for a single ad that would feature all of Google's major consumer products. But it just didn't feel right. They tried making more edits to the ad, but it was hard to follow and lacked emotional impact. Eventually Zack went to Tyler and said, "This is not working. It's not landing."

Tyler and Zack stayed at the office late one night to regroup and rethink. They asked: Why isn't this working? Are we trying to force too much into a single ad? What can we do differently? As they questioned their approach, it became clear that they were trying to do too much. Tyler said, "Let's simplify; let's start with just the search product." They decided to produce four distinct commercials, each focusing on a different Google product but with a singular message. They mapped out four commercials instead of one: sports, career, family, and connection. This would create a much better result but was no small change. They would need to tell four separate stories, expand scope with their ad agencies, deal with cost implications, and involve additional stakeholders. They pivoted. Zack recalled, "At Google, they tell you to expect a moving target. At this point, our worst enemy would have been stubbornness—to just keep going with the plan we had. But the old plan had gotten us lost." With this new approach, they were back on track.

Zack made the rounds, presenting the work in progress, listening, and gathering feedback—not faux feedback that creates agreement and closure but real feedback that invites change and causes rework. Even after a rough meeting, Zack maintained positivity, looking for learnings that would make the idea stronger and gleaning direction to keep the project moving forward. Tyler recalled, "Zack would come out of meetings where his ideas just got killed, and instead of being discouraged, he would have a smile on his face and be ready to take another swing at the project."

After dozens of rounds of edits, the ad called "Take the First Step" was ready for prime time. It debuted during the National Basketball Association (NBA) playoffs to rave reviews. The next three ads came together with fewer edits and aired over the next two months. The multiapp ad campaign not only hit the key performance indicators, it nearly tripled expectations for return on investment.

Zack didn't try to oversell his ideas or stick to the original plan. He and the team advocated for their work but then asked for feedback and adjusted until they hit the target.

Do you stick to what you know or change your game? If you want to have impact amid moving targets, ask for guidance and adjust your aim.

THE MENTAL GAME

Being reactionary is often seen as a negative quality, but actually, Impact Players are reactors—responding to changes in their environment and the feedback they are given. By being reactive (but not reactionary), they adapt to a changing environment, much like a chameleon changes color to fit its surroundings. And although stability is often viewed as a professional virtue, most players pull too hard to the center, avoiding change and sticking to what they know and where they are comfortable.

The top contributors we studied were agile learners. Their managers consistently noted two behaviors that set them apart: (1) how quickly and eagerly they learned when presented with a new challenge and (2) how curious and open they were to new ideas.[4]

Impact Players were able to adapt because they were confident in their ability to learn. But they were also comfortable enough with themselves that the prospect of failure—an inherent risk of learning—didn't compromise their self-worth. It is a posture of confidence—the belief that *I have value that can grow and evolve.*

The foundation of this outlook is a belief—widely known as a growth mindset—that *ability can be developed through effort and good teaching.* Carol Dweck's influential work has shown that with a growth mindset, students understand that their talents and abilities can be developed through effort, good teaching, and persistence. As Dweck teaches, people holding this mindset don't necessarily think everyone's a genius, but they believe everyone can get smarter if they work at it.[5]

With a growth mindset, we see ourselves as capable of learning and changing. We interpret feedback as vital information we need to make adjustments. Challenges and obstacles serve as the training grounds for growth and feedback. When we don't embrace a growth mindset—what Dweck refers to as a fixed mindset—we resist change and avoid challenge. We cling to the status quo, where we are safe.

Our ability to handle feedback, particularly correction or criticism, is also influenced by our assumptions about our identity, particularly whether we see our self-worth as intrinsic or conditional. Seen as conditional, we assume *other people's view of me determines my worth.* In this belief, our value as a person is determined by our performance at work or outward success in life. Thus, work provides meaning, ascribes value, and can lead to what the journalist Derek Thompson termed workism: the belief that work is not only necessary to economic production but also the centerpiece of one's identity and life's purpose.[6]

But associating our full identity with our occupation, even work we love, is dangerous, not only to our sense of well-being but to the quality of our work as well. When our identity is wrapped up in our job, criticism carries an extra sting and failure poses a greater threat. Our sense of self-worth rises and falls with the highs and lows of our career, the status of a particular project, or the results of a performance review. Feedback, correction, and change are threatening.

In contrast, intrinsic worth is the belief that *I have inherent value and ability*. When we see ourselves as inherently valuable, we are more willing to try something new, knowing full well that we may perform badly. In this mental model our self-worth remains independent of our work performance. We don't need to be deemed worthwhile by others; we just are. We understand that although we may love our work and derive satisfaction from it, we are not our work, and our work doesn't determine our worth as a human being.

Maintaining this psychological separation can be challenging, especially for those who are passionate about their job or consider their work a calling. But when we can separate our self from our work, we increase our ability to deal with moving targets and cope with the vicissitudes of life. Feedback becomes information, not condemnation or validation. Changing and evolving is extending, not compromising, ourselves. We approach change with confidence, believing we have the ability to learn, but if we fail in the process, we aren't a failure. And although we feel secure with ourselves, we are open to change. As one manager said, "Her confidence comes from the fact that she's trying to better herself. It's confidence with humility." This type of genuine self-assurance increases our adaptability by enabling us to:

1. **Solicit and act on feedback.** Understanding our intrinsic worth creates the psychological safety we need to both receive corrective feedback without feeling threatened and accept confirming feedback without being lulled into complacency.
2. **Behave in new ways.** We can more readily abandon old patterns of behavior and experiment with new practices when our self-esteem isn't dependent on the outcome of the experiment.

3. **Handle ambiguity.** In uncomfortable situations, we can have low situational confidence (i.e., "I don't know what I'm doing") but high self-confidence (i.e., "I can ask, adapt, and figure it out").
4. **Learn from failure.** When we don't internalize mistakes, we more readily admit when we are wrong and let go of faulty assumptions.
5. **Learn from everyone.** Instead of relying on managers as a single source of guidance (or to determine our worth), we can take input from multiple sources and figure things out ourselves.

As this learning cycle spins, we increase both the value and the impact of our contribution. Herein lies the power of this mindset: when we are confident in our inherent value, we can focus on sharing and growing that value rather than trying to prove our worth.

In short, confidence enables us to change and grow. When we are comfortable in our own skin and understand the elasticity of our abilities, we need not fear change. We seek information that enables us to adapt intelligently. As Marie Curie said, "Nothing in life is to be feared, it is only to be understood."

THE HIGH-IMPACT HABITS

When the world of work is changing fast, the critical skill isn't what you know but how fast you can learn. Savvy leaders know they need more than just a team of smart, capable people; they seek out players who have both the confidence and the humility to learn.

In asking 170 managers from the most innovative organizations what their employees do that they most appreciate, learning behaviors were at the top of the list. They include being curious and asking good questions; asking for feedback, admitting mistakes, and fixing them quickly; and being willing to take risks and change. Interestingly, humility and a willingness to learn increase our credibility. Leaders appreciate learners. In contrast, working with defensive and deflective staff members—those who blame others for their mistakes or listen to their manager's feedback, only to proceed as if the conversation had never happened—can be infuriating. The chart below lists ways to build (or kill) your credibility when dealing with moving targets.

Building Credibility with Leaders and Stakeholders

CREDIBILITY KILLERS	Blaming others for your mistakes
	Agreeing to someone's face but disagreeing behind their back
	Listening then ignoring feedback
CREDIBILITY BUILDERS	Being curious and asking good questions
	Asking for feedback
	Admitting mistakes and fixing them fast
	Being willing to change and taking smart risks

See appendix A for the full ranking.

Like many leaders, I have managed employees with sharply different learning orientations. The first I'll call Quinn. Quinn was a skilled listener. When he detected incoming feedback, he perked up and locked into the conversation, listening intently. He would ask, "Is there anything more?" to make sure he understood. He would then repeat back the key points, nearly verbatim, so I would know my message had been received. I left the conversations full of hope. But after a few of those conversations, I soon realized this dream employee was more of a nightmare. He had ostensibly heard the feedback, but then generally did nothing differently. When I looped back, he offered compelling explanations of others' failings and arguments to justify his actions. The subtext of these explanations was "My work is fine; you just don't see it." Though he put on a good show, Quinn was actually a master of the art of placation and distraction.

And then there is Shawn Vanderhoven, who is equally skilled in the art of listening. But Shawn doesn't just listen to appease; he listens to adjust. When I first started working with Shawn, I was struck by how many questions he asked. Initially, his questions were about hitting the right target, such as "What are you trying to build?" or "What does success look like?" But once he understood the goal, his questions would shift. After submitting a project, he would ask, "Are you getting what you need? Do you need me to do something differently?" On the rare occasion when his work was off the mark, it was easy to tell it to him straight, without injecting feel-good caveats to pump him up. He would respond, "Let me try again," then deliver a bull's-eye the next morning. In nearly five years of working together, I've rarely approached Shawn with corrective feedback—not because he didn't need it (we all do) but because he always beat me to it.

When people seek guidance—then act and adjust quickly—they show their leaders that a small investment in feedback can reap big dividends. We'll explore how the practice of asking, adjusting, and closing the loop allows the Impact Player's learning cycle to spin faster and garner greater investment from their stakeholders.

Habit 1: Ask for Guidance

The Impact Players in our study showed greater levels of coachability, or responsiveness to guidance, than their peers did. This may be due in part to their willingness to either take the lead or follow others depending on the situation (the central idea explored in chapter 3). In a study conducted by PsychTests, researchers asked individuals to identify themselves as leaders, followers or adapters (those willing to lead or follow, depending on the situation), then measured each group's openness to coaching. Those who identified as followers were consistently the least coachable. Dr. Ilona Jerabek, the president of PsychTests, said that self-described followers "seem to have a self-confidence issue. Being criticized makes them feel weak, incompetent, or incapable."[7] Though they may have appreciated their manager's positive intention, they still interpreted coaching as an indication that they weren't good enough. Self-described leaders ranked higher. However, interestingly, the adapters who could lead or follow were the most coachable and willing to learn, displaying the capability to admit faults, handle criticism, and ask for help.[8] This is consistent with our findings: the typical professionals in our study sought praise and validation, while the high-impact contributors sought guidance and information that would help them adapt.

Get in Tune

It's easy to watch for signs of affirmation; but staying in tune with our stakeholders (and working on the right agenda) requires that we search for gaps: unmet needs, mismatched expectations, unflattering data, and contrary points of view. Astute professionals keep an ear to the ground, paying attention to changes in the environment, watching for new trends, particularly those they might have missed. Rosabeth Moss Kanter wrote that excellent leaders "listen, include many viewpoints, learn from critics, and remain aware that trends could shift quickly. And then they are better armed when they act quickly and decisively."[9] To hit the mark, we need the information that tells us we may be off course.

Even conscientious professionals fall out of tune periodically, much like musical instruments. Instruments, such as a piano, require infrequent tuning (every six months or after it has been moved); however, others, such as a violin, require tuning every time they are played. Violinists expect to start with an out-of-tune instrument. No one would fault a violinist for arriving at the concert hall with an out-of-tune violin, but if the violinist failed to tune the instrument before performing, the musician probably wouldn't be invited back.

To tune an instrument, a musician must first compare the pitch of their instrument with a reference pitch from a tuning fork, digital device, or other musician, then adjust the instrument until the two pitches match perfectly. Hearing the subtlest differences in pitch requires a developed ear, and making the minute mechanical adjustments requires practice. Tuning an instrument can be difficult for new players, but it's a skill that can and must be learned.

Similarly, professionals usually need a reference point to recognize where they may be off pitch. Getting ourselves into tune can be frustratingly difficult, especially at first, but with practice, it becomes second nature. Critical to this process is information and insight from others to help us get back on track. Though the term feedback often carries the connotation of criticism or judgment, technically speaking, feedback is simply information to help the recipient recalibrate. Feedback can be this simple: Am I hitting the target? Where am I missing the mark? What should I be doing more or less of?

Ask for Feedback

The top contributors in our study didn't seek constant validation; they sought guidance. Though receiving cheers and medals might cause us to feel valued, at least for a time, receiving guidance—specifically, information to help us change course or improve—is what makes us valuable. Yet getting access to this critical "performance intel" is harder than it sounds. Corrective guidance can be difficult to receive because our brains have defense mechanisms, essentially mental helmets that protect against potentially damaging blows to our egos. Sheila Heen and Douglas Stone, Harvard Law School professors and the authors of *Thanks for the Feedback*, explained a key reason we resist feedback: "The process strikes at the tension between two core human needs— the need to learn and grow, and the need to be accepted just the way you are. As a result, even a seemingly benign suggestion can leave you feeling angry, anxious, badly treated, or profoundly threatened." [10]

Providing feedback is difficult for the giver as well. Most people are uncomfortable communicating criticism and worry that people will react emotionally, shut down, or ignore the feedback and waste their time. They might also fear that their feedback will do more harm than good, a concern that has been corroborated by several studies. [11]

The Impact Players we studied received more feedback than others because they made it easy for people to correct them. They solicited advice and asked for feedback before their managers and other stakeholders thought to give it. Proactively asking for feedback has the same effect as offering to do something before your boss asks you to, a practice that managers appreciate most and that ranks number one on the list of credibility builders (see appendix A). By asking early, we can get ahead of the feedback cycle, preventing frustration buildup and preempting a host of performance problems. Feedback isn't seen as punitive; it becomes vital intelligence. When we operate like a musician who is continually tuning their instrument, the beneficiaries of our work don't need to tell us we are out of tune.

Are you getting the feedback you need? Are you asking for guidance before you stray too far off course? Employees' constant requests for feedback can be wearing for managers; however, asking at the right moments (e.g., after you've taken a new approach or sensed that you've missed the mark) has the opposite effect. When contributors ask how they can improve before the boss tells them what to do differently, they make their boss's job easier and can now do their job better.

GETTING FEEDBACK WHILE WORKING REMOTELY

It's easy to fall out of tune when you work remotely because you don't receive the feedback that comes from casual hallway conversations, and it's hard to get feedback during virtual meetings through body language alone. Try these two strategies:

1. When sharing your written work, include a set of questions to prompt feedback, such as "What is one change that would significantly improve this work?"

2. When giving presentations or leading meetings virtually, have a plan to get guidance before, after, or even during the meeting. Before the meeting, you might ask, "What's the most important outcome to achieve?" Afterward ask, "What did I miss?" You can even invite people to provide real-time feedback through the chat or Q&A function to help you know to speed up, slow down, or clarify a key point.

Focus on the Work

Perhaps the greatest issue with receiving feedback is interpreting it as a judgment of ourselves rather than information about our work. This can be particularly challenging for knowledge workers, whose work output is often a direct reflection of their thoughts and ideas.

When I set out to publish my first book, *Multipliers*, I was like a foreigner in new territory. I hadn't written anything professionally other than a few business reports and verbose emails. Fortunately, I knew a few authors who might be willing to offer a newcomer like me some much-needed guidance. One of those people was Kerry Patterson, a brilliant and wickedly funny author of four *New York Times* bestselling management books. Kerry had been one of my college professors, and I'd later worked for him as an intern. As my manager, he had given me stretch challenges and always let me know where I stood with him, so I knew his feedback would be invaluable.

I sought Kerry's advice early on, acted on his guidance, and kept him informed of my progress. When I told him I had a couple chapters written, he offered to provide feedback. I anxiously sent off the chapters and awaited his feedback, expecting to hear from him in perhaps a week or two. I was stunned when I received a call from him just two hours later. He had read the material and was excited to share his impressions. I can't recall everything he said, but I clearly remember him saying, "Wow, it's clear you've done your homework" and "Girl, can you write!" I was elated. He didn't have time to go into the details right then but suggested I come by his office so we could go through the chapters paragraph by paragraph. I scheduled two hours with him for the following week; he confirmed our appointment, requested I send another chapter for him to read, and signed off, "It will be fun to see you." I sent another chapter, and a week later I excitedly flew across two states and drove to his office.

After exchanging pleasantries, we sat down at his conference table, where printouts of my three chapters lay waiting. He admitted he hadn't had time to read the latest chapter but said he would just read and react to it on the spot. It can be unnerving to have someone critique your writing, but it's particularly unpleasant when the criticism is delivered in real time. With the flair of a stage actor, Kerry began to read aloud while I sat across the table. Suddenly I realized this wasn't going to be the fun meeting I'd expected.

He read a paragraph, paused, thought for a second, and said, "That's terrible." He then expounded on the various shortcomings of the passage. He read another couple of sentences and said, "I disagree. I don't think that's even true." For the next ninety minutes, he proceeded to shred my work as if I weren't even in the room. Meanwhile, I furiously took notes and tried to stay calm enough to absorb the feedback. What he was telling me was helpful, but it still stung—and not like a shot in the arm. It felt like I was being beaten up by my hero. When Kerry finished, he looked up at me to gauge my reaction. He had been focused on the pages in front of him; now he was earnestly looking to me for an indication that his feedback had been helpful.

I blurted out, "Kerry that was so, so painful." He cracked a mischievous smile. For emphasis I added, "Honestly, the only thing that would have made that worse for me was if I was also standing on the table naked while you ripped apart my work." We shared a good laugh. I couldn't help but ask about what felt like a bait and switch: "Whatever happened to 'Girl, can you write!'?" His expression softened as he explained, "I meant that. I'm giving you my toughest feedback because your work is really good and deserves it."

In the end, I left his office feeling built up, not torn down. I realized I had arrived with the wrong mindset. Ostensibly I had come seeking feedback, but the truth is that I had really been hoping for a second helping of praise, with a few pointers thrown in for good measure. Fortunately, this wise mentor offered me something more valuable: correction and guidance. This great thinker and writer had made an investment in me.

Back at my office, I reviewed the feedback and revised the work, applying his insights not only to the specific sections he had reviewed but everywhere I could. After the book was published, I wrote to Kerry and thanked him for having enough confidence in me to beat up my work (without a shred of mercy, mind you). He had the letter framed and hung in his office, apparently the only letter to receive this honor.

Kerry hadn't been giving *me* feedback; he had been critiquing *the work*.

When we can separate ourselves from our work, we can make the work better. Focusing on the work rather than the person lowers our defenses, allowing more information to get in. Where do you need to remove yourself in order to improve your work? If you want to grow faster, assume your worth and focus on the work. When we are more clinical about feedback, we become learning machines. And when we ask for guidance often, we establish an autotune process that keeps us continually in touch and tuned in.

Being defensive is the natural, default response to criticism. How can you increase your receptivity to correction? How might you let others know you are open to guidance and willing to act? How could you switch from a defensive posture to an offensive strategy?

Habit 2: Adjust Your Approach

An old maritime legend tells of a battleship navigating through cloudy conditions by night: The captain of a ship looked into the dark night and saw a light in the distance. Immediately he told his signalman to send a message to the other vessel: "Alter your course ten degrees south." He received a prompt reply: "Alter your course ten degrees north." The captain was furious and sent another message to the obstinate commander: "Alter your course ten degrees south." Again the reply came: "Alter your course ten degrees north." The captain sent a final message: "Alter your course ten degrees south. I am a battleship." The reply was "Alter your course ten degrees north. I am a lighthouse."

Though that conversation never actually occurred in recorded maritime history, similar conversations happen every day in the workplace. One party has established a clear course and set their sails accordingly. Another party sees things differently, and now the two are set to collide. Who changes course?

Deep Shrestha is a lead programmer on the Salesforce Technical

Services team. The senior director of the division, Marcus Groff, said, "The guy has a real motor. He takes on challenges with a sense of joy and does things out of pride. He's fearless."

Early in his career, Deep's fearless zeal meant he occasionally locked horns with his colleagues. He started his career as a programmer at a software company called Bullhorn (coincidently but aptly named). As a routine part of his job, he received support requests from the customer service team. For the most part, he would review the customer's problem, find the glitch, and fix the code. But occasionally, he would receive tickets from support staff that were confusing or unfounded. Once, having received a particularly bogus service request, he was so frustrated that he stormed upstairs to customer support, found the support analyst, questioned him, and then let him know how stupid his request was. The manager of the customer support department called Deep's manager to tell him that Deep had been disrespectful. Deep admitted in hindsight, "I may have implied that he was a tad idiotic." Deep apologized, but did so three months later via email.

Deep had been the de facto architect for Bullhorn's products when Salesforce acquired the small software company. It was work he took great pride in doing well. Now that Deep was part of Salesforce, his product would need to be integrated into a suite of applications and work seamlessly with all the other products in the suite. A meeting of the various product architects was called to determine how the products would collectively handle customer purchase transactions—specifically, how they would be logged in the database. Deep had a simple but effective design in mind, which he shared with the group. The team pushed back on his ideas and pointed out the limitations of his approach in worst-case scenarios, such as incomplete transactions and server failure. Another architect recommended a far more complex design, which Deep saw as a complicated overkill and a waste of resources. He continued to argue for a simpler design, but the others were as unconvinced about the merits of his design as he was of theirs. They were at a standoff.

Deep left the meeting feeling frustrated, defensive, and stinging from their critical feedback. But this was not the first time his ideas had been shot down. He had learned years earlier that reacting too quickly to feedback was a mistake, akin to marching upstairs and giving an unsuspecting support analyst a piece of his mind. So he did what he had learned to do in such situations: he took a walk. He had discovered that a walk helped him create a buffer space to clear his head and, as he calls it, find his mind—the part that was calm and could listen and learn.

He set out on his walk in anger but returned to the office with a clear head. He revisited the problem but with empathy, putting on his colleagues' shoes and seeing the issue from their perspective. Now immersed in their logic and assuming best intent, Deep asked himself: "What are they not getting from me that they need?"

He realized that he had missed a key factor: the user experience. How would users react if their purchase transactions failed and the system didn't have the data to provide a clear communication of the transaction status? Would they wonder if they had been charged before they canceled the transaction? Now seeing all sides, he agreed to their approach and changed his product design.

Deep recalled, "It was a learning experience for me. Because we took the other approach, the product is more resilient." So is Deep, whom colleagues now describe as highly collaborative and "as willing to run with one of his teammate's ideas as his own." Most professionals tend to stay the course, while the most valuable professionals are willing to adjust their approach as needed.

Let Go

Leadership expert John Maxwell once said that change is inevitable but growth is optional. During our interviews, we consistently heard managers describe typical contributors as capable but unwilling to embrace change. One manager said, "I have to pull teeth to get him to move forward." Another said, "I have to sell her on what I need her to do. It's exhausting. I've come to dread one-on-ones with her." Though those employees were smart and capable, they struggled to let go of their existing routines and move beyond their established skills and ideas.

On the other hand, Impact Players adapt with such consistency that it's one of the five factors in the Performance Guarantee discussed in chapter 4 (see page 112).

Releasing our grip on our existing way of working sometimes requires us to take a break, hit the reset button, and resume. Deep Shrestha's practice of taking a walk can provide this type of reset. Not all of these walks literally involved walking, he said: "I just do something to not think about it for a bit." The method is irrelevant; what matters is creating separation to let go of old ideas and emotional reactions. "The goal is to slow my reaction and create a buffer space so I can find my mind and think objectively." When I asked Deep to name this practice, he thought for a moment and answered, "Reset walks."

When we reset, we find our right mind. We can't change course until we can see clearly.

Fine-Tune Your Approach

Though the business world is fascinated with reinvention, disruption, and transformation, there's danger in making big changes. Abrupt behavior changes can appear inauthentic or take us further off course. Instead of making big changes, fine-tune your approach by making a series of small adjustments in the right direction.

Jonathon Modica, a former HR leader at Adobe, exemplifies this ability to shift directions. When assigned to a high-profile project developing a new program for two senior business leaders, he started a meeting by framing the conversation: "I have some hypotheses to run by you." When one of the executives poked at his idea, he didn't become defensive or overreact. Instead, he stopped, leaned back, and said, "Help me understand what you want to see differently." He asked a series of clarifying questions to help understand the issues and objectives. After the meeting, Jonathon took in their feedback and began testing each suggestion until they discovered an approach that fit best.

He left such an impression that the two executives later asked his manager, "When do we get to work on another project with Jonathon?"

Jonathon didn't overreact or overcorrect. When taking in new feedback, you can avoid overcorrection by asking yourself: "What is the smallest change I can make that will get me closer to the target and make a noticeable difference?" As Peter Sims wrote in *Little Bets*, "Once a small win has been accomplished, forces are set in motion that favor another small win." Making a series of small corrections will build momentum and help you avoid major disasters.

Admit and Recover from Mistakes

Whoever said "Fail fast, make mistakes, and learn" probably didn't have wedding gowns in mind.

I was just seventeen years old when a bridal store hired me as its alteration seamstress. I had been sewing since I was young, and having made prom gowns and a tuxedo, I was fearless with a sewing machine. Most of the alterations were fairly simple, but when Kathy, a petite size 6, fell in love with a size 12 sample dress, my skills were put to the test. I disassembled and completely remade the dress. It fit perfectly, to her delight and mine.

The big screwup came when Kathy arrived to pick up her dress four days before her wedding. The store manager asked me to do a final pressing. She shouldn't have had to ask me. I knew I was supposed to press the dresses I altered, but I hated steaming and pressing them; it was sweaty work, and I considered it below my skill level. Begrudgingly, I fired up the iron and began. As I placed the iron on the bodice, I watched in horror as the polyester fabric and lace overlay started to shrivel. I quickly pulled away the iron to find a gaping hole in the bodice of the wedding dress! I stopped breathing as my eyes tried to process what my hands had just done—not just to the dress but to a bride getting married in four days. How could I have possibly done this?

It was such an egregious mistake that someone could be tempted to fabricate some story about an iron gone wild. However, this was entirely my fault, and there was no way to cover it up. So when I walked onto the store floor where the bride-to-be waited, I greeted her and said matter-of-factly, "Kathy, I just melted a large hole in the front of your wedding gown. It's really bad. But I will fix it, and it will be perfect again in two days." As you might imagine, Kathy was horrified. But to my greater surprise, she didn't scream or cry (though it would have been justified). She listened to my plan and expressed her confidence in my ability to fix the dress.

After school the next day, I drove across town, bought exactly the right materials, and then re-created the burned-out bodice panel. This time, I pressed it carefully, taking pride in this unglamorous work. When Kathy picked up her dress two days later, she showered me with praise—to her credit, not mine. That botched bodice and forbearing bride taught me a few secrets about how to recover well from mistakes: the best approach is to readily admit the mistake, take full ownership, fix it quickly and completely, and then do a little more.

Admitting mistakes and recovering quickly is one of the top ten differentiators between Impact Players and under-contributors.[12] Though admitting you were wrong is rarely easy, it's more easily done through a growth lens. With a fixed mindset, a mistake is a failure and a confrontation of one's own limitations. With a growth mindset, it is a chance to improve a product, repair a relationship, and ultimately restore confidence—either in ourselves or with the people around us.

When a distinguished professor of biomedical engineering wrote an article that contained some questionable conclusions, medical experts erupted on the internet to correct him. Instead of justifying his argument, he extended an immediate mea culpa on Twitter that read: "I was wrong. Thanks to all those who offered constructive criticism." When you have misstepped, the following process will help you restore confidence.

1. **Recognize the gap.** We can recognize some mistakes by the chorus of critical feedback telling us to change course. However, when we've misread a situation or behaved in an inappropriate way, we

often hear nothing. The only way to recognize these things is to ask people who will tell us the hard truth.

2. **Admit your mistakes.** When we hide or downplay mistakes, it leaves people questioning both our capability and our connection to reality. When we talk frankly about our mishaps, the conversation shifts from blame and cover-up to recovery. And when we readily admit our mistakes, it gives others permission to come clean, too.

3. **Fix problems fast.** Numerous studies show that fixing emergent snags both quickly and well can actually yield a net increase in customer satisfaction. Don't just own the mistake; fix it fast and completely.

4. **Solve the whole problem.** Every job has its unattractive, low-level work. While prima donnas cherry-pick the glamorous work (and leave holes for others to close), the most valuable professionals solve the whole problem, from top to bottom. Those who tackle the entire job later find themselves entrusted with bigger jobs.

Admitting our mistakes not only keeps us out of trouble; it's the key to maintaining self-awareness and understanding our impact on others. The Nobel Prize–winning economist Paul Krugman wrote:

Everyone makes bad predictions; God knows I have. But when you keep getting things wrong, and especially when you keep getting them wrong in the same direction, you're supposed to engage in some self-reflection—and learn from your mistakes. Why was I wrong? Did I give in to motivated reasoning, believing what I wanted to be true rather than following the logic and evidence? To engage in such self-reflection, however, you have to be willing to admit that you were wrong in the first place.[13]

When we admit mistakes early and fix them quickly, we let people know we're learning and that their feedback was a good investment.

Habit 3: Close the Loop

Braden Hancock is a cofounder and the head of technology of the promising Silicon Valley start-up Snorkel AI, a machine learning company spun off from a prestigious lab in Stanford University's Computer Science Department. Braden has a ridiculously impressive résumé, especially for a young professional: internships at the Air Force Research Laboratory, Google, and Facebook; research assistantships at Johns Hopkins University, MIT, and Stanford University; an undergraduate degree in mechanical engineering; and a PhD from Stanford in computer science.

People wonder what's behind his string of achievements. Braden is, of course, really smart and extremely hardworking. He's also genuinely humble and nice—I mean deep-down, real-deal nice. But it's more than just smarts, effort, and affability. Braden achieves more because he seeks more guidance than his peers, and managers and mentors invest in him. Here's why.

When he was young, Braden wanted to be a mechanical engineer and do cutting-edge research. Luckily the Air Force Research Laboratory was located in his hometown of Dayton, Ohio, and he landed an internship there. He didn't simply show up and do his assigned work; he asked his manager, John Clark, a passionate research scientist, for more. When John gave him extra-challenging work, Braden would head off to the lab's world-class library to investigate. Dr. Clark said, "I know scientists who have worked at this lab for decades who have never been to that library."

Braden again worked for Dr. Clark following his college freshman year. Braden asked for a challenging project that might earn him a scholarship for graduate school, so Dr. Clark assigned him the problem of reducing the strength of shock waves inside a jet engine flying beyond the sonic barrier, a project typically reserved for advanced graduate students. Dr. Clark defined the problem and offered guidance. Braden then worked independently to solve the problems, head-ing to the library when he needed to know more. When he reached an impasse, he looped back to Dr. Clark with questions.

Braden submitted the project for a prestigious national award for scientific research. When the judge announced that Braden, a college freshman, had received the national award, the judge had tears in his eyes, and explained, "It is so much more than he should have been able to achieve based on his education." Braden stays in touch with Dr. Clark, letting his mentor know how those internships and projects have led to new opportunities.

Despite a lack of computer programming experience, Braden later secured an internship at Johns Hopkins, working under the direction of Mark Dredze, an associate professor of computer science. Braden completed an online programming course before arriving so that he could hit the ground running; once in the lab, he used natural language processing techniques to analyze social media for shifts in public sentiment on public health issues such as gun control. He sought direction, solved problems, and asked for specific guidance when he got stuck. As he made progress, he looped back to the professor to agree on next steps. That internship opened a new career pathway that led to a doctoral program in computer science at Stanford University. At each step, Braden looped back, letting Dr. Dredze know where his guidance and mentoring had taken him.

In his doctoral program, Braden looked for an adviser and quickly noticed Chris Ré, a star professor and technology entrepreneur. Dr. Ré gave Braden the same advice he gives all graduate students: come to the weekly lunch meeting where current lab members discuss their projects, listen in, and look for a fit. Some grad students listened in but were disappointed that they weren't assigned projects; others found roles in projects that fit their preexisting interests and skills. Braden's approach was different. Noticing that a second-year graduate student, Alex Ratner, was someone Dr. Ré relied on heavily, Braden offered to help Alex. Braden did what he had always done: quickly solve the first problem, offer ideas for next steps, ask for guidance when stuck, act on it, and then report back. After a few cycles, he was working on the hottest project in Dr. Ré's lab, creating the technology that would become Snorkel, where Braden (aka Dr. Hancock) now works alongside Dr. Ré and Dr. Ratner.

There's a pattern in how this engineer and entrepreneur has obtained and maximized opportunities: He looks for people doing great work and then works on projects they are excited about. He does his homework, solves problems, and then does more. He consistently closes the loop, letting his managers know the job got done and what became of their advice. It is a purposeful and authentic way of contributing that activates a mentoring gene in others and triggers an investment cycle. As Braden makes an impact, his mentors make another investment in him.

Dr. Dredze acknowledged how satisfying it is to watch someone grow and said, "I was recently on a webinar when the subject of Snorkel came up. I jumped onto chat to tell people that Braden Hancock was one of my students!" Dr. Clark said, "He's such a good person. You want the best for him. Nice guys don't always win, but Braden wins, and I hope he keeps winning." He continued, "Braden isn't someone to squander an opportunity. He's the kind of guy you give pearls to."

Managers are willing to invest, but they want to invest in a closed-loop system, not a black box. When you ask for guidance and then close the loop, you let people know that their investment in you has yielded results.

Certainly Braden entered the workforce having had a strong education and access to opportunity. But these practices took him further. Wherever you start, closing the loop can take you further, too.

THE DECOYS AND DISTRACTIONS

While Impact Players are adjusting to the shifting winds of change, professionals operating in the Contributor Mindset are seeking stability and hunkering down. In this mode, we keep doing what has worked in the past. As one manager said, it's a difference of learners versus knowers. We steer clear of unstable, unsettling conditions and discount disquieting information. We become wary of things such as customer-driven innovation, new technologies, reorganization, surprising new job responsibilities, and 360-degree feedback. When taken to an extreme, we start avoiding the people who can give us much-needed corrective guidance, such as one SAP employee who didn't like the feedback she was getting from her boss, so she simply didn't come into the office the days her boss was there.

This tendency to avoid uncomfortable situations is a reflection of a fixed mindset, a belief that *my basic capability is set and doesn't change very much.*[14] When we hold a fixed mindset, the goal becomes looking smart and doing our best never to look dumb. This mentality causes otherwise smart, capable people to stick to what they know best or, when feeling most vulnerable, insist they know best. This drive to perform well can lead to two very different orientations to feedback; one is avoidance, the other is obsession. Both extremes contain decoys—practices that seem helpful but actually erode the value of our contribution.

Stick to Strengths

"Go where you are celebrated, not where you are tolerated" seems like good career advice. Everyone enjoys working where their unique strengths are seen and appreciated. It is certainly more pleasant to wade in a stream of affirming feedback than it is to trudge through criticism and correction. But when we follow the applause, we lose touch with reality and avoid situations that expose our weaknesses. In playing to our strengths, we may stop playing games we aren't sure we can win. We might even try twisting the game to our advantage, like the Swedish footballer and goalkeeper who literally moved the goalposts a few inches, making it harder for his opponents to score against him.[15]

Leaders should certainly seek out and use the native genius of their team members, but playing solely to our strengths can limit our ability to grow. In an environment of constant change, we all need to keep growing. Our most valuable contribution will come as we assume that real strength is the ability to adapt and adjust.

Game Face

When we are struggling to keep up with the pace of constant change, it's tempting to project a false sense of strength. We want to appear as if we have the situation under control, so we come to work with our game face on: We say the right things, use the latest terminology, and act as though we know what we're doing. I've certainly nodded my head and acted like I knew what I was doing when I really didn't. However, the problem with this classic fake-it-till-we-make-it strategy is that while it may inspire confidence initially, it suppresses learning and dissuades others from giving us the coaching we need. The fake smile or false bravado creates a feedback barrier, the false impression that we don't need guidance.

Instead of trying to portray confidence, project a clear understanding of a tough situation and demonstrate a willingness to be coached. Acknowledging the size of a challenge and the gap you need to close will actually increase your colleagues' confidence in you. And admitting what you don't yet know but intend to learn opens the gate to the feedback and coaching you need to be game ready.

Feedback Frenzy

But what happens when we swing to the other extreme, seeking feedback constantly, continually asking our boss, "How am I doing?" We can become so feedback-dependent that our desire for reaction borders on self-obsession. The problem with this overeager approach to feedback is that it is usually personal, as in "How am *I* doing?" rather than "Is this work hitting the mark?" To our colleagues, these requests seem more like pleas for affirmation than requests for feedback. This all-about-me approach is exhausting for managers. Instead of guiding everyone's work, they are feeding one person's ego.

A better approach is to get a regular flow of feedback on your work, not as a special request for attention but as a natural by-product of the work process. And don't just ask your manager. Your manager is just one source of information, so seek guidance from multiple perspectives. Most important, instead of asking people for feedback on your performance, ask for information and insights that will help you do the work well.

MULTIPLYING YOUR IMPACT

During our interviews, dozens of managers lamented that their employees weren't changing or fixing their issues, only to admit later in the interview that they had never actually talked with the person about the issue. Why would managers withhold this vital information? When it's too frustrating for managers to give feedback, they stop giving it. You see, the real problem isn't that most players aren't asking for feedback, it's that they aren't receiving it.

The inability to receive correction not only limits an individual's growth, it limits an organization's ability to change. When seeking

VALUE BUILDING: ASK AND ADJUST

Impact Players seek feedback, receive more guidance, and get seen as coachable players

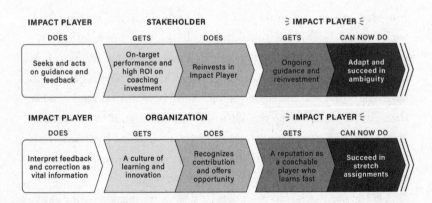

affirmation rather than feedback becomes a norm inside an organization, the culture resists its own transformation efforts. The aspirations of the organization are drowned out by the internal PR machine that shouts, "We are doing a great job!" Simply put, when we stick to what we know, we get stuck. Individuals and entire organizations can become pigeonholed in roles that limit their growth.

In contrast, with Impact Players, a little coaching goes a long way. Because they seek and act on feedback, they hit the target and receive a steady stream of guidance that helps get the right job done, develop more innovative approaches, and adapt in new and ambiguous situations. Their way of working not only up-levels their game, it raises the bar for everyone else on the team—an idea we'll explore further in chapter 8.

In reflecting on the lessons of his prolific acting career, Jason Robards, Jr., mused, "We grow each day or don't grow. . . . We're a different person all the time." [16] Top contributors and difference makers are constantly changing, ever adapting.

A finish line isn't an endpoint; it's a transition, a passage to something new. Michelle Obama captured this truth in the title of her memoir, *Becoming*. In the final words of the book she wrote, "I am still in progress, and I hope that I always will be. For me, 'becoming' isn't about arriving somewhere or achieving a certain aim. I see it instead as forward motion, a means of evolving, a way to reach continuously toward a better self. . . . Becoming is never giving up on the idea that there's more growing to be done." [17]

As we grow, we often need to slow down, catch our breath, and take account of where we've been so we can progress. We may need to follow Deep's example and take a reset walk. Where might you need to shed what you know and evolve your beliefs? Where do you need to let go of what has always worked to uncover an approach that will work better in the current reality?

Sometimes the smallest of adjustment is all we need to stay on course. Instead of pursuing big changes, master the art of small change. Invite input and seek correction. Ask for guidance and take action, then occasionally double back to let your guide know that with their help, you found your way. It will remind them that they've made a good investment and that their seeds of wisdom fell on fertile soil.

THE PLAYBOOK

This playbook contains tips for aspiring leaders to exercise and strengthen the assumptions and habits necessary to ASK AND ADJUST.

Smart Plays

1. **Ask for guidance, not feedback.** Because feedback is associated with evaluation rather than improvement, people tend to get better feedback in both quantity and quality when they ask for advice or guidance rather than feedback.[18] Instead of asking people for feedback on your performance, ask for information and insights that will help you do the task well. Use questions such as: "If I want to do X really well, what advice do you have for me?" "What insights do you have that would help me do a better job next time I do X?" "What should I do more of?" "What should I do less of?" "If I did just one thing differently next time, what would you suggest?"

2. **Walk it off.** Even for the most confident learners, feedback can still hurt and inflict injury on our ego. Much like an athlete, we can shake off the sting of a minor injury by walking it off. The following tactics can help you create some space between receiving and responding to feedback and will help prevent overreaction.

   • **Take a reset walk.** Literally, walk it off and clear your head.
   • **Talk it out.** Talk through what you hear with a friend or colleague before responding.
   • **Assume positive intent.** Consider the best intentions of the person

giving you feedback. Assume that they are on your side and are helping you improve your work.

- **Regroup.** Ask for time to process the guidance you've received and come back with a plan. Be sure to show appreciation for the feedback.
- **Be authentic.** Admit that your initial reaction is to feel defensive. Let them know that you intend to understand and act on their insight and will process it as soon as your amygdala calms down and you can lower your defenses.

3. **Circle back.** Don't leave people wondering what you did with the feedback or guidance that they gave you. Show its full effect and give an account of what you've done with their investment in you. You can close the loop by saying: (1) This is the guidance you gave me, (2) This is how I acted upon it, (3) This is what ensued, (4) This is how this experience benefited me and others, and (5) This is what I plan to do next.

When you close the loop, others can see how their investment in you yielded success and continues to accrue benefits for you and others, and they'll be more likely to make further investments in you.

Safety Tips

1. **Help others speak up.** People at all levels can feel uncomfortable offering someone else corrective guidance. Try making it safe for others in these ways.

   - **Invite.** Let them know that to hit the mark, you need to know where you might be missing the mark.
   - **React.** Don't get defensive, don't make excuses, don't retaliate. Just listen and ask clarifying questions.
   - **Respond.** Thank people for their insight and let them know how it will help you hit the mark.

2. **Publicize your progress.** For starters, let people know what you've done as a result of their individual feedback. Take it further by making your general learning a matter of public record. Let your colleagues know (1) what you are hearing from internal or external customers, (2) what insights you've gleaned, and (3) what adjustments you are making based on those insights.

Coaching tips for managers: You can find coaching practices to help your team members ask and adjust in "The Coach's Playbook" at the end of chapter 8.

CHAPTER 5 SUMMARY: ASK AND ADJUST

This chapter describes how Impact Players deal with moving targets and invitations to change and why they adapt and learn faster than their peers.

	CONTRIBUTOR MINDSET	IMPACT PLAYER MINDSET
Practice	Stick to What They Know Best	Ask and Adjust
Assumptions	My basic capability doesn't change very much, so change is a threat *(caution)*	I am valuable and can grow and evolve *(confidence)* Ability can be developed through effort *(growth)* I have inherent value and ability *(inherent worth)*
Habits	Seek validation Do what you're good at	Ask for guidance Adjust your approach Close the loop
Implications	This mindset limits an individual's professional growth and an organization's ability to change.	Individuals build a reputation as coachable players who up-level their own game and raise the bar for everyone on the team. This strengthens a culture of learning and innovation, helping the organization stay relevant.

Decoys to avoid: (1) Sticks to strengths, (2) Game face, (3) Feedback frenzy

Unrelenting Demands

CONTRIBUTORS	⋛ IMPACT PLAYERS ⋚
"She requires a lot of my time. I have to provide her a lot of support with things she should be able to do."	"He frequently comes to me and says, 'What can I take off your plate? How can I make your job easier?'"
"She makes everything harder for herself and others. She may get the job done, but there is a lot of damage in her wake."	"She avoids drama. Things don't get to her. She is compassionate but refuses to be an actor in any soap opera."
"When I have to have a one-to-one with him, it's an effort. It's draining. I don't look forward to it."	"She exudes positive energy. It's just big fun working with her."

Chapter 6

MAKE WORK LIGHT

There seems to be some perverse human characteristic
that likes to make easy things difficult.
—**WARREN BUFFETT**

The Great Alaskan Earthquake of 1964 was the most powerful quake ever in North America and the second most powerful ever in the world. It ripped open swaths of south-central Alaska, collapsing structures, creating chasms, and spawning tsunamis in twenty countries.[1] The epicenter was just outside the metropolis of Anchorage, home to 45,000 people.

Genie Chance was an Anchorage resident, wife, and mother of three who worked as a part-time reporter for the local radio station. When the megathrust quake hit at 5:36 p.m. on March 27, she was in the car with her son on an errand. As they drove to town, their car began to jerk and bounce. They saw parked cars slamming together, pedestrians struggling to stand, windows exploding, and a massive rolling of the road. Genie recognized that it was no minor event. When the four and a half minutes of convulsions and confusion ended, Genie's reporter instincts kicked in. She drove to the police and fire departments to gather details for a quick report. Then she and her son went downtown, where they witnessed the extent of the devastation. A new five-story department store had collapsed, and two entire city blocks had fallen into a chasm where the ground had ripped open.

Genie Chance's story is chronicled in Jon Mooallem's book *This Is Chance!* Mooallem wrote, "Genie knew that the citizens of Anchorage were scattered around, cut off from each other. The electrical grid was down. Most phone lines were dead. There'd be no way to know exactly what had happened or how thoroughly their world had been jumbled."[2] Genie made a quick trip home, and after she found her other children safe, she got to work.

The radio station began broadcasting on auxiliary power, and Genie used a portable radio unit in her car to make her first report. She provided the information she had and asked listeners to check on their neighbors. She offered the police and fire chiefs her radio to use for broadcasts; instead, they gave her the broadcasting job. She would become the voice that held the city together, as Mooallem put it. The electricity was out, and the temperature was below freezing; people were trapped in homes and buildings, and Genie's calm voice of hope would prevent mass hysteria, unite a community, and carry it through its most challenging time.

Initially, she provided essential information from local authorities. She listed locations of public shelters and read instructions for purifying water. Soon she was doing more than reporting the news; she was coordinating the initial emergency response. Officials and volunteers passed Genie notes, and she called for help: "All electricians and plumbers of Fort Ridge, go to Building 700 immediately." She connected resources with the people and places most in need of assistance. Members of the community came together—a loosely organized but highly effective mass of first responders. As people were rescued and damage was repaired, Genie assured listeners that the most volatile situations were under control.

The physical dangers began to subside, but people were rattled emotionally, still worried about loved ones. Genie started relaying thousands of messages, (e.g., "A message to Kenneth Sadler, Mrs. Sadler is fine. A message to Walter Hart at Kenai, Lee Hart is fine. Tim Murphy and Bill Somerville at Point Hope, your families are A-OK.")[3] With every report, Genie's real message was "You're not alone."[4] "Even amid all that devastation, people seemed happy," one researcher observed. "People felt a connection to one another, a kinship that's often lacking in ordinary life, and this togetherness seemed to make their problems more bearable."[5]

Genie Chance remained on duty and on-air for fifty-nine hours (sans a few naps), serving her community with devotion, intelligence, and strength. A colleague described her reports as "instrumental in avoiding panic confusion" and noted that she encouraged others and remained calm while "assuming such heavy responsibilities for such a long period of time, and without her voice showing the strain."[6] Mooallem wrote, "The information was a form of comfort, but so was the voice delivering it." He added, "She became known as the voice of Alaska, a stand-in for the resourcefulness and composure of an entire state."[7] Genie Chance's reporting lightened the air in a heavy time and made the community's arduous work more bearable.

Consider your work: Do you tend to make easy things difficult, or do you make hard work easier for everyone on the team? When things are tough and the load is heavy, the most valuable players on teams make work lighter. Though they may not be able to reduce the workload, they make the work process easier and more joyful. They are like a bouquet of helium balloons.

This fifth and final practice is about how top contributors and leaders deal with pressure and unrelenting demands. We'll explore how some people manage to take the work out of work and why Impact Players create a positive and productive work environment for everyone on the team—including themselves. We will meet a brilliant set of high-value, low-maintenance superstars from around the globe, in Waldorf, Germany; Boston; Dubai; and the San Francisco Bay Area. After exploring how these all-stars make hard work easier, we'll circle back to Anchorage to consider the enduring impact of people like Genie Chance.

As you dig in, you'll discover ways to be easy—easy to work with and easy for others to engage you at your best. Above all, we'll explore why being seen as low maintenance is as vital as being considered high performance, especially now, when both leaders and teams face non-stop demands and constant strain and burnout, which can spread like wildfire and threaten huge swaths of the workforce.

THE CHOICE:
GET WEIGHED DOWN OR PROVIDE LIFT?

Our workload can feel like a mounting debt that grows perpetually and follows us everywhere we go. Most professionals feel this at some level: there is too much work to get done each week, too many new tools and technologies to master, and more information than we can process, let alone retain—and that's just the day job. In 2019, full-time employees in the United States averaged 8.5 hours of work time on weekdays, and more than a third of them worked on any given weekend or holiday.[8] *Harvard Business Review* reports that the average executive, manager, and professional works a seventy-two-hour work-week.[9] The high-pressure workloads that were once seasonal have become normalized. One corporate manager said of their workload, "It's like hiking uphill while carrying a child and a dog, and every time I stop to catch my breath, someone puts another rock in my backpack."

Yet our *actual* workload accounts for only a portion of the burden we experience at work. In one survey, over half of respondents said that their primary source of work-related stress didn't have to do with their workload; rather, they cited stressors such as people issues, juggling work and personal lives, and lack of job security.[10] Workplace politics and drama create friction, and complex collaborations and endless meetings dominate time. Another study found that US employees spend, on average, 2.8 hours per week dealing with workplace conflicts.[11] A study by Rob Cross, Reb Rebele, and Adam Grant estimated that over the previous two decades, the time spent in collaborative activities has increased by 50 percent or more, generating a deluge of additional meetings and email traffic that tax collaborators and can put an organization into gridlock.[12] These factors constitute a phantom workload and can lead to burnout.

Meanwhile, the same technology that enables us to work anywhere also urges us to work everywhere and at all hours. The Center for Creative Leadership found that employees who carry a smartphone report interacting with their jobs for 13.5 hours each day on average.[13] In the last two decades, work has been like rising floodwater seeping into our homes, with professionals who work a second shift caring for family members experiencing the highest levels of stress. The blurring of work and home reached its peak in 2020 when the world took shelter en masse from the threat of COVID-19. The abrupt shift to working from home was a tidal wave that left some treading water juggling too many jobs and others stranded on metaphorical islands, working in isolation.

Our work, both the real work and the phantom workload, can feel inescapable and exhausting. According to a 2019 Gallup study,[14] eight in ten full-time employees feel burnt out. It would be one thing if we were spending extra hours and energy conquering difficult challenges with a team, but much of that energy is spent unproductively focused on insurmountable obstacles and obstinate coworkers. While mastering challenge is exhilarating, dealing with unproductive conflict is simply exhausting. We waste too much of our energy and intelligence dealing with office politics and conflicts and high-maintenance colleagues.

Without realizing it, we can add to the weight of this problem. When the pressure is on and the workload increases, typical contributors seek help rather than offering to help, becoming dependent on their bosses to relieve their burden. As they do, they put another rock in their manager's pack. Some are truly difficult to work with and taxing to their colleagues. But most don't actively foment conflict; they simply contribute to the stress by participating in the clatter on the periphery of the actual work and adding to the noise.

For example, Isle[15] is a highly capable and hardworking chief operating officer for an engineering division of a global technology company. Isle is usually the last person to leave the office. She's conscientious and completes all her work, but she likes to fix and finish other people's work as well. She tells her boss, the head of engineering, "The quality of their work was so bad, I had to fix it." That person usually finds out that she's disparaged them, and in turn looks for ways to undo her attempt to redo their efforts, and her boss is often sucked in to arbitrate. Her boss observed, "She may get the job done, but she annoys five people in the process. She acts as if she's adding value, but it's antivalue."

When people begin creating more noise than value, they become an additional burden to their leaders and colleagues, which, in turn, makes work harder for them as well. Yet other people, faced with the same workload and unrelenting demands, help lighten the load. While others create a tax, the most vital players offer a time rebate. They make hard work easier; the work doesn't necessarily become easier, but the process of working becomes easier and more enjoyable. They provide lift, not by taking on other people's work but by decreasing the phantom workload. They foster a light environment that lowers stress and increases the joy of work, both of which reduce burnout. These critical players reduce drama and politics, reinforcing a culture of collaboration and inclusion. Meanwhile, they develop a reputation as a high-performing, no-nonsense player who everyone wants to work with. As they make work easier for their colleagues, work gets easier for them as well.

Here is what the practice of making work lighter looks like in action.

Cathy Ward is the global chief operating officer of SAP Innovation Services in the United Kingdom. Karl Doose is the business manager on her staff. Most executives at SAP have a business manager who does financial and business analyses to help ensure a profitable and smooth operation; however, not everyone has a business manager like Karl Doose.

Karl was just twenty-three years old when he assumed that responsibility. Despite his youth, he sees his role as critical to the business and behaves accordingly. As he started his new job, he looked up "chief of staff"—a role a notch or two higher than his—to better understand what that job entails. He then created a three-slide presentation for Cathy. On slide one, he articulated what he believed his role would look like when done exceptionally well. On slide two, he assessed his current capabilities. On slide three, he outlined his development plan.

Karl said, "My job is to make my boss successful. If it is important to her, it's important to me. If she looks good, I look good." Hence, Karl doesn't just do his job as business manager; he's continually thinking about her job and what she needs for the team to be successful. He doesn't wait for Cathy or anyone else on the team to ask for an analysis. He looks ahead on Cathy's schedule and predicts the information and analyses she'll want based on what she's needed in the past. For example, if she has a client review upcoming, he puts together a slide deck before she asks and emails her, saying, "You've got a client review next week. These charts should help."

Part of Karl's brilliance is his ability to metabolize data quickly and distill information into the most relevant points. Cathy said, "Karl listens to understand the problem and then comes back, sometimes just thirty minutes later, with something that hits the mark, has the right tone, and looks great, too." He understands that by communicating briefly and clearly, his ideas have greater reach and value to others. For example, if he finds a thirty-page white paper that would be of interest to Cathy or the rest of the team, he sends it with a note: "I appreciate you won't have time to read this, so here are the five salient points." The speed at which he learns and the efficiency with which he communicates is "constantly saving time for the business," according to Cathy.

Synthesizing critical information is done not just for his manager; it's a strength that Karl shares freely with others on the team and beyond. For example, Cathy had just finished a full day of meetings in Germany when she received an urgent message from the company's head of product development. He had an important presentation to the SAP board of directors and wondered if her team could help him create an executive summary. Word had gotten out that her team excelled at this. Cathy briefed Karl, who had also just finished a full day of meetings. He was excited by the invitation and had energy for the challenge. Cathy flew back to London. When she landed an hour later, she found an email in her inbox with Karl's new presentation attached. Karl had sorted through the executive's detailed presentation, pulled out the key messages, and crafted a new set of slides. Cathy said, "It was a total transformation. The presentation was pitch perfect." The same day, Karl received a message from the head of development: "Karl, I didn't know you until this morning. . . . Personally, I have become your fan—how could you turn such a mundane PPT into such an elegant pitch so quickly? Thank you, and I will look forward to working more with you."

Karl makes work light for everyone, not just his boss. Cathy said, "It's easy to engage Karl like a peer, because that's how he operates." As a result, he is given opportunities, learns about the business at a su-percharged rate, and is seen as ready to be promoted. He was recently promoted to chief of staff, something that was easy to justify because he was already operating this way.

When workloads bear down, do you seek relief from your boss and push work to your colleagues, adding to their burdens? Or do you help make work lighter for all?

THE MENTAL GAME

When workloads spike and persist, managers typically seek external reinforcements—additional head count—to cover the work. Their logic is: *Our team has more work; therefore, we need more workers.* Though new recruits can provide relief, additional head count also increases the managerial burden; there are more people needing direction, more issues to resolve, more one-on-one meetings, higher coordination costs, and often more drama.

Impact Players aren't like the reinforcements dispatched from recruiting. They work as structural reinforcements, much as crossbeams and rebar-reinforced concrete columns fortify structures to withstand greater loads. While other colleagues add to the load, they make work light. The way they approach work enables an entire team to carry a heavy load.

Impact Players interpret unrelenting demands as an opportunity to support and help others. Their orientation to help begins with a sense of belonging, a notion that they are not only on the team, they are wanted in the group, their unique strengths are recognized, and their work is needed and valued. They hold the fundamental belief that *I am an important part of the team*. They assume they are valued members of a community, as are their colleagues.

Lionel Lemoine, director of solution consulting for Adobe's Western EMEA region, builds community and creates a sense of belonging, not just on his team but across the entire office. Lionel's manager, Chris Taplin, said, "Lionel is easy to approach. He creates great energy in the office. The people around him can feel that he cares about what they care about." Lionel is known to keep a bowl of chocolates on his desk—the workplace equivalent of a welcome mat. Lionel, who is French and works in Paris, admits, "I love chocolate. I always keep ten different flavors." This is fine chocolate, the really good stuff. People stop by Lionel's desk for coffee, chocolates, and discussion. It's light, it's friendly. The bowl of chocolates says, "Come, sit down, talk to me, you are welcome here."

Contrast this with an accounting professional at a major event company who also had a bowl of chocolates prominently displayed on her desk. She didn't keep it light and friendly like Lionel did; rather, once she ensnared her colleagues with chocolates, she sucked them into self-indulgent ranting. Her colleagues soon learned this display of generosity was a trap. The chocolates were her web, and the visitor her prey. The message was more like "Right now, I own you." Instead of building community, she was building her own involuntary support system.

When people feel that they belong in a community, they become more active and operate with a heightened sense of obligation to the community. This is what the researcher and advocate Ash Buchanan refers to as a benefit mindset—an extension of a growth mindset in which we not only seek to grow and fulfill our potential but do it in a way that serves the well-being of all.[16] Buchanan wrote, "In a benefit mindset, we understand we are not separate individuals going it alone.

We are interdependent beings who belong to a massive global ecosystem." [17] The belief is: *I can improve well-being for all.*

This belief is at the core of how Lionel Lemoine leads and collaborates. Lionel said, "I work from a mindset that I am useful and I can have an impact." He explained the rationale for his approach: "I feel more impact when I help others succeed, when I help people address issues or move a project." There's more than just altruism at work here. Lionel acknowledges, "If my boss is successful, it also makes my life easier in the company." His manager feels that support but also knows that Lionel is looking after the needs of all his stakeholders—his boss, his staff, and his internal clients—and remarked, "I know he will do what is right for Adobe." In fact, Lionel signs off his emails with "for Adobe."

These two orientations, a sense of belonging and a desire to benefit the larger community, form the belief that *my efforts can make work better for everyone on my team.* With this outlook, a challenging workload is not our burden to bear alone. We are neither a spectator of nor a contributor to others' struggles. We can draw on our strengths to lighten the workload and make work easier for all.

THE HIGH-IMPACT HABITS

When work is challenging—particularly in times of change, uncertainty, and crisis—team members who are easy to work with are at a premium. And those who make work easier for all are indispensable.

What did managers tell us they appreciate most? "When people help their teammates" came in at the number three spot on the list. This behavior is not only endearing; it's a necessity, much like it is for parents of a large brood of children. They can't possibly help all their children at once; they need the older children to help the young ones. Further, managers want to work alongside people who are easy—easy to get along with, easy to understand, easy to engage—and people who are cooperative, moving forward with ease. Wouldn't you? If you had your druthers and could choose from a talent pool of equally smart, capable people, wouldn't you pick the easy one?

Conversely, team members who create confusion, disruption, or drama are an unwelcome tax on the manager and a liability to the team. In essence, managers want their staff members to help them get the team's work done and not create additional work; to lift their burden, not add to it. See the chart below for ways to increase (or simply not decrease) your credibility as you deal with a heavy workload. In the next section, we'll explore three ways Impact Players make work light, both for themselves and others.

Building Credibility with Leaders and Stakeholders

CREDIBILITY KILLERS	Continually asking about your next promotion or raise
	Sending long, meandering emails
	Bad-mouthing colleagues, creating drama and conflict
	Asking to revisit decisions that have already been made
	Leaving out inconvenient facts and the other side of the story
	Showing up late to meetings, multitasking, then interrupting others
CREDIBILITY BUILDERS	Helping teammates
	Bringing good energy, having fun, and making others laugh
	Cooperating with leaders
	Getting to the point and telling it straight
	Doing your homework and coming prepared

See appendix A for the full ranking.

Habit 1: Be Low Maintenance

Managers often described typical contributors as highly capable but time consuming. These might be the person who exhausts their manager's time rather than extends it; or the person who makes a good point but requires a lot of words to do so. They are like a massive, gas-guzzling Hummer automobile: it will get you there, but it consumes a lot of resources in the process. One such manager said of an employee, "He is knowledgeable and a good performer, but there is an awful lot of drama and baggage. And it isn't worth it."

On the other hand, managers described high-impact contributors as high performance and low maintenance—like the ideal car that performs exceptionally, requiring little effort to achieve and maintain that performance. Our survey data indicated that Impact Players consistently demonstrate low-maintenance, low-drama behavior at rates 4.5 times higher than typical contributors and 21 times higher than under-contributors.[18] These powerhouses can carry a huge workload, but they don't make work any harder than it has to be. As William James, the "father of American psychology," wrote, "The art of being wise is the art of knowing what to overlook." Likewise, the secret lies not just in what these players do but in what they don't do: they don't complicate matters, create friction, or overcommunicate. They favor value creation over politicking. Like Karl Doose, they are agile and easy to work with. Much like a favorite car, they are dependable, efficient, and economical, getting a lot done but requiring little oversight.

Low Friction

According to the managers we interviewed, Impact Players steer clear of noisy, taxing, and fruitless efforts like finger-pointing, complaining, showboating, and land grabbing. They eschew politics and dramatics that foment conflict but don't produce results. Each of these is an unproductive activity, a friction point that slows progress or stymies collaboration. They can be counted on to virtually never engage in these, thus creating another type of performance guarantee—an efficiency factor.

The most vital, valuable contributors take a low-friction approach to work. They reduce resistance by streamlining work, reducing conflict, and eliminating the drag created when we become overly attached to our ideas. They may have strong opinions and take a stand, but their opinions are held loosely, which allows them to change direction more easily. It's as if they have a sign in their office that says OPEN FOR FEEDBACK (NO MATTER HOW CONVINCED I MAY SOUND). Consider several Impact Players profiled earlier in the book.

Paul Forgey (the supply chain director at Target profiled in chapter 3) was described as "Mr. No Drama." His vice president said, "Paul doesn't let rumors or politics get in the way of the work. You always know where you stand with Paul, but he's willing to learn and change directions."

When Fiona Su (the planning manager at Google's Media Lab in chapter 4) and her boss, John Tuchtenhagen, were at odds regarding a new media strategy, Fiona wanted John to see that although she had a point of view, her heels were not dug in. She presented her ideas to him in draft form, using handmade flash cards rather than a slick digital presentation. She tore scrap paper into quarters and handwrote her ideas in simple form, using only keywords and basic visuals. They talked through each of the ten rough-cut ideas with ease and created a plan they both supported.

Zack Kaplan (Google's brand marketing manager in chapter 5) didn't discourage his colleagues from critiquing and giving feedback on the ideas he presented. Even after difficult meetings, he celebrated the team's progress and thanked his colleagues for strengthening the ideas.

THE IMPACT PLAYER EFFICIENCY FACTOR

An Impact Player can be counted on to almost never:

1. Get involved in internal politics
2. Cause drama or contention with colleagues
3. Waste time

| 4. Complain, blame others, and hold on to negativity |
| 5. Show off, seek credit, or compete with teammates |

This low-friction approach prevents Impact Players from becoming stuck and enables their leaders to move faster and more freely. As one Adobe manager said, "He makes my job easy or really just frees me up for dealing with the other people who don't do the same."

Economy of Words

These contributors deliver high performance, but they do so economically, getting high mileage from their efforts. They speak with purpose, not impulse, and practice frugality—using fewer words to say more—especially in team settings. They may have a lot to say, yet they don't always say it. Rather, they contribute intentionally, remaining aware of when it's time to play big and when it's time to play small. They don't throw all their ideas out at once but instead dispense their thoughts in small but intense doses, targeting the issues on which they can have the most significant impact.

Monica Padman, the cohost of the *Armchair Expert* podcast profiled in chapter 1, admitted that she had to grapple with the tension between weighing in and holding back during interviews. When talking to interesting people, it's natural to want to weigh in and score intellectually. Still, she's learned to check her intent and ask herself: Am I saying something because it's necessary or because I simply want my voice heard? Padman reflected, "You do not have to say everything that comes in your head. . . . I think we all feel like we have to tell everybody exactly what we're thinking at all times. . . . No, I can think it and it can be an interesting thought and it's okay that they're not going to hear it." Creating maximum impact requires knowing "when to come in, when not to" as Padman noted.[19]

Is your voice being fully heard, and does it have weight? Are you making yourself easy to understand? If you want to increase your influence, use fewer words and limit the number of times you contribute in a given meeting. Focus your contribution where your ideas and comments are relevant, unique, and evidence-based. To be sure your point lands, be succinct. Using the Play Your Chips Wisely Smart Play on page 197 will help you economize your contribution and provide dual benefit: you will create more space for others to contribute, and your words become that much more influential.

Impact Player Pro Tip

If you want your words to have more weight: (1) say it once, but say it clearly; (2) present an opposing view to add credibility; and (3) add a short preface to let people know an important idea is coming (e.g., "I have an insight that I'd like to offer.").

Always Ready

If you've ever owned an unreliable car, you know how stressful it is when it doesn't start. You've felt the constant weight of hoping it will work when you need it. In stark contrast, if you've driven a dependable car, you've experienced the peace of mind of knowing with surety that it will start. Being ready to go when needed is a crucial feature of a low-maintenance car. The same holds true in our professional work: always being ready to step up or step in increases the value of our contribution.

Impact Players maintain a work-ready posture; they show up to meetings prepared to be called on and ready to contribute. If we want to have a voice in matters, we need to be prepared to contribute extemporaneously—to present a plan, report on a situation, weigh in on a critical decision, or step in for an absent colleague—without forewarning. When we are seen as reliable and ready, we become impactful in moments that matter.

American football player Jack "Hacksaw" Reynolds, known for his intensity, epitomized this readiness. The rest of the team would meet for breakfast on game days wearing T-shirts and sweatpants, then later suit up in the locker room. Not Hacksaw. He arrived at breakfast in full uniform: Pads on. Helmet on. Eye black on. Hands taped. While speaking at the Bill Campbell Trophy Summit, his former San Francisco 49ers teammate Ronnie Lott recalled, "He was saying to us, 'Hey, man, I'm ready to play right now. Let's play the game.'"[20] The most valuable players can be put in at a moment's notice.

If you want to get in the game, be game ready.

Habit 2: Lighten the Load

Andy, a finance manager for a tech company, was asked by his manager to analyze the division's spending patterns. He crunched the numbers and emailed his manager the spreadsheet with the message "Please see attached workbook," then checked the task off his list. Yet his manager felt as though Andy had just added to his to-do list. The manager said, "Well, now he gave *me* homework. He gave me the numbers but did no qualitative analysis."

Contrast this with Hilary Caplan Somorjai, an astute, talented professional I was fortunate to work with at Oracle Corporation. As the global head of human resource development, I had a demanding executive job that came with an abundance of side projects for the company's management committee. I had my hands full at work and at home, with two young children and another on the way. I had to make trade-offs to make it all work. I had always been an avid reader of management journals, but there was no longer enough time in my days. I stopped reading almost anything other than email messages and children's bedtime stories. However, I knew I needed to stay abreast of best practices and new ideas to be effective in my job. Hilary had her own workload, but she understood my challenge. She stopped by my office one day, brought up my predicament, and then asked, "Would it be helpful if I read for you?" She told me she would read *Harvard Business Review* and the *Wall Street Journal* each day and then send me a summary of the relevant articles. This had nothing to do with her job; it was an extraordinary offer, far outside any of her formal responsibilities, and presented in an unassuming manner. I gratefully accepted. That occurred well over twenty years ago, but I can still feel the relief.

The financial analyst had added to his manager's burden, whereas Hilary helped me carry mine. Impact Players not only do their job well, they help their colleagues do their jobs well, too, which decreases the manager's worry load. When they lighten the load for their bosses and colleagues, they benefit as well.

Lend a Hand

Consider the career of Karen Kaplan, who thought she was taking an easy job; but by making work easier for others, she earned her way to the top of the company. When Karen applied for a job at the advertising agency Hill Holliday in 1982, she was looking for a light, low-impact job that would give her time to study for the LSAT and get into law school. The receptionist job she was offered would be perfect. But when the founder extended the job offer, he said, "Congratulations, Karen, you are now the face and the voice of Hill Holliday." She remembered, "I was stunned. He seemed to think this job was significant, so I figured I would take this role seriously and work wholeheartedly." At the front desk, Karen didn't have a boss per se, so she decided to become the "CEO of reception," ensuring the entire front office ran smoothly. For example, when airline tickets from the travel agency arrived via courier, instead of just phoning people and letting them know to pick up their tickets, she delivered them. Then she offered to book the travel arrangements.

Soon Karen was given bigger jobs and working for overwhelmed people carrying heavy client loads. She offered to take some of their workload, and most gladly accepted. One boss tended to nap during client meetings, so she agreed to lead the sessions for him. Soon she was running major pieces of business—and then entire operations. Within twenty years she was the president, and in 2013, she was appointed chairman and CEO of Hill Holliday. In reflecting, she said, "My favorite bosses were really smart but a little lazy. They let me take work off their plate, but when I needed help, they could give me great guidance." By helping to shoulder the burden of leadership, she developed the mind and character of a senior executive, readied herself for advancement, and became a trusted choice to lead the company.

Offer Their Genius

Jhon Merca, a young content creator working in the United Arab Emirates who goes by "Jruzz," had worked for the Dubai-based training and consultancy firm Biz Group led by CEO Hazel Jackson. Like the best leaders, Hazel had made a practice of discovering her team members' *native genius*—a term I use for what people are naturally and astonishingly brilliant at. Native genius is what people do easily, without much conscious effort, and freely, without needing to be paid, rewarded, or even asked. When her team had met to discuss how to best utilize each person's native genius in the company, they gave Jruzz the moniker "Creative Comic," for the jovial, imaginative energy he brought to his work in their media department. Years later, when Jruzz started his own video production company (with his former employer Biz Group as his favorite client), he named the company after his native genius. When I met Jruzz, he was wearing a black-and-turquoise polo shirt with his company name, "Creative Comic," embroidered above the left breast. When I asked about it, he beamed. "This is my native genius." It was his way of advertising to the world "This is who I am and what I do: I'm creative, I'm fun, and I'm funny. Don't just hire me; let me put my creativity to work for you." He made it easy for others to see and use his genius.

How can you make it easy for your boss and your colleagues to tap into your best work and use your talent at its fullest? You certainly don't need to embroider your native genius on a shirt or use it as your company's name, but you might need to give your colleagues some guidance and simple instruction. Think of this as a *User's Guide to You*. Like a good product manual that tells users what the product is designed to do and how to use it, a User's Guide to You will let people know what you do well—your native genius—and how to utilize you at your best.

When we work within our native genius, we get the job done easily and brilliantly, which means we create the largest impact with the least amount of effort, and work becomes lighter for all. Additionally, when we lend a hand and offer our genius, our reputation grows along with our influence. How can you offer your genius so others can easily utilize your best self?

Habit 3: Lighten the Atmosphere

People enjoy working around Impact Players because they offer help and are easy to work with. While some players create a heavy, humid environment, they provide a light breeze. They help other people do their best work and create a sunny atmosphere, which helps eliminate the phantom workload. Though myriad factors contribute to a positive work environment, here are three of the ways Impact Players improve the environment and make work easier and more pleasant for all.

Bring Levity

If the workplace were a theater, Impact Players would be all comedy, no drama. In tense situations, they bring much-needed levity, making hard work fun and lighthearted and eschewing the political game playing that sucks the life out of our work lives. Some are real comedians who get everyone laughing, like that witty colleague down the hall who drops little wisecracks to break the tension, but most just possess a good sense of humor. Numerous managers from science to sales functions described their high-value contributors as "fun," "funny," "laughs at himself," "makes me laugh," "makes us all laugh." These good-humored colleagues laugh their way through difficulties, ward off despair, and unite people through humor. One manager told us, "He is outcome-focused and delivers, but he's also so funny, self-deprecating, and endearing. People feel really valued when they work with him."

In their book *Humor, Seriously*, Stanford University professors Jennifer Aaker and Naomi Bagdonas made the case that humor is one of the most powerful tools we have for accomplishing serious work. They asserted that humor makes us appear more competent and confident, strengthens relationships, unlocks creativity, and boosts our resilience during difficult times.[21] In both their research and my own, we found that top executives appreciate working with people with a sense of humor (this might just be because there are a lot of days when it sucks to be the boss). Our study showed that "having fun and making us laugh" was number eight on the list of things managers most appreciate, while Aaker and Bagdonas found that 98 percent of top executives prefer working with employees with a sense of humor and 84 percent believe they do better work.[22]

And just in case you aren't convinced that it pays to have a sense of humor: In his book *The Levity Effect,* the management consultant Adrian Gostick drew upon multiple workplace studies to conclude that humor strengthens relationships, reduces stress, and increases empathy and that those who work in a fun environment have greater productivity and interpersonal effectiveness and lower absenteeism.[23]

While some of these stellar contributors lighten the environment with their humor, others turn challenging times into elevating experiences—more like the fun of climbing a tall mountain together than the fun of being at the beach together. Others may be more like Mary Poppins, who proclaimed, "In every job that must be done, there is an element of fun." They create a sense of buoyancy by turning quotidian work into games and making chores more bearable.

For example, when Hannah Datz took over as the presales leader at SAP North America, she inherited a disjointed group of roughly a hundred individuals from various acquisitions. They were a collection of unconnected people with very different backgrounds, and morale was low; Hannah knew she needed to make real changes to the team's culture, and fast. She mixed the acquired groups, split them into new teams, and gave each team a project: develop a creative story line for one of their product solutions. Each team's output would be relevant and useful for the entire group, but Hannah also introduced an element of fun that her group embraced wholeheartedly: each team had to present it to the group in a competition format. Sara Jones, SAP's global vice president and Hannah's boss, said, "I've never seen so much come from an intracompany project. They now have eleven research projects completed, and when I see these people in the office, there is team spirit and camaraderie." Employee attrition is typically high after an acquisition—often as high as 40 percent. Under Hannah's fun and productive leadership, the group retained ninety-eight of the hundred acquired employees.

Recognize Others

In their book, *Leading with Gratitude*, Adrian Gostick and Chester Elton assert that performance improves when leaders express gratitude for their team members."[24] But the benefits of gratitude work both ways. Gratitude reduces anxiety and depression, strengthens the immune system, lowers blood pressure, and creates higher levels of happiness.[25] Focusing on, exercising, and expressing gratitude can mitigate the negative effects of stress in and out of the workplace.[26] What's more, gratitude is contagious: when we express gratitude in the workplace, we can create a ripple effect that drives the organizational culture toward positivity.[27] With the Impact Player Mindset, we celebrate our colleagues' successes as much as our own. We shine a spotlight on outstanding work and let people know their work is appreciated.

Zack Kaplan, the brand marketing manager at Google mentioned previously, not only does stellar work, he recognizes when his teammates do likewise. His former manager Tyler Bahl explained that Zack is constantly appreciating the work others are doing and is fond of giving his colleagues digital "high fives"—a formal recognition program Tyler's team used. Tyler said, "For the last six years, I've kept track of the high fives awarded by people on my team. Zack has sent sixty-nine high fives in the space of six months." Putting that into context, Tyler pointed out, "Zack has sent more in six months than others have sent in six years. I know people who took six months just to send thank-you notes for their own wedding." This practice snowballs for Zack: people love working with him. When asked, Zack said, "I like getting them, so I figure other people would too," and then shared a notion he learned watching his mother, Karen Kaplan, grow from CEO of the reception desk to CEO of Hill Holliday: your candle loses nothing when it lights another.

Be Human

The managers we interviewed indicated that their top contributors promoted well-being and safety for others at much higher rates than their peers—with Impact Players doing this an average of 2.3 times more than typical contributors.[28] The stories told by managers didn't paint a portrait of a busybody, alarmist, or do-gooder. The Impact Players promoted well-being by imbuing a sense of humanity into the workplace, treating people as a whole, and recognizing that each of their colleagues carries stress (as well as joy) far beyond their responsibilities at work.

Sue Warnke is the senior director of content experience at Salesforce. She is one of those vibrant people who can shoulder multiple responsibilities with success and have energy to spare; she's a strong leader and a meaningful contributor and still goes beyond, working to make Salesforce a more inclusive place. She's also the mother of three adolescent children, the youngest of whom struggled with a perplexing mental condition. When his condition escalated in early 2020, Sue took a leave of absence so both she and her husband, who was already caring for the family at home, could focus fully on their son during that challenging time. Before she left, she shared her story on the company's internal website. It was a heartfelt message in which she shared her family's struggles in the hope that others experiencing similar situations wouldn't feel alone. More than thirteen thousand of her fellow employees read, shared, or commented on her post; it was an expression of humanity that resonated around the world.

A month later, after her son's condition improved, Sue returned to work. She was sitting in a meeting when two employees walked in, holding a rod the length of a broomstick from which hung hundreds of origami cranes. The cranes were strung together in columns, forming what Sue described as a breathtaking curtain of color. Before she understood what was happening, more people walked in with a second curtain of cranes and an enormous box of more unstrung cranes. Why paper cranes, and why so many?

One of the thirteen thousand employees who had seen Sue's blog post was a woman named Lynn Levy. While Sue was away caring for her son, Lynn decided to string cranes for Sue's son. It's an ancient Japanese tradition called *senbazuru*, which means "one thousand cranes" and symbolizes peace and healing for someone in pain. Lynn's idea sparked a minimovement at Salesforce. Teams began meeting to fold cranes during lunch breaks and team meetings. They talked and laughed and connected as they folded. Lynn tracked it all with charts and encouragement, hoping she could get to one thousand cranes before Sue returned in March. Employees began mailing her cranes from all over the world: Munich, New York City, London, Denver, Dallas, Surrey, Singapore, and New Jersey. At one point, Lynn made trips to the mail room three or four times a day. Soon there were not just one thousand cranes but two thousand and then three thousand. Employees in San Francisco gathered to string them together. The final number was 3,122 cranes from hundreds of participants.

The crane is an apropos symbol of support because of its double meanings: the bird's wings create lift for flight, while the construction crane lifts the heaviest of loads. Sue described the impact of this gesture:

> I looked at the sea of color yesterday evening, and I imagined the many hands who folded them. A human being taking a moment out of their day to love another human being they may not even know. And I heard their voice as a community, folding, talking, sharing, and laughing together. Many said that the folding parties were some of the best moments they've had at Salesforce. I see these cranes of every color and made by employees of every background as a representation of deep beauty and compassion and diversity.[29]

When we consider our colleagues as humans, not resources, we form connections that enable others to carry their burdens with greater ease.

We also create community and build the collective strength to endure hardship and withstand crisis. Jon Mooallem paraphrased the work of two sociologists who studied the human effects of natural disasters:

> In ordinary life we suffer alone. Any struggle, any pain winds up isolating us from other people or even making us resentful of everybody else, who seem to somehow have it easier. But in a disaster, an entire community suffers together. Trauma and even death, the stuff that we suppress in daily life, spills out as a public phenomenon for everyone to see . . . and all those who share in the experience are brought together in a very powerful, psychological sense.[30]

Mooallem concluded that the best force for counteracting chaos is connection.

Speak Up

Though Impact Players make work lighter for others, including their leaders, and create a positive work environment, that doesn't mean they steer clear of heavy topics. They use their influence to raise difficult topics and to speak up for colleagues who may lack a voice in the organization. But they do more than cry foul; they bring leadership and facilitation to otherwise difficult issues.

That was the case when Leyla Seka, a senior vice president at Salesforce who had worked for the company for more than ten years, became concerned that women in the company were being paid less than their male counterparts and felt an obligation to do something about it. She teamed up with Cindy Robbins, the executive vice president of human resources; together they met with Marc Benioff, the company's founder and CEO. As they shared their concerns, Benioff was initially skeptical; something so contrary to the company's values would be hard for any leader to acknowledge. Eventually, he agreed to an audit of the company's then seventeen thousand employees. The audit uncovered disparities, and as a result, the company spent $3 million to award salary increases to 6 percent of the company, including both women and men.[31]

Seka and Robbins raised a difficult topic, one that certainly didn't make their CEO's life easier. However, by speaking up, they made it easier for him to see the disparity and ensure the company was living its values. We, too, may need to use our influence to make it easier to have difficult but important conversations, especially those that enable everyone to contribute at their fullest and be valued for their contribution.

THE DECOYS AND DISTRACTIONS

Professionals who operate with a Contributor Mindset aren't necessarily difficult employees. They may not be drama queens, problem children, or taxing people; they simply consume management attention, adding to the burden their leaders and colleagues already feel. However, when we assume that greater demands pose a threat to our well-being and conclude that *I need help from my leader*, we are seen as dependents, not leaders.

Face Time

It's easy to assume that getting more face time with your leaders is a good way to get ahead. It's like a scene out of *Mad Men*, the TV series that chronicles the work lives of the advertising executives of the 1960s on New York City's Madison Avenue. In this world, you curry favor with the boss or the client by stopping by their office regularly, engaging in small talk, or going for drinks after work. The assumption is that relationship trumps outcomes and spending time with your boss signifies your importance and assures success.

However, the data show that managers spend a disproportionate amount of their time with low performers (26 percent of their time, according to one study[32]). As you might guess, they resent it. As one NASA manager described an old-school, schmoozing mission manager, "He chats with you, assuming you want to talk with him about these tangents. He figures if the relationship is strong, you'll overlook the problems." The manager admitted that whenever he saw the man's name on his meeting calendar, he tried to get out of the meeting. And he's not the only one; SpaceX staffers called to complain that the mission manager was wasting their time and threatening the mission, and the manager was forced to do damage control. Instead of seeking more face time, strive to be low maintenance but visible. Use the face time you do have to find out what's important right now (the W.I.N.), negotiate what you need to finish strong, and get guidance to ensure you hit the target.

Play Big

We can reduce our influence by playing too big. When we speak too often or are too verbose, people stop listening. We become like white noise; our voices fade away, relegated to background chatter. We are particularly vulnerable to overcontributing when the stakes are high and we're passionate about a topic. We may think people are still listening—most still nod their heads politely—but we've been tuned out, much like a dog that barks at everything and everyone. The secret to being heard is contributing intentionally and knowing when to play big and when to play small. If you want to maximize your impact, dispense your opinions in small but intense doses (see the Smart Play on page 196).

FAILED PLAYS

Four common ways to misplay your chips and reduce your voice and credibility:

1. **The Ditto**: Piling onto someone else's comments with empty agreement

2. **The BTW**: Veering from topic with the seemingly irresistible tangent

3. **The Double Down**: Repeating your point for emphasis

4. **The Monologue**: Trying to figure out what your point is by talking it out in a rambling monologue

Full Disclosure

Most professionals appreciate that the workplace has become more casual—not just a relaxed dress code but an environment where we don't have to leave our authentic self at the door. However, we all know someone who has taken "casual Friday" a little too far and shared way too much. Instead of being a whole person (and acknowledging the other facets of and interests in everyone's life), they spew their whole life onto their colleagues. One manager described someone who shared too much: "We all heard about his joint custody woes and how poorly his ex-wife was raising the kids. It was like he dumped all of the glasses of his life into one." The glass overflowed and made others on the team uncomfortable. You may not need to be buttoned up at work, but don't show up to the team-building rafting trip in a Speedo. Creating a personable workplace doesn't require full disclosure. We can recognize that people have full lives outside work without sharing or asking about all the details (see the Safety Tip "Prevent overexposure" on page 199).

Cheering Section

Several years ago, a colleague and I collaborated to organize a global leadership forum in Asia. It was a bold, challenging endeavor. As we achieved each milestone, my partner praised my efforts and expressed his sincere delight in each success. Initially, it was affirming, but it became wearisome when I realized I was doing the heavy lifting while he was just cheering me on. I shared my concern. He agreed, actually, and then elaborated, "But what I bring is hope and belief—belief that we can do this and belief in you." Ah, that explained things. I told my lovely colleague that while I appreciated his support, I already had plenty of self-confidence. What we most needed was for him to pull more weight himself. To his credit, he did—and then we both cheered as we delivered a successful program. It's admirable to cheer for our colleagues while they do difficult work, but it's far less inspiring when they need us out on the field. And when someone's being mistreated or there's a breach of ethics, it is time for speaking up, not cheering up.

Don't be a cheerleader when your coworkers really need a teammate or an advocate.

MULTIPLYING YOUR IMPACT

In tough times, when we cast ourselves as dependents rather than reinforcements, we not only cause strain and frustration for our leaders, we nudge them down the path of diminishing others. Our requests for assistance encourage them to operate in know-it-all mode and pull them into micromanagement, the number one characteristic of leaders I refer to as Diminishers.

When taken to an extreme, this dependence mentality turns to entitlement, the assumption that *other people owe me the help and resources I need*. This is draining for managers and has a corrosive effect on team culture, destroying cohesion and collaboration as entitled employees suck energy and resources away but fail to contribute to the broader community. As others pull away from the takers, factions are formed, politics proliferate, and toxicity creeps into the culture.

In contrast, consider the value proposition created by Impact Players (represented in the chart on page 195). By being easy to work with, they do great work faster and without fuss, which means everyone gets a time rebate. And as they use their strength to help the struggling players on the team, they free their managers up to lead rather than micromanage. The individual gets seen as a deputy to their leaders and stakeholders, which means they gain valuable leadership experience and influence. So when they advance to more senior and more challenging leadership roles, they are ready for them—and others want to work for them.

Furthermore, by creating a positive environment in which people feel included and want to belong, they help shape the organization's culture, reinforcing the values of collaboration and inclusion and reducing the toxic effects of burnout. As a by-product, they build a reputation as low-maintenance, high-performance players people want to work with. They are picked first for important jobs and included in the most critical initiatives.

VALUE BUILDING: MAKE WORK LIGHT

Impact Players make hard work easier and get seen as leaders and no-nonsense players

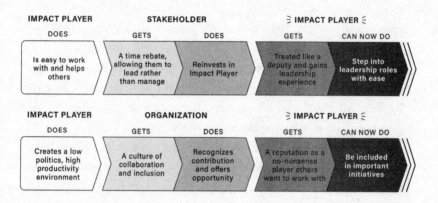

American football is a grueling sport. Players face off against opponents determined to not only stop their progress but also literally tear them down. Perhaps no player shoulders more pressure than the quarterback, who must read the field, locate open players, and make split-second decisions while massive opposing linemen charge directly at him. A quarterback might not expect that one of those opponents would be the one to lighten his load.

Yet that was precisely what happened to Steve Young. Young was a Hall of Fame quarterback for the San Francisco 49ers and two-time NFL MVP; his opponent Reggie White was a fearsome defensive end and the NFL's all-time leader in sacks—198 quarterback takedowns by the time he retired in 2000. He was strong, fast, and big—six feet, five inches and three hundred pounds big. White was loud, too—growling and screaming as he advanced on the field. Young said, "Reggie just threw people out of his way. I'd drop back to pass, and I could hear Reggie coming for me."

Young explained what made Reggie White such an amazing player:

in the middle of all that intensity, adrenaline, and competitiveness—that insanity—Reggie was mindful of Steve's well-being. Young said, "He was exploding with everything he had, trying to get his job done. Then all of a sudden he would grab me and then roll around and make sure that *I* fell on top of *him*." Yes, he did his job; however, he also did what he could to prevent injury to Steve. Young continued, "And then he would want to talk. 'Hey, Steve, how you doing?'" Steve would reply, "Well, Reggie, right now, not so good." Or Reggie would ask, "Hey, how's your dad?" [33]

Work can be intense, but it can still be light. If that giant of an athlete could make a heavy hit more bearable for an opponent, it's surely possible within a team of coworkers. Impact Players—be they on the sports pitch or at work—make heavy work lighter.

As work creeps in scope and permeates every facet of our lives, there's no room for a shadow workload, but there is every reason to make work easier, smoother, less injurious, and more joyful. We may not be able to reduce our caseload, but with the right mindset, we can lighten the phantom workload for all. And as we make challenges more bearable for others, we might find that our work experience improves and our load lightens as well.

THE PLAYBOOK

This playbook contains tips for aspiring leaders to exercise and strengthen the assumptions and habits necessary to MAKE WORK LIGHT.

Smart Plays

1. **Get to the point.** People who are easy to work with are usually easy to understand. They get to the point and express their ideas clearly. If you want to sharpen your point, try any of these techniques:

- Write your point out as if it were a 140-character tweet.
- Add an executive summary to your written reports or oral brief-ings. This could be a paragraph with the key points or just a single sentence with the conclusion. When delivering your report, start with the executive summary and then add detail as needed.
- When forwarding a long email chain to a leader (or any other col-league), provide a summary of the idea exchange included in the email chain. Then add your question or request.
- Score a three-pointer by summarizing your thoughts (or a larger conversation) in three clear points.

2. **Play your chips wisely.** Before an important meeting, give yourself a budget of "poker chips," where each chip represents a comment or contribution to the meeting and is worth a specific number of seconds of talking time. Use your chips sparingly, weighing in when you have an insight that is:

- **Relevant.** Is this issue immediately relevant to your boss or stake-holder? If it isn't on the specific agenda for the meeting, is it something that is on their broader agenda (one of their top three priorities)?
- **Evidence based.** Is the insight based on data or other evidence? Are you presenting a balanced point of view with data that also tells the other side of the story?
- **Unique.** Is your point additive to what has already been said, or is it just restating a point that has already been made? Do the ideas or insights reflect your unique role, perspective, or skills?
- **Succinct.** Is your point concise and clear? Some people may need to play their chips more sparingly, while others may need to dis-pense their ideas more liberally. Either way, a chip—whether a physical chip in your pocket or an image held in your mind—serves as a talisman, reminding you to contribute intentionally and valuably.

3. **Discover your native genius.** If you aren't clear about what your na-tive genius is, you can get a rapid 360-degree perspective by sending an email or text to six friends or colleagues. Make it easy for them to respond by using this template:

Hi. I would appreciate your input. I'm trying to better understand how I can use my "native genius" at work, meaning what I do naturally, easily, and freely. From your perspective, what do you see as my natural genius? If you need a prompt, here are a few questions to get you thinking:

- What do I do better than anything else I do?
- What do I do without effort?
- What do I do without being asked?
- What do I tend to do better than people around me?

Thank you. Your input will help me understand how to contribute at my fullest.

4. **Create a User's Guide to You.** If you feel as though you are being used like a hammer when you're actually a Swiss Army knife, you might need to let your team know how best to use you. Create a User's Guide to You that includes: (1) Native genius: What does your mind do easily and freely? (2) Uses: What are various ways your native genius could be applied at work? (3) Instructions and care: What type of information, feedback, and support do you need from others to do your best work? (4) Warnings: Where do you tend to get stuck or derailed, and how can people help you stay on track?

Safety Tips

1. **Communicate your native genius.** When communicating your native genius, remember to:

- **Clarify your intent.** Explain what is meant by "native genius"—it's people's natural brilliance or gift, what they do easily and freely and extremely well. Let people know that you really enjoy and excel at work that draws on your native genius and that you are eager to use it to contribute in more significant ways.
- **Don't be a prima donna.** Don't demand to work only within your native genius. Just because you have identified your native genius, doesn't mean that you shouldn't have to work in areas that you aren't naturally good at or particularly interested in.

- **Give it time.** When asking someone to consider additional ways to utilize your native genius, give them time to think. Try to break up the conversation into several steps: (1) share your intent, (2) discuss your native genius, (3) discuss new applications for your talents.
- **Make it a two-way street.** In addition to discussing your native genius, take the opportunity to recognize and be interested in the native genius of others on your team, including your boss.

2. **Prevent overexposure.** Most everybody wants to be treated as a whole person, not just an employee; however, everyone has a different comfort level with mingling work and personal life. If you are someone who is comfortable talking about your personal life, use these safety measures: (1) share only what you would be willing to share publicly, (2) share but never inquire (this allows others to reciprocate voluntarily), (3) continue only if your sharing is appreciated and reciprocated. If a colleague doesn't reciprocate, it might be a sign of an unwelcome gift.

3. **Ensure your help is helpful.** You don't want to be the party guest who arrives early and offers to help with last-minute preparations but requires so much instruction, attention, and validation that you become an encumbrance or nuisance. Try these three tips to ensure your offers to help are a blessing, not a burden: (1) Instead of asking, "What can I do to help?" ask, "Would it be helpful if I did [this thing] for you?" (2) Instead of asking, "How do you want me to do it?" ask, "Are there any specific requirements I should know about, or should I just use my judgment?" (3) Let the person know what you did and to tell you if they want you to do it differently.

Coaching tips for managers: You can find coaching practices to help your team members make work light in "The Coach's Playbook" at the end of chapter 8.

CHAPTER 6 SUMMARY: MAKE WORK LIGHT

This chapter describes how Impact Players deal with unrelenting demands and how they create a positive and productive work environment for everyone on the team.

	CONTRIBUTOR MINDSET	IMPACT PLAYER MINDSET
Practice	Add to the Burden	Make Work Light
Assumptions	I need help from my leader (*dependence*)	My efforts make work better for everyone on the team (*contribution*)
		I am an important part of a team (*belonging*)
		I can improve well-being for all (*benefit*)
Habits	Require attention	Low maintenance
	Seek help	Lighten the load
	Contribute to the stress	Lighten the atmosphere
Implications	This mindset increases the burden of already overtaxed leaders and teams, especially during difficult times.	Individuals develop a reputation as high-performing, no-nonsense players that everyone wants to work with. This reinforces a culture of collaboration and inclusion.

Decoys to avoid: (1) Face time, (2) Play big, (3) Full disclosure, (4) Cheering section

PART II

DEVELOPING THE

≥ IMPACT PLAYER ≤

MINDSET

Chapter 7

INCREASE YOUR IMPACT

Some think you become great on the big stage
under the bright lights. But the light only reveals
the work you did in the dark.
—JEFF BAJENARU

Thus far, we've explored the anatomy of the Impact Player Mindset,
we've examined the mindsets and behaviors of Impact Players, and we
know what greatness looks like. In this chapter, our focus will shift to
you and what you can do to strengthen this mindset for yourself—
not just changing your behavior but changing the beliefs behind your
behavior. We will begin with a fairly extreme example, someone who
exemplifies this ethos but who earned it the hard way: by overcoming
true adversity, wrestling with new beliefs, and making difficult behavior changes.

Fernando Carrillo is the CEO of a nonprofit organization, a podcast host, and an Anglican priest who lives in London, England. He's
affable and optimistic and puts his heart and soul into his endeavors.
He does great work and does it with an attitude that brings others
along with him. Guests on his *London's Leadership* podcast are im-
pressed by his preparation and well-informed questions and can feel
that they and their ideas are valued. Collaborators with his nonprofit
organization, WellWater, appreciate his positivity and proficiency and
the way he creates a sense of belonging and purpose for his team. One
collaborator said, "He maintains good humour through tough challenges and lifts the spirits of us all."

Fernando seems like a natural Impact Player, but that way of think-ing wasn't his birthright. The mindsets and practices were hard won, and the road to change was arduous and long. Fernando was born in a Miami prison where his mother was incarcerated; his father was soon out of the picture. At the age of four, with his mother in rehab, Fer-nando was brought to London to be near extended family.

Fernando quit school at fifteen, without job qualifications, with-out prospects, and without much adult support. By seventeen, he was incarcerated in a young offenders' institute. He assumed his situation would improve once out of prison, but after his release, things only got worse. He fell deeper into the world of drugs and crime, and by age nineteen, he was heavily addicted. At the peak of that mess, he was awake for five days without eating or sleeping. He spent four months in rehab and left with a plan to live a different life: be clean, get a job, and study at university. But as soon as reality hit, his willpower buck-led and he stumbled; when faced with uncertainty and stress, the only coping mechanism he knew was escape. For the next two years, he ric-ocheted between rehab and relapse. With each misstep, the belief that he was unloved, alone, and a failure who would never be good enough was etching itself deeper into his belief system.

Fernando found work in a restaurant kitchen. The rigidity of the schedule gave him much-needed routine and a reason to remain on track. He was living in a drug-infested environment and still vulner-able to relapse, but he was accumulating small successes. Evidence that he was capable was piling up, and he was starting to believe he could change, learn, and adapt. When a friend invited him to church, he accepted. At the small church, which served the Latin American population in London, he was enveloped by a supportive community. He still struggled with the complexities of addiction, but a mentor emerged who became his life guide and taught him what it meant to be responsible and what it felt like to be loved unconditionally. Fer-nando enrolled in a college preparatory course and found success as a student and a pathway to university. Each success strengthened his budding growth mindset, and he began to see new possibilities. As his focus shifted from his challenges to the needs of those around him, his perspective changed, too. He began to think that he could contribute to society and make a real difference in the world.

As his own life stabilized, he turned his attention to youth facing the struggles he knew all too well. He began mentoring young men and discovered a passion for service. Feeling an emerging sense of his own strength, he began stepping up and into stretch situations. With the help of a friend, he opened a gym for troubled teens in an under-resourced area of London. He completed a bachelor's degree in international business with Spanish from the University of Westminster and then a second degree in theology. He began working as a student pastor at Holy Trinity Brompton, a vibrant Anglican church located in the heart of London. To help young people channel their skills toward community service, he founded WellWater, which aims to raise leaders who help eliminate poverty in the world. Meanwhile, he continued his studies and earned a master's degree in Christian leadership from Middlesex University. On a quiet Sunday morning in September 2020 in London's St. Paul's Cathedral, Fernando was ordained into the ministry of the Anglican Church.

As Fernando will tell you, this radical change in behavior was precipitated by several profound changes in his mindset. It began with a change in his identity. "I went from feeling meaningless to knowing I was meaningful," he said. "I knew my worth and that I had something to give." That new identity was shaped by his newfound spirituality. Every morning he read a set of declarations about himself that reflected his inherent worth and true identity. As he anchored his work in a deep belief that he, as a person, was valuable, he began to see his own capability differently as well. Now in his late twenties, he recalled, "I can't remember the exact day, but I do remember waking up and feeling capable. I felt strong and able to face bigger challenges."

As he better understood his own strength, he began to interpret challenges and adversity differently. He saw extreme challenges less as threats and more as opportunities for growth. This is, perhaps, best exemplified in his orientation to feedback. He explained, "I've been on a long journey to be able to receive feedback." Previously, he avoided feedback because it simply hurt too much. He took it personally, as an attack on his identify and an affront to his capability. He said, "Negative feedback affirmed negative beliefs I had about myself. It reminded me that I was an outsider, that I could never be good enough, and that I was fragile." Over time, his attitude shifted. Reading his self-declarations daily affirmed his strength and gave him the confidence to change his behavior. Today Fernando has a very different relationship to feedback. He said, "Now I seek feedback all the time. I'm desperately looking for people who can tell me how I can improve and how I can do better. It's the best opportunity to grow."

Fernando continues to develop young leaders who can change the world—through WellWater, through his podcast, and through his church service. His work is fueled by the belief that everyone can be a leader, no matter where they are or where they've been in the past. Meanwhile, he hasn't stopped working on himself. He meets with his mentor weekly and writes in his journal daily. He works with an executive coach, coaches other leaders, and was recently accepted into Marshall Goldsmith 100 Coaches, a community of highly accomplished executive coaches, authors, and leaders who use their talent to make good people and organizations better.

Carving a path to new behavior takes time. The road may have occasional epiphanies or transformative experiences; however, these changes are usually gradual, occurring in almost imperceptible increments. But each successive step strengthens nascent beliefs and reinforces new behaviors. As Fernando said, "The more you walk down a path, the more natural it becomes. Almost without knowing it, it just becomes the way you live."

While we have little control over our circumstances, both in life and in the workplace, we can control our reactions and make changes to our behavior and beliefs. There are numerous models for how to change our patterns of thought and action. Most experts argue that behavior is predicated on belief, that we must first change our mindsets and then new practices will follow. Others suggest that experimenting with new behavior may lead to new mindsets. But there is one thing that everyone agrees on: changing our beliefs and modifying our behavior isn't easy, nor is changing how others see us. This chapter will offer you a few ways to make hard changes a little easier. We'll begin by helping you get out of the weeds and down to the root of the Impact Player Mindset.

MASTER THE UNDERLYING BELIEFS AND BEHAVIORS

In my experience coaching leaders, I've noticed that failure to change is typically due to an overabundance of ambition, not a lack thereof. We generally fail by trying to adopt too many new behaviors at once. In his book *The One Thing*, Gary Keller wrote, "You can become successful with less discipline than you think, for one simple reason: success is about doing the right thing, not about doing everything right." [1] The same holds true when attempting to adopt the various attitudes and practices of Impact Players. Though you may feel inspired by many of the individuals profiled in this book and convinced that operating in similar ways can create greater value for you and your colleagues, trying to exemplify all the mindsets and behavioral characteristics we've discussed can be overwhelming and almost certainly doomed for failure. Let me assure you that you do not need the full package to be counted among top contributors. In fact, the Impact Players in our study typically exhibited three or four of the five practices (on average 3.17 out of 5, to be precise). But even trying to develop three of the practices or implement a number of Smart Plays can be daunting.

There is a more powerful and sustainable approach to developing the Impact Player Mindset. Instead of trying to simultaneously implement myriad outward behaviors, focus on one of the fundamental internal practices. We call these the master skills—two core competencies that all the high-impact contributors in our study seem to possess. Just as physical competencies such as speed and hand-eye coordination are foundational in a wide variety of sports, the master skills are foundational for all Impact Player practices. When practiced authentically, these master skills naturally produce the right behavior. The first master skill is seeing through the eyes of the people and communities that are served by your work; the second is seeing opportunity where others see threat. We'll begin by exploring how changing perspective naturally changes action and impact.

Master Skill 1: Changing Your Perspective

When faced with a problem, it's natural for bright, action-oriented professionals to assess the situation, take charge, and act swiftly. However, they can easily hit the wrong target. Too many professionals are stuck in their own head, working on what *they* deem most important, not seeing beyond their own perspective. Their intention is positive, but they are looking through the wrong point of view. When vision is limited, so is impact.

To increase our impact we must know what is valuable to others. We must train our minds to view situations through others' eyes. We must see through the eyes of those who benefit from our work. Our vision won't necessarily improve by looking harder, squinting and straining to see more clearly; we improve our optics by changing our perspective and observing a situation from a different angle. As James Deacon said, "What you see depends not only on what you look at, but also, on where you look from."

This is a principle I learned from a favorite professor, J. Bonner Ritchie, who was not only an influential mentor to many but became an influential player in the promotion of world peace by becoming a student himself.

A New Point of View

J. Bonner Ritchie was a professor of organizational behavior at the Brigham Young University Marriott School of Management but was a Scholar in Residence at a satellite campus in Jerusalem, located on Mount Scopus on the eastern edge of the historic city. He had been living and working in East Jerusalem for several months teaching leadership to students and running training programs in the local community. One day while driving home, Bonner took a shortcut through a Palestinian section of East Jerusalem called Issawiya. As he drove through the neighborhood, a group of teens surrounded his car and began throwing rocks—not pebbles but rocks large enough to serve as weapons. The road was narrow, and he had no way out. Several of the rocks crashed through the driver-side window, and he felt the impact against his shoulder. He looked down to see his white shirt covered in blood. He managed to back his car up the hill and leave before the situation escalated. He drove home and then to the hospital, where a doctor removed thirty pieces of glass from his arm and face.

After a day of recuperation, Bonner, now wrapped in bandages, made another visit to Issawiya to "get more information from [his] assailants."[2] He had been angry two days before when the rocks were flying, but today he was headed back to the village for understanding, not reprisal. He took a translator with him, and this time, he walked to the town instead of driving. He asked to speak with the *mukhtar* (mayor) and explained that he wanted to talk to the boys and understand their intent. The mukhtar apologized for the situation and gathered three rather nervous boys. Bonner explained that he wanted to be friends with them and then asked, "Why? What made you do this?" The kids explained that his car had the yellow license plates of Israel (as opposed to the blue plates of Palestine), adding, "We appreciate what you do, but your car deserved to die." To the boys, the plates were a symbol of occupation. Bonner listened and talked with the boys and others in the village at length. Reflecting on the situation later, he wrote, "I listened to their frustration and hopelessness, and while not accepting the logic for violence, I understood their need for freedom and independence. We became friends instead of enemies."[3]

That experience was one of many that created deep relations between Bonner and both the Jewish and the Arab communities in Jerusalem. The three boys from Issawiya visited him occasionally at the university center and brought him gifts. He continued to work at the university and ran leadership workshops that brought together leaders from both the Arab and Jewish community. He developed a reputation as a thoughtful leader who built bridges—someone who could see both sides but never took sides.

In the spring of 1993, Bonner got a surprise call from a staff member to Yasser Arafat, the leader of the Palestine Liberation Organization (PLO), who told him that Arafat had heard of Bonner's reputation as a bridge builder and wished to meet with him at the PLO headquarters in Tunisia. Just days later, Bonner was blindfolded, taken on multiple car rides, and driven through secret tunnels before he was eventually taken to meet Arafat. Arafat greeted him and explained the situation. Arafat had been offered the first chance at peace talks with the Israelis. However, half of the members of the PLO executive committee were vehemently opposed to the idea of peace with Israel. Arafat was to meet the Israeli prime minister, Yitzhak Rabin, in one week and asked Bonner to spend the next several days with his team and help open their minds to peace. Bonner did, and the following week, Arafat and Rabin began peace talks and then in the fall signed the 1993 Oslo Accords.

Instead of merely tending to his own wounds, Bonner worked to improve his vision—to understand how another group saw his presence and to consider another vantage point. Though the peace accord was made possible by the work of countless people, Bonner was able to make an important contribution because he was willing to see the world through someone else's eyes. That broader view allowed him to play an influential role.

What can you do to expand your understanding and improve your vision? Are you relying on a one-sided view of value, or are you seeing through your stakeholders' eyes? When we choose to see what others see, we improve our optics, and when we make what is important to others important to us, we get the vector right and increase our impact.

When we look through our stakeholders' eyes, what's important to them becomes clear and increases our understanding of their priorities and needs. We have a better angle from which to see the real job that needs to be done. When we understand the real needs and priorities and encounter a leadership vacuum, we don't get trapped waiting for an invitation, we step up and take the lead. When we understand the burdens our leaders carry, we don't stop by their office to clock more face time; rather, we step in to make work light for them. In short, when we change our perspective, we can increase our impact.

The following chart shows how the master skill of perspective taking helps invoke a number of the Impact Player practices. Further, it illustrates how this improved vision allows us to spot and avoid the traps that trip up typical contributors.

IMPACT PLAYER MASTER SKILL: PERSPECTIVE TAKING

Perspective taking leads to other high-impact practices

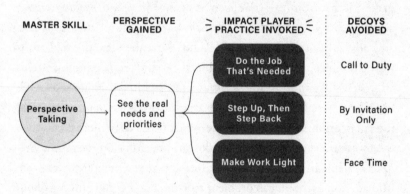

MASTER SKILL	PERSPECTIVE GAINED	IMPACT PLAYER PRACTICE INVOKED	DECOYS AVOIDED
Perspective Taking	See the real needs and priorities	Do the Job That's Needed	Call to Duty
		Step Up, Then Step Back	By Invitation Only
		Make Work Light	Face Time

Here are a few simple ways to change your perspective and get a better angle on the action:

Zoom out. Try pulling back from your position in the organization or work process and viewing your situation through a wide-angle lens. Ask yourself: Who are the other players, and what do they need from me to be successful? Who are the people downstream who are affected by my work? Who are the people who benefit most from the work I do? What would benefit them most?

Change seats. Instead of zooming out, zoom in, but through someone else's perspective. You might do this by simply asking: What does this situation look like from your perspective? What do you see that I might be missing? How do these problems affect you personally? What is a win for you? Or you might literally change seats to better understand your stakeholder's perspective on a situation. You could take a different seat in a meeting or sit in a meeting you don't normally attend. You could tag along on a customer visit, spend a day as a user of your own product, or volunteer to handle someone else's workload while they are away. Doing so will help you understand and improve the experience for those you work for.

Listen longer. Most of us know that impactful work typically begins with curiosity, empathy, and listening, but are you listening long enough to gain the understanding you need to create a big impact? Michael Bungay Stanier, the author of *The Coaching Habit*, asked, "Can you stay curious a little bit longer and rush to action and advice a little bit slower?" Paulo Büttenbender, the SAP software architect from Brazil mentioned in chapter 1, epitomizes this approach. Like most business application architects, Paulo researches his clients' needs, comes in with a point of view about what existing application module will fit their business requirements, and then interviews clients or users to make sure he fully understands their needs. While listening, most architects make the mental switch from information gathering to problem solving, and begin thinking about fixes and offering solutions. What sets Paulo apart from most architects is how long he listens—"I usually listen for a full week," he told us. Even though he comes prepared and is knowledgeable about software solutions, he keeps listening, suppressing the natural impulse to share his expertise or switch into problem-solving mode. It's a conscious effort; he explained, "I try to spend the entire time with them understanding the problem and not giving any solution. I wait to the next time slot before I share a solution." He admitted that it can be really hard to listen for four to five hours a day for five days straight, but the payoff is worth it. As his colleagues and clients know, the software he designs is better, more keyed into their needs, and more impactful.

In what way would your work improve if you held back and listened more? Could you increase your impact simply by changing seats, getting a new perspective, and staying curious a little longer?

Master Skill 2: Changing Your Lens

One of the many lessons I learned from Professor Ritchie is that managing ambiguity is an essential function of good leadership. In times of uncertainty, the best leaders create stability for their team by absorbing ambiguity. They need to be comfortable with uncertainty—so much so that they can sit in its company long enough to transform unknowns into opportunities. This comfort with uncertainty (and its close cousin adversity) was one of the hallmarks of the Impact Players we studied and the key differentiator between them and their peers. In fact, the five everyday challenges introduced in chapter 1—messy problems, unclear roles, unforeseen obstacles, moving targets, and unrelenting demands—were like a Rorschach test. In the same situations, most people saw threats to avoid, but Impact Players saw opportunities to add value. Frances Hesselbein, a former CEO of the Girl Scouts of the USA, captured this mindset when she declared, "We see change as a challenge, not as a threat."[4]

The ability to interpret challenging situations as opportunities rather than threats can have a profound impact on one's ability to cope effectively with stress. The cognitive psychologists Richard Lazarus and Susan Folkman refer to this as "appraisal," or the way in which an individual responds to and interprets stressors in life. They assert that during primary appraisal, an individual interprets an event as either positive or dangerous to their personal goals. During secondary appraisal, the individual evaluates their ability or resources to cope with a specific situation.[5] For example, if we view the lack of a formal leader on a team as an opportunity, we see a chance to fill the leadership vacuum. When we deem ourselves sufficiently capable of leading a group of peers, we step up and take the lead. However, if we appraise the same situation as a threat, we defer to leaders, hoping they will deal with the uncertainty and provide direction.

The difference between these two worldviews is much like the difference between a convex and a concave lens. Seeing ambiguity as a threat is like looking through a convex lens that causes light rays to converge at a single focal point, which tends to be ourselves. When we use a threat lens, we become myopic: we look inward, consider the situational impacts, and tend to see ourselves as standing alone, lacking control or organizational backing.

THE THREAT LENS

Through this lens we become myopic, seeing ourselves alone and lacking control

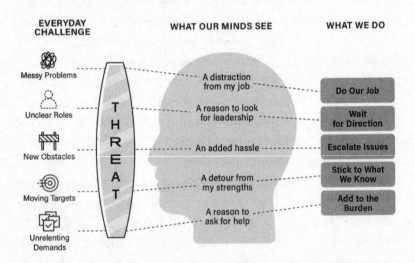

When ambiguity is viewed through the lens of opportunity, the resulting image is more expansive, and we tend to see what is happening around us. This is similar to the effect produced by a concave lens that disseminates light rays. With the opportunity lens, we view a broader context; we can see the upside as well as downside of our choices and the benefits to our stakeholders.

THE OPPORTUNITY LENS

Through this lens we take a broader view, seeing options and reasons to take action

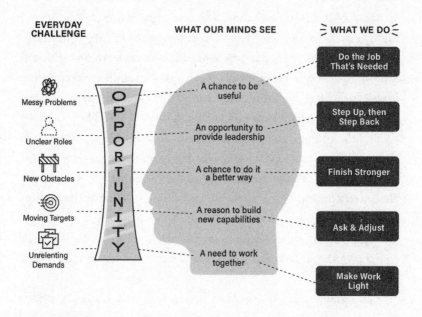

EVERYDAY CHALLENGE

Messy Problems

Unclear Roles

New Obstacles

Moving Targets

Unrelenting Demands

OPPORTUNITY

WHAT OUR MINDS SEE

A chance to be useful

An opportunity to provide leadership

A chance to do it a better way

A reason to build new capabilities

A need to work together

WHAT WE DO

Do the Job That's Needed

Step Up, then Step Back

Finish Stronger

Ask & Adjust

Make Work Light

Risky Business

Let me return one last time to my experience managing the Leaders Forum at Oracle and to a time when I was able to reframe a risky situation into valuable opportunity. We were midway through the first weeklong program. Everything had been going well, but now the participants were tackling a real, mission-critical project using what they'd learned about the company's strategy. That's when I detected rumblings of dissent. The class leaders pulled me aside and clued me in: the group felt that rather than working on the assigned project, they could make a far greater contribution by giving the company's top executives feedback on how to improve the company strategy.

This was more than a slight change in plan. We had invested substantial time and resources into preparing the project, and the top executives were expecting solutions the next day. Plus, it was a dangerous deviation. Improving the company strategy seemed noble, but this could easily spiral into a gripe session and exposé. Top executives rarely appreciate surprises, and emperors seldom like hearing that they have no clothes.

An outside consultant whom I deeply respected cautioned me, "I highly advise against this. Keep the team on track." My team members noted that this was more than just high-stakes learning—this was "you-must-be-high" kind of stakes. I could certainly see their point; it was fairly clear how this could end badly, especially for me. However, there were significant upsides to consider. It could help us really tighten the strategy and make it more understandable for everyone in the company. Actually, that was what the executives really wanted the leaders to do—to share the strategy across the company. As I considered their request, I envisioned the possibilities: What if this mutiny is actually a sign of commitment? Could this detour lead to a breakthrough? What if the detour is exactly what we need? Is it possible to manage the situation so it produces a huge win rather than a total disaster?

The senior executives couldn't be reached, and I was the closest thing to adult supervision. Should I choose the safe path or take the rockier road that could pave the way for greater progress?

I decided that allowing the group to wrestle with the company strategy and walk in the senior execs' shoes was the best way to hone their strategic thinking skills. The group was thrilled (and perhaps a bit surprised) when I told them that they were free to redefine their work. However, I also made it clear that with freedom came obligation. "Be creators of value, not just critics of the status quo," I cautioned and then added, "I am trusting you; do not let me down." It was clear to me that the benefits of the new approach outweighed the risks, but I needed to make sure the senior executives who clearly outranked me would agree. I scrambled and called each of the three executives at home. It was too late to ask for their permission, so I shared my rationale and asked that they keep an open mind. Yes, they were slightly annoyed at first, but they were also intrigued.

The group worked late into the night and delivered a compelling presentation—analysis *and* answers. Having been prepared, the senior executives responded perfectly. There were a few uncomfortable moments, but the ripples stirred by those emerging leaders became a wave of change that delivered a clearer, more compelling strategy. The would-be mutiny was transformed into a movement because we took the unpaved path.

When we change our lens from threat to opportunity we can turn risky situations into rewarding experiences.

Reframe Threats as Opportunities. You can use cognitive reframing (a psychological technique to identify, challenge, and change the way a situation is viewed[6]) to help you see opportunity in otherwise threatening situations. Changing deeply engrained beliefs, especially when fear is involved, may require deep work and the help of a coach or therapist. However, with practice, reframing situations can become as simple as changing the filters on a photo taken on a smart phone; for example, swapping the noir filter with a vivid option. Use these four steps to help you reframe threats as opportunities:

1. **Recognize ambiguity.** Watch for the situations fraught with uncertainty and difficulty in which Impact Players tend to think and respond radically differently from others. These five situations (messy problems, unclear roles, unforeseen obstacles, moving targets, and unrelenting burdens) can serve as signals to pause and check which lens you are using.
2. **Check your lens.** Pay attention to your thoughts and reactions. Check for signs that you are looking at the situation through a threat lens, by using either the chart on page 214 titled "The Threat Lens" or the following questions.
   - Am I concerned primarily with the downside risks rather than the upside possibilities?
   - Am I pulling inward rather than looking outward?
   - Do I believe that I lack ability, power, or resources rather than see sufficient levels of capability and resources in myself?

3. **Reframe the situation.** Consider what the situation would look like through an opportunity lens. Identify the situation that currently feels threatening to you and ask:
   - How would an Impact Player see this as an opportunity to add value?
   - How can this have a positive impact on my own goals?
   - What capabilities and resources can I tap into to navigate the inherent ambiguity?
4. **Replace with an opportunity lens.** Now consider what you would do differently if you saw this situation as an opportunity. You can use the chart titled "The Opportunity Lens" to identify the Impact Player beliefs and practices to employ or simply ask: As I look through the opportunity lens, what beliefs and behaviors naturally follow?

Reframing uncertainty as opportunity will help you act boldly, yet simply reframing a situation may not be enough. These situations often involve legitimate peril (at least professionally), so you'll want to take the risk out of otherwise risky situations. For instance, in the above example when I called the Oracle executives at home to explain my rationale and reset their expectations, I was derisking a potentially dangerous situation.

Changing our response to situations beyond our control begins with reframing how we view and interpret stressful situations. Changing our perspective and our lens allows us to see clearly and take the right path. However, to sustain our efforts, we need more than beliefs; we need proof that the Impact Player Mindset actually delivers greater value and increases influence and impact.

TAKING SMART RISKS

Three ways to take risk out of risky moves and turn uncertainty into opportunity:

1. **Acknowledge the risk.** Identify potential dangers, keep your ear to the ground, and watch for signs of trouble.

2. **Set expectations.** Clue people in, inform them of both upside and downside risks, and let them know what you need from them.

3. **Set boundaries.** Establish thresholds and stop-loss points to minimize negative consequences, and have backup plans ready.

GATHER SUPPORTING EVIDENCE

Many of our attempts to change get off to a great start, but few achieve a strong finish. Why? Because we try to fuel change with sheer willpower rather than validate our progress with evidence of improvement.

One of my former colleagues had received a barrage of feedback that he was a strong leader but a weak collaborator, especially when it came to supporting his colleagues. He heard the feedback and knew the issue would be career limiting, so he made a plan to address the problem. He typed himself a reminder note, printed it in 72-point bold font, and taped it to the wall in front of his desk. It read: FIND SOMETHING THAT NEEDS TO BE DONE AND DO IT WITHOUT SEEKING CREDIT.

Not long after the sign went up, I noticed him making a conscious effort to help others. His actions were feigned and awkward, but he was doing the right things. Within a couple weeks the sign came down. I interpreted it as a hopeful sign that he had discovered the joy of teamwork and no longer needed the constant prompt. However, not long after, he returned to his old ways, pursuing his agenda and insisting on the spotlight. He had tried to "fake it till you make it," but he never made it because the weaker, nascent mindset was overpowered by an old assumption: *I will get more credit by being the leader.*

Harvard's Robert Kegan and Lisa Lahey refer to this dynamic as "immunity to change." In a *Harvard Business Review* article entitled "The Real Reason People Won't Change" they wrote, "Even as they hold a sincere commitment to change, many people are unwittingly applying productive energy toward a hidden competing commitment. The resulting dynamic equilibrium stalls the effort in what looks like resistance but is in fact a kind of personal immunity to change."[7] On the outside, my colleague had been acting in a supporting role, but his commitment to supporting his colleagues was competing against another deeply entrenched assumption. He couldn't see how supporting others would lead to success for himself, so he reverted to his old belief. He had the will, but he lacked proof and gave up.

The eighteenth-century Scottish philosopher David Hume said, "A wise man . . . proportions his belief to the evidence." To this end, we'll cover three ways you can use evidence to build an Impact Player Mindset and strengthen your reputation as such. The first is to collect evidence to support experimental behavior.

1. Experiment and Collect Evidence

Nascent behavior and beliefs are fragile and will be overpowered by older assumptions until they are strengthened by supporting evidence. The supporting evidence forms a buttress around the budding mindset, much like a brace around a sapling provides stability until the tree is strong enough to stand on its own. Instead of relying on willpower to stick to your commitments (or hanging a sign over your desk), you can make further and more durable gains by gathering evidence and building a case for the incipient mindset or behavior. As Kegan and Lahey suggested, once we understand what existing assumptions may be preventing us from committing to new behavior, we need to actively seek experiences that cast doubt on the validity of our old assumptions and prove the utility of new ones.[8]

When you try a new practice or attempt to adopt a new belief, think of it as an experiment; instead of jumping in headlong, think like a scientist who, having formulated a hypothesis, conducts an experiment to test the assumptions and gather evidence to either support or contradict the theory. Because the Impact Player framework was developed using the scientific method, much of the work has been done for you. These mindsets and behaviors have proven effective for the Impact Players in our study. However, you need not take my word for it; run your own experiment. Treat these practices as hypotheses and prove them for yourself.

For example, Andrew Ritchie, a business strategist in New Zealand, decided to test out the hypothesis that saying less in a meeting could lead to greater impact. He experimented with this idea by trying out the Smart Play called Play Your Chips Wisely (page 197) during his company's quarterly strategic planning meeting. These meetings are all-day intense sessions filled with robust debate, and as one of the company's strategy experts, Andrew is normally one of the most vocal contributors.

Andrew identified three topics on which he knew he absolutely needed to contribute his perspective and play a chip. Two chips would be used on two projects he wanted to push forward, and one would be saved for a critical topic he wanted discussed. He planned his chips in advance, preparing to share his unique perspective and supporting evidence using bullet points to help him be succinct. When a colleague messaged him asking why he was unusually quiet, he responded, "I'm playing my chips wisely." He got a thumbs-up response.

He played his chips with surgical precision, and by the end of the day, the two projects he advocated for were approved and the topic was debated as robustly as he hoped. Additionally, because he was really listening to other people's perspectives, he could more clearly see the various agendas at play and noted, "I miss this subtext when I am deeply engaged in the debate."

Andrew shared the results of his experiment with us; by playing his chips sparingly, he not only achieved the outcomes he was looking for, he gained new perspectives and insights as well. The evidence was compelling enough for him to try the approach again. The experience challenged his old belief that constant advocacy increased his influence.

Gather Evidence. When you experiment with an Impact Player behavior or mindset, take the smallest viable action and then collect evidence. Use these questions to gather evidence and understand the effect (and efficacy) of the new behavior.

1. What will you do differently?
2. How did others react differently to your action?
3. Did it produce the outcome you were hoping for?
4. What are the signs that it worked better than what you've done previously?
5. What are the signs that it was less effective than what you've done previously?

Repeat the experiment until you have overwhelming proof that the new belief is accurate, or adjust your approach to fit the situation. Make note of the assumption that was strengthened or proven true. Unless an experimental practice yields better results, we will eventually revert to old, trusted assumptions and patterns of behavior. When you experiment with new behavior, look for evidence that weakens the grip of old assumptions and bolsters the case for new, more powerful beliefs and habits.

2. Elevate and Evidence Your Contribution

Philosophers have raised questions regarding perception and meaning with this simple (and likely familiar) thought experiment: If a tree falls in a forest and no one is around to hear it, does it make a sound? Similarly, we might ask: If someone makes an important contribution and no one notices, was the contribution valuable? Perhaps, but value must be both received *and* perceived by the customer or stakeholder.

Throughout this book I've spoken of the tragedy of under-contribution—when smart, capable, hardworking people fall for decoy value and consequently dilute their impact. Yet the greater tragedy might be the unseen Impact Player—the high-contributing individual who embodies the ideals of Impact Players but whose work is overlooked or taken for granted. They might be the unsung heroes who work behind the scenes or who are from underrepresented populations that lack the advantages of people from well-represented populations. Too often their work goes unseen and their voices unheard. Clearly the onus for building an inclusive organization is on the organization's leadership. Further, the managers bear the responsibility to look beyond surface characteristics to see the diverse talent on their team (a topic we'll address in chapter 8). However, it certainly doesn't hurt to help your leaders and stakeholders see your capability more clearly. So what might you do to ensure your work is not overlooked and that others see the true value and impact of your contribution?

Elevating the Intel Inside

Intel Corporation faced a similar problem: customers couldn't see the value of one of its most valuable products. It was early in the 1990s, and the personal computing revolution was in full force. Companies and people everywhere were buying PCs and laptops from IBM and a host of manufacturers of IBM-compatible computers such as Compaq and Toshiba. Encased in each of these computers was a microprocessor, an integrated circuit that is the central processing unit of a computer, essentially its brain. Intel Corporation was the market leader in microprocessors, with approximately 85 percent of all IBM-compatible PCs running on an Intel microprocessor,[9] so the explosion in demand presented a huge opportunity for Intel. But it also posed a problem.

Intel's processors had a great reputation with computer manufacturers and tech nerds who understood and appreciated their technical superiority and quality. However, PCs were increasingly being purchased directly by end users, most of whom wouldn't know a motherboard from a mainframe. Intel needed to cultivate a similar renown among end users and help them understand that a computer with an Intel 486 processor would run faster and do more and that it was worth more than computers with other processors.

Thus was born Intel Inside, a landmark branding campaign. The logo was simple—the words "Intel Inside™" encased in a circle. Manufacturers were incentivized to include the "Intel Inside™" logo on their computers. The logo enabled them to quickly differentiate the quality of their product and gave non-techies an easy way to understand the value of computers with the Intel microprocessor.[10] The Intel Inside campaign turned Intel into a household brand name. Consumers now thought twice about buying a laptop that didn't have Intel Inside. The high-performance microprocessors were delivering real value; it was merely hidden to the consumer. The campaign ensured that that value was seen and understood.

People aspiring to greater impact may need to do the same.

Make Your Contribution Evident. Like Intel, you may need to help others see the value of your contribution to be appropriately recognized. You need not launch a multimillion-dollar campaign or engage in shameless self-promotion or branding. But you may need to publicize your contribution more actively, especially if your work is done quietly or behind the scenes.

Observing the subtle signals of a skilled waiter in a fine restaurant can illustrate how to do this well. A good waiter works efficiently and in the background but comes into the foreground at critical moments (and often just before delivering the bill) to let you know the work he's done on your behalf. He might say, "Just to let you know, I've put a rush on your order to ensure you get to the theater on time." His tone is not forceful; it's informative, it's evidence-based, and it's a savvy way to remind patrons of the quiet but valuable work being done on their behalf.

Many people who work in support roles report that they feel truly fulfilled by the satisfaction of helping others. However, even if you have a strong internal anchor, when your good work isn't noticed and appreciated by others, you can become pigeonholed, overlooked for growth opportunities, and more vulnerable to employment redundancies. Even the saints of the workplace deserve to be recognized and appreciated.

There are numerous ways you can tactfully draw attention to your efforts (see the inset below for a fuller list). Doing so might be as simple as providing an FYI, such as "I took care of the list of escalated issues from yesterday's task force meeting, so you don't need to worry about them." If your work involves a routine process, try innovating the process. When you succeed with a new approach, people notice

---

ELEVATING YOUR CONTRIBUTION

Tips to help others see the impact of your contribution:

1. **Provide an FYI.** Let other people know what you've done to make their work easier. Don't overdo the details; just let them know what they don't need to worry about because you're on the job.

2. **Add a surprise.** Do more than is expected of you; people will take notice.

3. **Innovate and share.** Improve a process, then share the innovation with your colleagues or group. Your work will be recognized, and your colleagues will benefit too.

4. **Share evidence of success.** Periodically share the compliments and kudos you receive (or have your customers and collaborators share it directly), or simply let people know what you've done—not with self-promotion but just the plain facts.

5. **Build champions.** Build mutually supportive relationships with your peers and stakeholders. Champion one another's successes and talk each other up to your shared stakeholders.

6. **Promote the work, not yourself.** Separating your sense of self from your work makes it more comfortable to share (and hear) news of success.

what's new and improved. When it fails, they also notice and better appreciate the old approach. If your work is often unseen, you might let one of your colleagues or your manager handle a few of your unseen duties while you are out on vacation.

Debra Steppel is a senior vice president who manages all back-office technology and marketing functions for a financial planning company. She's also an executive who juggles domestic responsibilities. When she was forced to spend several months on pregnancy-related bed rest, her husband did more work around the house, including the family's laundry. When he realized that carrying a large basket of laundry up and down two flights of stairs was harder for his petite five-foot-tall wife, he continued doing the family's laundry and has done so every week for the last twenty years. Debra reflected, "Some things must actually be personally experienced to fully comprehend the depth."

In addition to ensuring our own contribution is visible, we can and should do the same for our stellar but unassuming colleagues. This is especially true if our colleagues are members of underrepresented groups and in situations in which we have greater power or access. We can amplify their voices to ensure their ideas are heard rather than hijacked and attributed to someone else. We can endorse them publicly, refer to their accomplishments, and mention things we've learned from them. When they are not in the room, we can reference them and suggest their perspective be taken into account. The leadership author Kevin Kruse nicely captured the importance and promise of allyship: "By amplifying and advocating for underrepresented colleagues in meetings, you'll help ensure all voices are heard, with the added bonus of helping everyone know that they are influential and valued members of the team."[11] When the contribution of all people is acknowledged, we not only use all the talent available but incent everyone to contribute at their fullest.

ESTABLISH THE IMPACT PLAYER PERFORMANCE GUARANTEE

People who bring the power of *always*—those who do the entire job the right way *every single time*—increase their credibility and influence. To establish this powerful guarantee, come out of the gate strong: on your first piece of work for a boss or a client, get the job done completely, without reminder and without alienating others. As you repeat this cycle, you'll become known as someone who can be counted on to finish strong and make work light for others—and you'll be seen as a risk-free, high-yield investment for your colleagues' and stakeholders' time and resources.

3. Build a Case for Your Growth

In addition to helping others see what we do, we may need to help our colleagues and bosses see who we are, especially when we'd like them to notice our professional growth. In my experience as an executive coach, I've seen many people make rapid change only to find that their reputation changed slowly and sometimes not at all. Carol Kauffman, founder of Harvard University's Institute of Coaching, estimates that the lag time between when someone makes a meaningful behavior change and when others acknowledge that change can be months. With superficial improvements the lag time may be only a month or so. However, when the person's previous behavior was perceived as negative, it can take six months to a year before others acknowledge the new behavior. Why is this?

Most of us are bombarded with more information and change than we are able to process. Jeff Dieffenbach at the MIT Integrated Learning Initiative said, "While change is accelerating, one thing that is definitely not is the neuroplasticity of the brain. In other words, the rate of change in the world may have surpassed the speed at which the human mind can process those changes." [12] Furthermore, even when your colleagues notice your new behavior, they may not be willing to see you differently just yet, especially if you've been a source of grief in the past. In their mind, they may have already labeled you as difficult, recalcitrant, or even self-centered. They've put you into a penalty box and may not yet be ready to release you.

How can you help your colleagues, bosses, and clients see and appreciate your growth? In addition to being patient, you may need to market your efforts and use evidence to strengthen your case. The way companies announce upcoming product upgrades and service improvements provides a useful example. Typically, when a retail store undergoes renovation, the store management alerts customers immediately, typically displaying a large COMING SOON banner. They might include an illustration of the new, improved storefront or layout and a sign saying PARDON OUR MESS. By establishing an expectation of progress, customers are more tolerant of the messy middle and more likely to notice the improvements when the new store is unveiled.

Open a Folder

Likewise, if you want your colleagues to notice your improved ways of working, let them know what's coming. Telling them what to expect prompts them to create a new mental folder—much like a case file—in which they can collect evidence of your behavior change. For example, let's say Yuri's boss sees him as someone who escalates problems rather than finding solutions on his own. If Yuri addresses the issue in solitude, his manager is unlikely to notice (after all, the manager would have to to notice the absence of Yuri's escalations). Instead, Yuri communicates his intention to "finish strong" and maintain ownership of the problem until it's fully solved. In the next staff meeting, when Yuri briefly mentions a problem but tells the team he's handling it, that incident is put into the folder. The following week his manager learns that Yuri's been working with an adjacent team to fix a process problem without being asked. That goes into the folder as well. Yuri might even pop his head into his manager's office with a courtesy FYI on a situation. The next week he responds to an email with "I'm on it." His manager now has a folder full of evidence and is piecing together a new narrative: Yuri is a strong finisher, not a rapid escalator. Now Yuri is not only working differently, he is being seen differently as well.

Changing your reputation is as important as changing your underlying behavior—and it deserves thoughtful effort. So don't just change your ways; market those changes to key stakeholders. Let key people know what's coming soon so they can open a folder to collect data. You will reduce the time it takes for their perception to catch up to reality.

Of course, there are cases where the perception gap is simply too big to close. Or you may have lost the energy needed to turn around the situation. In such circumstances, you may need more than a new approach; you may want to make a fresh start somewhere else.

TAKING CHARGE

Throughout this chapter we've discussed a number of changes you might make to more fully embrace the Impact Player Mindset. But adopting this high-impact, high-value way of working is not about remediation; it is a matter of growth and advancement. Simply put, as we build this mental muscle, we take charge of our contribution. We can be liberated from micromanaging bosses because we are actively managing ourselves. We put ourselves in a position to contribute at our fullest and make our most valuable contribution. As the humanitarian and author Bob Goff said, "We're not held back by what we don't have, but by what we don't use."

In order to take charge of his contribution, Fernando Carrillo, the Anglican priest, podcaster, and CEO, had to first take charge of his life. But even professionals at the very top of their game can play bigger, and those having the time of their life still have room—and desire—to contribute in more impactful ways. Such was the case for Bradley Cooper, known around the world for his starring roles in dozens of hit movies, including *The Hangover*, *Silver Linings Playbook*, *American Hustle*, and *American Sniper*, as well as the voice of Rocket, the mutant raccoon, in *Guardians of the Galaxy*.

In 2016, Cooper was in the top echelon of actors—he had received four Academy Award nominations, was the highest-paid actor in Hollywood, and had twice been listed on *Time* magazine's "Most Influential People" list. But he felt he was underutilized and had more to offer. The *New York Times* journalist Taffy Brodesser-Akner wrote, "By the time he finished 'American Sniper,' he had been feeling like he'd done enough acting. He loved it, he *loves* it. He still plans to do it. But it was time to do more. 'I guess I felt like I wasn't utilizing all of myself,' he said."[13]

Despite his success as an actor, it wasn't easy landing a director role. The journalist continued, "Some people told him that he was an actor and nothing else. Within his acting work, people would just try to cast him in roles that were exactly like the ones he'd just played. . . . Then he pitched *A Star Is Born* to Warner Bros., and whatever happened in that room made the Warner people hand over $38 million before marketing costs." *A Star Is Born*, Cooper's directorial debut, opened in 2018 and received eight Oscar nominations, including Best Picture. Not a bad debut—after all, he was just getting started as a director.

Most of us want a job where we can make a difference and contribute at our fullest on a daily basis. Though a certain level of routine diligence is necessary, there are critical inflection points in one's career arc when extra vigilance is in order. These might include at the very outset of your career, when switching jobs, when returning to the workforce after a hiatus, or when recalibrating after slipping into a negative, or merely mediocre, pattern of thinking and working. But perhaps none is harder or more critical than reupping our expectations of ourselves when we seem to be at the top of our game and convincing both ourselves and others that we can contribute in new and higher ways.

We can sit back and wait for someone to discover our true talent and capability, or we can get ourselves into the game. We don't need to be the boss to take control of our own contribution, and we don't need to be in the most visible job to decide to add value. The Impact Player Mindset is an invitation to contribute at your fullest. If the path to leadership and greater influence is still unclear to you, please accept this simple nudge: Just start. Start anywhere. By trying on the mind-sets and practicing the habits, you'll get a better read on your situation and build awareness.

You might be lamenting that you didn't understand these principles earlier in your career. But it's not too late. As the Chinese proverb teaches, the best time to plant a tree was twenty years ago; the second best time is now. So start now, but don't finish. Don't settle for just having a job; strive to do work that makes a meaningful impact in whatever position you play. The value you create will multiply, compound, and return to you.

CHAPTER 7 SUMMARY: INCREASE YOUR IMPACT

This chapter illustrates what individuals and managers can do to develop the practices illustrated in chapters 2 through 6. It offers two ways to make hard changes a little easier because changing your beliefs and modifying your behavior isn't easy, nor is changing how others see us.

1. **Master the underlying beliefs and behaviors.** Instead of trying to simultaneously implement myriad practices, focus on the two foundational competencies that Impact Players possess.

   - **Master Skill 1: Changing your perspective.** This skill involves perceiving situations and issues from another person's point of view and helps invoke a number of the habits of Impact Players. It allows you to spot and avoid the traps that trip up typical contributors. You can change your perspective by zooming out and changing seats.

   - **Master Skill 2: Changing your lens.** This skill involves seeing opportunity rather than threat in ambiguous and uncertain situations and is at the root of the Impact Player Mindset. You can change your lens by reframing threats as opportunities.

2. **Gather supporting evidence.** Instead of trying to fuel change with sheer willpower, validate your progress with evidence of improve-

ment. Then, gather and share evidence of your contribution so it is both received and perceived.

- **Experiment and collect evidence.** Treat the practices in this book as hypotheses to test out for yourself. Run an experiment and gather evidence to confirm the results.

- **Elevate and evidence your contribution.** To ensure your work is not overlooked, you may want to expose other people to the work you are doing behind the scenes.

- **Build a case for your growth.** If you want your colleagues to notice your professional growth, let them know what to expect. Tell them what's coming and help them open a mental folder in which they can collect evidence of your behavior change.

Chapter 8

BUILD A HIGH-IMPACT TEAM

A single person doesn't change an organization, but
culture and good people do.
—FRANCES HESSELBEIN

"The Dream Team." It was the name given to the 1992 US Olympic basketball team comprising some of the greats of the game: Michael Jordan, Magic Johnson, Larry Bird, Charles Barkley, Karl Malone, John Stockton . . . the list goes on. We've seen dream teams in other sports, of course—Brazil's 1970 men's football team that won the World Cup; the 1980 USSR Olympic ice hockey "red machine" team; and the US women's national soccer team, which won the Women's World Cup in 2019—but we've seen dream teams in all fields throughout history, dense concentrations of star talent working under the influence of strong leadership, such as the artists of the Italian Renaissance or the five-time Nobel laureates of the Curie family.

We also find dream teams inside our modern workplaces, such as the NASA rover team (profiled in chapter 4) or the *Saturday Night Live* cast anchored by the power duo of Tina Fey and Amy Poehler. If you're fortunate, you've worked on such a team or have had the privilege of leading one. The best leaders don't just stumble upon such teams; they know how to build a dream team, even under challenging circumstances.

At the close of the 2013–14 basketball season, the Philadelphia 76ers had won only nineteen of their eighty-two games, giving them the second worst record in the NBA that year. Off the court, they weren't doing any better—in the league of thirty teams, they ranked dead last for sponsorships, and sales of season tickets were an abysmal 3,400 in an arena of more than 20,000 seats. The organization needed to turn things around in a big way, and Scott O'Neil was brought in as CEO to make it happen. You may remember Scott from chapter 2; over the next four years, he led the organization through a major transformation. By the end of the 2017–18 season, the 76ers had won fifty-two games and were ranked fifth in the league. What's more, the team's sales performance had gone from last to first, leading the league in sponsorships, attendance, and client satisfaction and retention.

The development of the basketball team was at the heart of the change, but Scott knew that the back-office functions—the teams behind the team—would require significant improvements as well. He brought in Jake Reynolds as the VP of ticket sales and services and charged him with a daunting task: figure out how to sell tickets for a team that lost three times as often as it won. Jake led the Sixers' sales organization in its climb to the top—and incredibly, much of this improvement in sales came even before the team began winning.[1] How did they do it?

Jake is a passionate, all-in type of leader who gets his energy from people, from investing in them, helping them, and watching them grow. Scott called him "the best leader I've ever seen." Jake knew the Sixers' management couldn't control what was happening on the court, but they could control other factors such as people, processes, and culture. He was betting that this combination could beat out product. He assumed that if he and his management team "hired the right people, put them in the right positions with the right training and development, and immersed them in a fun, competitive, high-energy environment, they'd be successful."[2]

Jake made it fun to sell, even when the team was losing. He said, "You're selling one of two things: You're either selling championships, or you're selling hope."[3] They sold hope, and they did it with joy. The sales staff's pregame meetings were spirited with hoverboards, fog machines, raffles, and cheering sections. They felt more like NBA games than corporate meetings—an approach that resonated with a team composed almost entirely of millennial talent. Their day-to-day work environment was high decibel, with laughter and cheering filling the bullpen. In fact, they were forced to swap out clapping with snapping so that their neighboring departments could get some work done. In an article for *Sports Illustrated*, Jake was quoted as saying, "We walk a very fine line between having fun and having too much fun."[4] Jake made selling against the odds fun, and even as the team mounted losses, ticket sales grew.

It's typical for teams that aren't winning to reduce sales staff, but instead, the 76ers hit the accelerator, growing the organization from 28 to 115, the largest sales force in the NBA.[5] Jake carefully recruited talent with the right mindset, people who were competitive, curious, and coachable—what Jake called the "three C's." If he could bring in people who wanted to win, who wouldn't stop until the job was finished, and who would listen and learn, he figured the leadership team could teach them the rest.

As the organization ramped up, Scott, the CEO, encouraged Jake to upgrade his management team, trading out some of the existing team members for more experienced, capable leaders. Scott said, "We didn't have six months to wait and watch what people could do. I needed Jake to let some people go and build a true management team." There was one particular manager whom Scott wanted Jake to replace. Scott admitted, "I was riding Jake hard," insisting he let the individual go. Jake responded to that pressure with his own intensity. He countered, "I need you to trust me and let me do my job." Scott was surprised— but delighted to see that Jake was fully in the game. Jake continued, "I told you I have it covered. I've already replaced four managers, but I don't want to replace this one. I think she has potential. Let me work with her." He did, and as Scott proudly acknowledged, "She's one of our superstars today."

Developing the players on his team was (and remains) Jake's top priority; he estimates that he spends a whopping 50 percent of his time developing and coaching his team. In addition to countless hours of one-on-one coaching time, the entire management team gathers for an hour each week just to learn—they read and discuss an article, watch a talk, or listen to a podcast. (Coincidentally, the week I contacted Jake for an interview, his team had just discussed *Multipliers* and *Rookie Smarts*.) Jake is convinced that with every all-star team he's led, the most critical thing he did early on was creating a space where coworkers could learn from one another. Though he may be the head coach of his team, the team members all have license to challenge one another—particularly when someone needs a mindset adjustment. Jake said, "We go in and out of this mindset all the time. External forces can pull us away and throw us off center." That's true for all of us. If we're mindful, we can see it ourselves. However, it's easy to miss our own weak spots, which is why we need teammates to cover for us, challenge us, and hold us accountable to the commitments we made.

The Sixers' transformation was a multiyear process, and the back-office teams trying to deliver big numbers could have been disheartened by the discouraging scoreboards on the court. So Jake decked out the sales office with a scoreboard of their own. He created visible signs of progress: a leaderboard on the wall with names and faces of top contributors, banners hanging from the ceiling with the names of sales reps who had been promoted, mementos of top achievements. He and his management team distributed awards weekly, including an MVP award, which the sales reps themselves voted on, and promotion days, which occurred quarterly and felt as exciting as NBA draft day. The culture fostered competition, but the sales reps understood that they weren't competing with one another; they were competing to be the best in the world, as a group.[6] After each competition, Jake raised the bar and up-leveled the challenge. He understood what would happen if he stopped giving them new challenges: "When you plateau, you lose people."

Over time, some great players have left the 76ers organization for new opportunities, but the front-office team has remained strong because Jake and his management team built a culture that can handle challenge and can endure beyond a given season or set of contributors (Jake himself went on to a bigger opportunity as the president of the New Jersey Devils hockey team). "The culture of the Sixers' sales staff has been the main driver of their success," said Brendan Donohue, the NBA's senior vice president of team marketing and business operations. "It's vibrant, fun, and contagious, with a terrific group of hard-working professionals who want to be a part of something bigger than themselves."[7] The team had developed the mind and practices of Impact Players.

Most managers are thrilled to have just one or two Impact Players on their team, but the best leaders want an entire team of these stellar players. It may seem improbable, but a champion team isn't a stroke of luck or a magical coalescing of the right players at the right time. A dream team isn't just a dream; it results from carefully curating players with the right mindset, developing them as individuals and as a team, and nurturing a robust, healthy culture. It is an act of bold, aspirational leadership. It requires purposeful development and the right type of coaching.

This chapter is written with managers in mind. We'll explore how leaders can build a dream team, one with Impact Players who work together and a culture that lives longer than the stay of a single superstar. We'll consider what managers can do to (1) hire more of this talent on their teams, (2) strengthen the Impact Player Mindset in their members, (3) replicate this behavior across a team, and (4) build the right culture—one that's inclusive of diverse talent and celebrates those who could easily be "the missing Impact Players." Further, we'll consider the magic that happens when a team of Impact Players is working under the influence of Multiplier leaders and why it creates more than just a great place to work—it produces brilliant work.

We'll begin by exploring how managers can get more of this talent onto their teams.

RECRUITING IMPACT PLAYERS

Each of the characteristics discussed in this book is important and valuable; however, some are certainly easier to develop. Some beliefs are functions of deeply anchored personality traits—for example, the belief that you can control the outcomes of events in your life (aka internal locus of control)—and are harder to change; others are by-products of life experience and tend to evolve with new experiences and supporting evidence (such as resilience).

Put simply, the best strategy for building a team of Impact Players is to hire people who already have the qualities that are most difficult to develop and then actively cultivate the other qualities. Of course, this requires knowing which mindsets are the most difficult for an individual to develop. Though volumes have been written on the virtues of various mindsets and behaviors, there is little research available on their relative learnability. To better understand which mindsets and behaviors are the easiest to change and which are the most difficult, I turned to a set of professionals who have a helpful perspective on this issue—executive coaches. In particular, I queried my executive coaching colleagues in the MG100, a collaborative association of one hundred of the top executive coaches from around the world created by Marshall Goldsmith, the preeminent coach and prolific author.

We asked this group about their real-world experience coaching leaders around the world on the beliefs and behaviors represented in this book. We asked them about the approximate success rates of their coaching interventions: Did the individuals successfully adopt the desired behavior or mindset? Did they maintain it over time? Was it a minor or radical adjustment to their behavior and beliefs? We used their responses to rate the "learnability" of twelve behaviors and eleven beliefs in the Impact Player framework. Although more research is warranted on the relative coachability of Impact Player traits, we found clear patterns in their responses. For each mindset and behavior, there were individual cases where someone who was eager and committed had made significant improvement; however, in aggregate, interventions for certain mindsets and behaviors were consistently more successful. Their insights are reflected in the following table, which outlines three categories of learnability from the least to most coachable beliefs and behaviors.

THE COACHABILITY OF THE IMPACT PLAYER MINDSET

How easily people adopt Impact Player beliefs and behaviors,
according to top executive coaches

LEAST COACHABLE ⟵ ⟶ MOST COACHABLE		
Assumptions and Mindsets		
Internal Locus of Control: I can control the outcomes of events in my life **Informality:** I don't have to be in charge to take charge **Opportunity:** I see ambiguity and challenge as an opportunity to add value (rather than a threat) **Benefit:** I can improve well-being for all	**Intrinsic Worth:** I have inherent value and ability **Agency:** I can act independently and make decisions **Grit:** I can persevere and get this done *(Note: Easily adopted but harder to sustain for a long period of time.)*	**Growth:** I can develop ability through effort **Belonging:** I am an important part of a team **Proactivity:** I can improve the situation **Resilience:** I can overcome adversity
Behaviors		
Lead and Follow: Can take the lead, but can also follow the lead of others **Know What's Important:** Figure out what's important without being told **Bring Fun:** Bring a sense of humor, fun, and levity to make difficult situations easier	**Anticipate Challenges:** Anticipate problems and find workarounds **Stay Accountable:** Maintain ownership for outcomes rather than escalate issues to management **Perspective Taking:** Look at situations through someone else's perspective	**Seek Feedback:** Seek feedback, correction, and contrary views **Offer Help:** Offer help and support to their colleagues and leaders **Influence Others:** Involve others through influence (rather than authority) **See Big Picture:** Understand the big picture instead of just doing their piece

Understanding which of the mindsets is most difficult to change allows managers and organizations to both synchronize and optimize their talent acquisition and development programs. The insights we gathered from top executive coaches suggest that companies should hire candidates who are self-directed, community-minded, have a high tolerance for ambiguity, and are fun to work with, even in stressful times.

When these traits become table stakes, leaders can invest their training and coaching resources where they can produce real gains. This more focused approach to talent development helps managers break through a common barrier that prevents them from being active coaches. Talent development professionals often assume that if managers don't coach their employees, it's because they lack skills or time. Often, however, managers do attempt to coach but give up when they don't see improvement. If you want your managers to be active coaches, help them direct their coaching efforts where they see a clear return on their coaching investment.

Behavioral-based interviewing can help you identify candidates with a history of working with the Impact Player Mindset. This popular interviewing technique emphasizes a candidate's past approach to specific situations and is based on the assumption that past behavior is the best predictor of future behavior. Behavioral interview questions tend to be pointed, probing, and specific and are intended to solicit verifiable, concrete evidence as to how a candidate has dealt with an issue in the past.

You can use behavioral-based interviewing to determine how a candidate tends to react to one of the five situations that most differentiate Impact Players from others (see page 13). DDI, a leadership consulting firm, created the popular STAR format for interviewing, in which interviewers encourage candidates to describe a Situation, Task, Action, and Result. I suggest a slight modification: look for a SOAR, replacing "Task" with "Outlook." For example, you could use the following questions and criteria to determine how a candidate has dealt with messy problems and if she went out of her way to do what was most useful or simply did her job.

SOAR HIRING TECHNIQUE

Look for how the candidate handles one of the five everyday challenges

STEP	QUESTION	IMPACT PLAYER PROFILE	CONTRIBUTOR PROFILE
Situation	Can you tell me about a time when you noticed a problem at work that affected a number of people but didn't fall into any one person's job?	Has dealt with messy problems.	Hasn't dealt with or doesn't see messy problems.
Outlook	How did you think about this situation? What were your options for dealing with it?	Sees the situation as a chance to be useful.	Sees situation as a distraction from their real job.
Action	How did you handle it? What did you do?	Does the job that needs to be done (understands what's important and works enthusiastically where they are most needed)	Does their job (takes a narrow view and works in their designated position)
Result	What happened?	Focuses on the benefit to stakeholders	Focuses on the benefit to themselves

Ben Putterman, whom I mentioned in the introduction, is now the vice president of learning and development at the electric adventure vehicle maker Rivian. Ben used this behavioral-based interviewing approach during a recent hiring spree when he needed to hire ten new staff within just two months. Rivian is a high-growth, venture-backed company, so Ben was looking for individuals who could work with agility in the environment of rapid change and uncertainty that's inevitable in this type of business. He decided to drill into how each candidate had dealt with messy problems and unclear roles (two of the five everyday challenges that differentiate Impact Players from professionals operating with more of a Contributor Mindset). After conducting the first six interviews he noted, "I'm not sure I know yet how to spot the Impact Player, but it really helped me know who not to hire." As he continued interviewing, he not only heard sharp differences in the various candidates' approaches but also noticed differences in their body language. He commented, "The people who seemed to thrive in ambiguity leaned forward and smiled when I asked them about how they dealt with a messy problem. The candidates that found these challenges disruptive or threatening tended to lean backward and throw up their hands." After conducting this test he concluded, "I need people who can turn ambiguity into opportunity, so knowing what mindsets and patterns of behavior to look for is invaluable."

Leadership Pro Tip

Impact Players won't sign up to work with lousy coaches, so your best strategy for recruiting top talent is to be a leader who brings out the best in people.

DEVELOPING IMPACT PLAYERS

Sometimes you can recruit for the Impact Player Mindset and stack the deck in your favor; this is especially true if you work in an organization that is actively bringing in new talent (e.g., a rapidly growing start-up, a business with high employee turnover, or collegiate athletics). However, few corporate managers have the luxury of handpicking and assembling their dream team from the start. More often, they must create a dream team by conjuring brilliance from a group of inherited employees, an unruly cross-functional team, or a surprise summer intern who was a "gift" from a higher-up. In this case, it's the leader's job to grow the talent they already have.

Here, the leader's job more closely resembles the role of a wise parent than a talent scout. As a parent, you don't get to pick your team; you work with the team you have. Indeed, I would have enjoyed raising a bunch of Mensa geniuses with Olympic-level athletic potential and runway-model looks. However, each of my children, just like their parents, is a mixed bag. Wise parents don't try to contort their children into some unattainable ideal but rather help them grow their strengths and work around their weaknesses.

You may not have complete control over who is on your team, but by working with the talent you already have, you can build a team that thinks and acts like Impact Players, a team that is capable of winning. The playbook at the end of each chapter provides the curriculum—the assumptions and habits managers can use in coaching their players. However, player development involves more than just a playbook. Managers need to create an environment in which the right mindsets and behaviors can grow. As we saw with Jake Reynolds and the Sixers, if you want people to have a positive attitude, you need to create a positive environment.

Creating Safety That Enables Stretch

The best leaders cultivate a climate that is both comfortable and intense. They remove fear and provide the security that invites people to do their best thinking. At the same time, they establish an energizing, intense environment that demands people's best efforts. As Amy Edmonson, Harvard Business School professor, wrote in *The Fearless Organization*, "If leaders want to unleash individual and collective talent, they must foster a psychologically safe climate where employees feel free to contribute ideas, share information, and report mistakes."[8]

Still, a safe environment alone doesn't engender high performance. Edmondson went on to say, "Not only do leaders need to build psychological safety; they must set high standards and inspire and enable people to reach them."[9] The best leaders create the tension needed to achieve high performance, for example, establishing high expectations, providing candid feedback, and holding people accountable.

In other words, once leaders create a great place to work, they expect people to do great work.

What occurs when a leader creates only one of these conditions? What happens when a leader stretches people without first building a foundation of safety, trust, and respect? The onslaught of challenges produces debilitating anxiety rather than growth. On the other hand, when a leader fosters a supportive environment but never asks others to do something truly difficult, her people feel appreciated but stagnant. People perform and grow best with equal doses of safety and stretch.

Five High-Impact Coaching Habits

Creating an environment of both safety and stretch in which individuals feel safe to experiment and fail, yet challenged to perform at their best, is one of the fundamental tasks of managers, coaches, and mentors. It is also essential for building a team capable of dealing with ambiguity and adversity. Each of the five situations that most distinguish Impact Players involves inherent stretch, which means the leader needs to first create safety and then coach people through the stretch challenges.

The following five leadership habits will encourage the right behavior in a team—the first two establish an environment of safety; the last three provide stretch.

1. **Define the W.I.N.** If you want the people on your team to venture beyond artificial job boundaries and *do the job that's needed*, help them see what's most important at any given time. Sharing strategic imperatives or annual objectives is a good start, but we all know these goals tend to evolve as the environment changes. You can help your team know where to focus by defining the W.I.N. (What's Important Now) and keeping it front and center. For instance, when I was working as a vice president of Oracle University, the sheer volume of programs we ran made it difficult to keep our priorities straight. But we needed to shift our energy toward several new initiatives. Instead of calling a management meeting or distributing a document to all staff,

I posted three top-priority initiatives on the door of my office. The list was short, probably no more than ten words in total, and it wasn't fancy or framed. It was written in dry-erase marker on a whiteboard, but everyone knew what was most important and where they could be most helpful. Letting people know what's important doesn't require elaborate presentations or expensive communication campaigns—you simply need to share what's at the top of your mental to-do list. It doesn't need to be carved in stone—just make it obvious and keep it evergreen, so the organization can adapt as fast as needs change.

2. Redefine leadership. Innovation is increasingly becoming a team sport, requiring diverse perspectives and collective intelligence. These teams tend to be ephemeral. They form, collaborate, and disband quickly and must operate more like a team in a pickup ball game than in a sports league. Team members need to be able to step up and step down with equal ease. To participate in this fast, fluid model of leadership, less assertive employees (and those uninterested in careers in management) will likely need help stepping up. To get these reluctant leaders to *step up, then step back*, provide a path of retreat. Show them that being a designated leader can be a temporary assignment, existing for the duration of a project or even for just a single meeting, not a permanent job.

While some team members will need encouragement and support to step up and lead, other contributors need coaching to get them to step back and support others. A team manager (or senior executive) can help the latter group develop a more fluid leadership style by modeling healthy followership practices. Let them see you collaborating with a peer organization or contributing to a project led by someone below you in the management hierarchy. Show your team that you can work as passionately as a follower as you do as a leader and that excelling as a follower is not a dead-end job but part of growing as a leader.

3. Ask them to stay until the job is done. If we want people who work for us to *finish stronger*, we may need to insist that they finish one job before moving on to the next. Consider the powerful lesson Dan Rose, chairman of Coatue Ventures, learned while working for Diego Piacentini at Amazon, which he recounted on Twitter.[10]

In 2004, Dan jumped at the chance to join the new Kindle team at Amazon; Kindle was new and exciting, and he felt ready for a change. For the last two years, he had been running Amazon's cell phone store; he had steered his little piece of business away from potential shutdown and turned it into the fastest-growing segment at Amazon, but over time, its competitors had closed in, and growth had stalled. That's when the offer to work on Amazon's Kindle came, and Dan accepted. He wrote, "Not only would I have the chance to launch a new business, I could walk away from my current business and let someone else clean up the mess."

One week before he was scheduled to begin his new job, Diego Piacentini, the worldwide head of retail, called Dan into his office. "He explained you don't get rewarded with new opportunities when you're doing a bad job," Dan recounted. "He would allow me to join Kindle team, as soon as I got my current business back on track and hired a successor who was stronger than me."

Surely this was hard to hear. "Not only was my new opportunity on hold indefinitely, but it was also clear I was failing in my current role," Dan wrote. He spent the next six months fixing it. Once he had reaccelerated growth and found a strong successor for himself, Diego allowed him to join the Kindle team.

"A year earlier I had been on top of the world," Dan wrote. ". . . Everyone told me I was a rising star. Then things got hard and I tried to run away to a new job in a new dept. But great companies and strong leaders hold people accountable. . . . It's tempting to run away to something new. Resist that temptation—stay until your job is done, take pride in fixing what you broke, don't hide from problems, act like an owner."

When we hold people accountable for finishing their work, we send a powerful message that their work matters and that we believe they are strong enough to stay in the game, even when things get tough.

4. **Critique the work not the person.** People generally need two types of information to achieve top performance. The first is clear direction: What is the target, and why is it important? (In other words, the W.I.N.) The second type is performance feedback: Am I actually

hitting the target? Am I doing it right? Most managers treat feedback as a judgment, an assessment of someone's work, or a pronouncement of a person's capability. Too often, this leads them to withhold it. After all, most of us don't take pleasure in delivering bad news. But this avoidance can also occur when the feedback is affirming. Why? Most people feel uncomfortable being the sole arbiter of someone else's work. Think of feedback as critical information—data people need to calibrate and adjust their approach—rather than a critique. When feedback is simply much-needed information, the feedback is both easier to share and receive.

If you want your team members to *ask and adjust*, provide performance intel, and treat it like helpful information rather than personal judgment. As my teenage son Josh recently said to me when I brushed off his repeated suggestion that I change a setting on my smartphone, "I'm not telling you you're an idiot. I'm just giving you important information."

5. **State what you appreciate.** During research interviews, I was struck by the number of managers who could clearly and passionately articulate what employees do that managers most and least appreciate but who admitted that they had never communicated these differences to the people who work for them. These managers typically left the interview committed to sharing these insights with their team. Managers, if you want your staff members to *make work light* for you and others, make a practice of flagging behavior that you appreciate. When someone does something to make your work easier, say, "When you do *X*, it's easier for me to do *Y*."

For example, "When you provide a summary when forwarding a long, meandering email chain, I'm able to respond more quickly," "When you can laugh at yourself when you make silly mistakes, it makes it easier for others to shake off their own mistakes and learn quickly from failure," or "When you help colleagues who are struggling, it makes it easier for me to resist rescuing them and taking over their work." You probably don't want to post a full list of your pet peeves on your door, but you might want to create a simple User's Guide to You (see page 198) that lets people know what they can do to help you work effectively and thus provide the best guidance and support to them.

Elise Noorda is the president of a three-hundred-person youth symphony and choir run entirely by volunteers in Las Vegas, Nevada. Just a few weeks before a performance, the atmosphere was tense because the teenagers were acting like teenagers, which frustrated the adult volunteers; that, in turn, made Elise's management job even harder. Everyone was stressed by doing work that was supposed to be joyful. One night after rehearsal, while Elise was meeting with the adults, she spoke to Holly, a volunteer who managed the nightly midrehearsal snack break. "Holly, you're doing a great job," she said. "You feed three hundred people in ten minutes and make it fun. When you create a fun atmosphere during the break, it helps the rest of the rehearsal go smoothly." The next rehearsal fell on Halloween, and Holly took snack time to a whole new level: festive treats, spooky decorations, and a fog machine. The lightened atmosphere spread through the rest of the rehearsal. The entire team got the message and followed Holly's example, keeping everyone's tempers down and spirits up for the rest of the season. Elise said, "I let Holly know, in front of a bunch of people, 'Hey, I love what you're doing,' and it affected every area of our work."

When leaders can quickly huddle with their teams, coaching team members through dynamic situations is relatively easy. However, when teams are distributed and individuals are working remotely, it's easy for people to miss context, veer off agenda, or get stymied by obstacles. Managers can help their team members perform at their best work together with full force by providing these essential conditions:

1. **Context.** Anchor conversations and group meetings by reminding the team how it fits into a larger objective. Share the why of the work and let people know why their contribution matters. Think of it as the "You are here" marker on a trail map.
2. **Clarity.** When it's cumbersome to have quick conversations to clarify expectations, obstacles can get magnified causing employees to

defer to higher-ups. To help staff maintain ownership, provide a clear Statement of Work (SOW) (see Smart Play 1 on page 126) and use the Multiplier practice of giving 51 percent of the vote (see *Multipliers*, appendix E).

3. **Collaboration.** Remote employees typically have a surfeit of online meetings but a dearth of opportunities to collaborate deeply with their colleagues, so give extra attention to creating forums where tough issues get tackled and people's best ideas surface.

4. **Connection.** Remote work can be isolating, so be intentional about creating connections that build the relational capital you'll need later for difficult conversations and for tackling tough challenges together. Try the simple practice of "checking in before diving in" by allocating time in staff meetings to check on how people are doing; ensure everyone feels like a person first and an employee second. Try any of these questions to kick off a meeting: "What are you proud of?" "What's particularly difficult right now?" Or simply, "How are you doing?" Furthermore, it's easy to overlook what is going well when you don't see people regularly, so double up on appreciation by highlighting wins and giving positive feedback twice as often as typical.

Whether a team works side by side or spans the globe, when leaders create the dual conditions of safety and stretch, their employees can step out, step up, and finish strong. With the right coaching practices, employees learn faster, get stronger, and grow beyond what they thought was possible.

DEVELOPING A CHAMPION TEAM

As a corporate leader or social entrepreneur, you might be inclined to identify and celebrate a particular superstar or deem an individual the MVP of your team. However, you will build a stronger team by asking: *How can I get as many MVPs as possible onto my team? How can I develop an entire team of people creating value and playing with impact?* In this section, we'll explore strategies for building an entire team of all-stars, each an Impact Player in their own right, playing different positions, possessing unique technical or functional skills, but working together—not by acquiring new talent or even by coaching each player separately but by raising the sights of the entire team and letting everyone catch the fever.

Getting Off to the Right Start

Remember Jack "Hacksaw" Reynolds, the all-pro American football player profiled in chapter 6 who arrived at breakfast on game days in full uniform and game ready? His high standards were infectious and spread to his teammates. While speaking at the Bill Campbell Trophy Summit at Stanford University, Hall of Fame cornerback Ronnie Lott recalled the first time he met Reynolds.[11]

It was the first day of the San Francisco 49ers training camp. Lott was a rookie and a first-round draft pick from the University of Southern California (USC). Hacksaw had been playing pro football for over a decade but was new to the 49ers. Lott recalled, "I sat right next to him, and I look over, and he's got a hundred pencils, and they are finely sharpened. I'm like, 'Who is this dude?'" Then coach Bill Walsh walked in, stood in front of the team, acknowledged Lott, and announced, "We finally got our first-round pick, and he's signed his contract." The team welcomed the highly anticipated rookie. Walsh proceeded with the briefing and said, "We're going to take notes now."

Lott panicked because he didn't have a notebook. He turned to Hacksaw and asked, "Can I borrow a pencil and some paper?"

His new teammate shook his head, looked at Lott, and said, "No."

"Come on, man. You got a hundred pencils. You got to give me one."

"No." Hacksaw continued, "You know something? I love this game.

Man, I've given everything to this game. If you want to play with me, you better be prepared."

That hit hard. Forty years later, Lott still remembered what Hacksaw Reynolds said, how he said it, and how it made him—the hotshot rookie—feel. Lott spoke emphatically: "That moment taught me to be prepared. That I needed to earn it. That being great requires intensity and takes every ounce of your soul."

That season the San Francisco 49ers won their first Super Bowl. For Lott, it started with a contagious moment—the mindset of one great player rubbed off on another, and a passion for excellence spread across an entire team.

Replicating the Starter

Managers naturally want to replicate the Impact Player Mindset. Recall the words of Amanda Rost's manager in chapter 1: "If I could have built a statue of her and put it in the center of our sales floor as a shining beacon of how to be a sales executive, I would have." How do you get a positive mindset to spread across a team? How do you make a belief, behavior, or sense of energy infectious? Building a champion team is a bit like making sourdough bread (another San Francisco institution). Baking a loaf of this tangy, airy bread requires sourdough starter—some of the bacteria (*Lactobacillus sanfranciscensis*) that is already growing and living in flour and water (which can be passed down through generations or, with a little effort, cultivated in the wild). When starter is kept in a warm environment and frequently fed fresh flour and water, it grows and spreads.

Similarly, to replicate a set of mindsets or behaviors, you need starter talent—people who can serve as the model and catalyst. Like the sourdough starter, this person could be either transplanted or carefully cultivated. When the Impact Player starter is placed in close contact with potential-but-not-yet-high-impact contributors in a warm-but-not-heated environment and fed the right amount of support and reinforcement, the Impact Players' qualities spread. Eventually everyone rises.

I've observed this dynamic in my own team at The Wiseman Group. When Lauren Hancock joined our research team as a data scientist, I could see that she was a gifted analyst. Everything she touched got better—more rigorous and understandable. She had an infectious enthusiasm for making data-driven decisions. But as I worked closely with her, I could see there was more to her gift. Not only did she increase the rigor of the work, she did so without increasing complexity. Collaborating with her always improved my thinking and made my work easier—not just because she took work off my plate but because she could find the simplest way to make sound decisions. This was a gift that needed to be shared.

In a company meeting, I explained how Lauren had improved the research and made a simple suggestion: if you are working on anything that would benefit from a more scientific or systematic approach, partner with Lauren. Various team members began pulling her in, not to do their work but to help them think through a problem and craft the right approach to solving it. Jayson, who leads marketing, asked her to help him think through an important market research survey. Lauren helped him design a survey that not only would provide more scientifically sound answers to his questions but insights into questions he hadn't previously considered. Karina, who runs the research practice, had been staring at a spreadsheet, looking for the story in the data, and was just about to do the analysis brute force style (sorting through tedious detail by hand), when she remembered that Lauren had taken a systematic approach to a similar problem in the past. She called Lauren and asked her if Lauren could teach her how to do it. Lauren was on vacation in New York City and in a restaurant but was so delighted by the request that she stepped outside and walked her through the Excel code. When the COVID-19 pandemic hit and the economy began shutting down in 2019, Lauren taught a seminar on the fundamentals of macroeconomics and recession so everyone on the team could make sense of the incoming economic reports. She then worked with the practice directors to build scenario-planning models to help them make good decisions with greater confidence amid the uncertainty. Lauren did more than bring her brilliance to the team; she spread it around and raised the level of thinking for everyone. When it came to data-driven thinking, our work got better, and the workload became lighter.

The Impact Player starter approach works because humans are natural watchers and replicators of behavior, especially behavior that appears advantageous. Social Learning Theory, a model developed by Stanford University psychologist Albert Bandura, explains how behavior gets replicated across social units, such as workgroups and families. By observing this cause-and-effect dynamic, we can acquire large amounts of behavioral knowledge without having to experience it ourselves or build up patterns through trial and error.[12] Of course, certain conditions are needed for behavior replication to occur. First, learners must notice the essential features of the model behavior, and second, they need to remember it. Bandura wrote, "Observers who code modeled activities into either words, concise labels, or vivid imagery learn and retain the behavior better than those who simply observe or are mentally preoccupied with other matters."[13] Third, they need to possess the component skills to replicate it. And fourth, the new behavior must be sanctioned and reinforced by leaders.

Once you have the starter—someone on the team with the right mindset—and you bring them into contact with other team members, some of their attitudes and behaviors will spread naturally as their colleagues observe their behavior and its consequences (e.g., she took the lead, organized a group to solve a problem without being asked, and the boss publicly thanked her for her initiative). But can you accelerate the spread? Drawing from research in social science and epidemiology, on page 254 are six strategies that will help you increase the contagiousness of positive behaviors.

With thoughtful effort, leaders can spur and hasten the spread of desirable behaviors across a team or organization. Unfortunately, on the other end of the behavioral spectrum, the proliferation of bad behaviors requires little help. As Mark Twain said, "A lie can travel halfway around the world while the truth is putting on its shoes." It isn't clear if a lie actually beats the truth in a footrace; however, several studies, including one recently featured in *Harvard Business Review*,[15] show that bad behavior in the workplace tends to be more contagious than good behavior. One reason for this is that bad behavior is usually easier to replicate; it's often on the path of least resistance. As Yale lecturer Zoe Chance explained, "The single best predictor of behavior is ease, more than price, or quality, or comfort, or desire, or satisfaction. Overall, the easier something is to do, the more likely people are to do it."[16]

PROMOTING DESIRED BEHAVIORS
Ways to increase the contagion of Impact Player practices across a team

NAME IT	Associating a behavior with specific words or vivid imagery makes it easier to recall and discuss. The Impact Player framework in this book is meant to give you memorable labels and a common vocabulary to discuss within a team. But you can make it your own and use language that resonates with your team.
CALL IT OUT	Help people recognize the behavior in action. Point out people who evince Impact Player practices and double-click on the positive, culture-shaping behaviors. Draw a clear line between positive behavior and positive results.
INCREASE CONTACT	Behaviors will spread faster when people work in close proximity or with frequent contact. In a physical workspace, get Impact Players working side by side with others. In a virtual workplace, increase face time and collaboration, especially problem-solving sessions or settings where an Impact Player's thought processes are revealed.
MAKE IT LEARNABLE	When highlighting Impact Player behaviors, focus on practices and behaviors that are most easily learned and aren't dependent on additional technical skills or access. See page 239 for the mindsets and habits that are the most coachable.
STRESS TEST IT	Crisis situations present powerful teachable moments, so model the desired mindsets and behavior in stressful times. As Thad Allen, a former admiral in the US Coast Guard, said, "You are most valuable as a leader when you are most at risk and in a crisis because your people get to watch you under stress and learn."[14]

| PROMOTE IT | Reinforce desired behaviors with both private and public acknowledgment, and make a point of acknowledging the right behavior even when it doesn't initially achieve the desired results. Remove barriers that prevent Impact Player behavior and make it easiest for people to do the right thing. |

To build a champion team, you need to do more than just encourage the proliferation of Impact Player behavior; you need to actively quell contrary behaviors, particularly the practices that cause smart, talented professionals to contribute below their capability level and the limiting beliefs that have been inured in a team culture (see ImpactPlayersBook.com for the list of practices).

CONTAINING CONTRARY BEHAVIOR
Ways to decrease the spread of contrary practices across a team

NAME IT	Associating a behavior with specific words or vivid imagery makes it easier to recall and discuss. The labels for the Contributor and under-contributor practices and decoys can help you pinpoint and discuss the limiting behaviors (see ImpactPlayersBook.com).
EXPLAIN IT	When highlighting examples, be specific about the behavior but do not necessarily name the person involved. Discuss how the behavior limits outcomes and prevents your team from serving your customers, solving problems, or responding to opportunities. Let people know the warning signs, what they can do to avoid the behavior, and what they should do instead.
CALL IT OUT	Provide a way for your team members to assess their own behavior to know whether or not they need to take corrective action. You can point them to the Impact Players quiz at ImpactPlayersBook.com.
CONTAIN IT	If someone is a source of many bad habits, don't let them be a superspreader. Discuss the problematic behavior with strong players to help them steer clear and not get infected by the negative behavior.
DETER IT	Attach consequences to the behavior either by introducing negative consequences or withdrawing positive consequences. Ensure everyone understands them, and be consistent in following through with the repercussions.

Accelerating the spread of positive, high-impact practices and slowing the spread of detrimental influences help create an all-star team. And as any sports fan knows, all-star teams win championships, but they don't last forever. Similarly, although the right starter talent can have a viral and uplifting effect on a team, their presence may not persist. Let's return once more to the science of sourdough bread making. Sourdough starter is a growth agent and is programmed to grow exponentially in one phase. Every sourdough baker can recall walking into the kitchen one morning to find that their starter had broken out of its container and was now sprawling all over the countertop, eating everything in sight. Bakers regularly discard a portion of starter because they have what they need.

As top contributors grow, they need bigger arenas to play in. You may need to let them move on to a new opportunity where (with the right environment) their mindset and ways of working will spread across another team. But their effect continues to redound. When Impact Players depart, they don't leave a hole; they leave more talent, more starters.

SUSTAINING A WINNING CULTURE

As the cycle repeats, you will start to build something more powerful than a few strong players on your team and stronger than rule books and playbooks. You will create a culture—a set of norms and values about how work gets done. These are in the water and permeate the air, and they become ways of working that persist long after a single player leaves a team.

The resulting culture is a collective expression of the mindsets that produce extraordinary value: service, stewardship, strength, confidence, and contribution. The culture will teem with a sense of adventure and a productive combination of initiative and accountability—a willingness to venture out but also a drive to get it done. People will have the confidence they need to learn and innovate and the agility to adapt to moving targets. The organization will have the collective strength to tackle hard problems, navigate ambiguous situations, and pursue opportunities. Though strong, the culture will also value service—not servitude but a willingness to help colleagues and a penchant for excellent customer relations.

As a leader, what can you do to create a culture that produces Impact Players and fosters this high-value way of working? Further, how do you create the conditions that allow everyone to contribute their unique capabilities in meaningful ways?

Value Diverse Roles

Creating a team culture in which each person can contribute at their fullest is one of the fundamental roles of leadership and begins by valuing the diverse perspectives and capabilities that each player carries onto the field. What would happen on a team if the group operated as if every role was valuable and each person had something important to offer? Leaders would operate like Dr. Kelly, an emergency physician who believed that everyone taking care of the patient (the attending physician, house staff, nurses, and patients themselves) was an important part of the health care team and that anyone on the team could have the idea that would save the patient. Each person who worked under Dr. Kelly's leadership felt this. One of the more junior members of the team said, "People are willing to come forward with ideas because it's clear that our contribution is important and wanted." When employees feel respected and valued, they experience a sense of belonging, connect more deeply with the culture, and their ability to contribute increases.[17] If you want to build a champion team, build a diverse team and create an environment in which each person can offer their natural gifts, and then coordinate their efforts to deliver the best outcomes.

Elevate Unseen Contribution

It's no secret that in most organizations the playing field isn't really level. Certain groups of people are always working at a disadvantage. Yet increasingly research shows that inclusive organizations that harness diverse talent have a competitive advantage. Managers face a choice: either they can continue to invest in the same professionals, defaulting to the team members who look and think like them, or they can proactively look for the "missing Impact Players"—the potential superstars within populations that have experienced discrimination. Managers can use the Impact Player framework to consciously identify and fight bias in the workplace.

For starters, managers can share the practices that point people down the pathways that produce value and impact. They can also help unveil what we've referred to as the unwritten rule book, the often subtle dos and don'ts of how things get done, what builds credibility, especially how things work inside your organization. By making implicit rules and systems explicit, managers can increase access to networks, vital information, and high-profile assignments.

Managers can also take measures to ensure a more even distribution of what Joan C. Williams and Marina Multhaup called the glamour and housekeeping work of the organization. Their research showed that "women of all races report higher levels of office housework, and both women and people of color (of both sexes) report less access to the glamour work." [18] When certain people are consistently asked to carry the back-office load, their contribution can be overlooked and their impact underestimated. When high-profile assignments are more evenly distributed to all aspiring leaders, those individuals will be more deeply engaged and the organization will more fully tap the hidden capability in the existing talent pool.

Last, leaders can ensure that the people who may be working against systemic biases and disadvantages have the necessities to succeed. You may recall from chapter 4 that although we often assume that managers need budget and head count to be successful, what people most need is access to critical information, guidance, and support from key leaders (see page 115). The following practices listed in "The Coach's Playbook" at the end of this chapter will help ensure everyone has the necessities for success: *share the agenda, spot opportunities, define the W.I.N., give feedback, invite others in.*

The process of providing feedback warrants special mention. Several studies have shown that people in underrepresented groups tend to receive less guidance than their peers.[19] For example, women tend to receive less feedback[20] and less specific, actionable feedback[21] and are more likely to be given inaccurate performance feedback, in which the messenger obfuscates a negative performance review behind a positive personal description.[22] When people lack performance intel, they're more likely to miss the target and become the missing Impact Player.

Leaders also play an important role in ensuring that the contributions of those who work in background roles are recognized and receive their share of the spotlight.

Colleen Pritchett is the president of Americas Aerospace & Global Fibers business unit of Hexcel Corporation—global leader in advanced composites for aerospace and industrial markets. She leads an organization of thousands of employees, spanning the full range of job functions: R & D, supply chain, manufacturing, sales, administration, and others. As at most organizations, some functions are naturally in the spotlight; however, she and her management team make a point of recognizing great work being done across all functions, especially by those who work behind the scenes. When the supply chain team was feeling undervalued, the VP of sales held a roundtable discussion with them to communicate, "I recognize what you do. I appreciate it, and so do our customers." He then solicited their perspective on important sales issues.

Colleen herself is constantly looking for star employees who aren't receiving recognition. When she discovers one, she sends an email to let them know that she sees the good work they are doing—and she copies the rest of the management team, so kudos abound. Town hall meetings provide another forum for spotlighting unsung heroes. These everyday heroes are lauded with appreciation and respect from their colleagues, and the spotlighted behavior gets noticed and replicated by others.

Managers: to foster a culture where everyone contributes at their fullest, look behind the scenes and seek out the unsung heroes. Ensure they are seen and heard, then celebrate their work. Elevate hidden contributors and amplify the quiet voices, especially those lacking systemic power or ordinary privilege. Add an extra dose of inclusion when leading people or teams who are working remotely.

LEADING INCLUSIVE MEETINGS

These simple meeting practices can help ensure everyone's ideas are heard and their contributions are seen.

1. **Prime the pump.** Send agendas and discussion questions in advance to give people time to gather their thoughts.
2. **Acknowledge everyone.** Start meetings by acknowledging everyone in the room.
3. **Ask everyone.** When asking for input, ask each person for input. Don't let any one person speak twice until you've heard from everyone once.
4. **Yield right of way.** If two people are trying to talk during a team meeting, give the right of way to the one who is quieter, more junior, working in a remote location or time zone, communicating in a non-native language, or a member of an underrepresented group.

Build Unity

Diversity without unity is noisy and can descend into chaos. However, a team of diverse talent working with shared values and toward a common agenda is a winning combination.

When Robert Zemeckis, an American film director who has forty-five film credits, was speaking at USC, he was asked which of his movies was his favorite? He replied, "*Forrest Gump.*" Why? "Because we were all making the same movie," he explained. When Zemeckis read the screenplay, he quickly saw that this simple story about the relationships that hold our lives together had none of the typical plot devices and broke every rule of movie making, yet he couldn't put it down. Like millions of viewers, he was smitten with the spirit of Forrest Gump, a simple man of low intelligence who ends up doing extraordinary things and brushing up against great people and great leaders. The movie stars Tom Hanks, Sally Field, Robin Wright, Gary Sinise, and Mykelti Williamson. The titular character, played by Hanks, makes one think that anything is possible and that, according to Field, who played Forrest's mother, "Life is there to be had. It is just a matter of reaching out and grabbing it." [23] Not everyone loved the movie; in fact, viewers were generally polarized. However, the artistic team that created it was anything but divided.

What happens when everyone is working on the same agenda, applying their native genius to the most important work at hand? People feel appreciated, are eager to tackle new challenges, and are willing to step up and lead—or follow someone else's lead. People do great work, and the environment is a great place to work. When talented people are working on the same agenda and contributing to their fullest, magic happens.

THE COACH'S PLAYBOOK

This playbook outlines a set of coaching practices to help your team develop the assumptions and habits of Impact Players. The first section is organized by the five practices of Impact Players. It also offers tips for leading inclusively and maximizing the contribution and impact of your entire team, including teams working remotely.

Practice 1: Do the Job That's Needed

Elevate the job. Job crafting is a technique that encourages employees to shape their own roles, but it can also be used to help employees reframe their work and connect their actions to a higher purpose.[24] You can help people on your team develop a Service Mindset by asking:

- Who benefits from your work?

- How would their lives or work suffer if your work wasn't done?
- In what way do they benefit? How does this benefit our larger community?

You can find additional resources in the work of Amy Wrzesniewski[25] or Tom Rath's book *Life's Great Question*.[26]

Elevate a value. Identify one of your leadership values or one of the organization's cultural values that is particularly important to you, such as transparency, and elevate it to the status of sacred value—something you'd go to war over. Let people know why it's important to you and the business (e.g., "We need the brutal facts to make sound decisions").

Provide context. Remind people how the current work or conversation fits into a larger objective. Explain what you're doing now and why it matters. Think of this as the equivalent of providing a "You are here" marker on a trail map.

Share the agenda. Instead of telling people what to do, describe the most important outcomes. Describe (1) what success looks like, (2) what a completed job looks like, and (3) what is off limits.

Spot opportunities. Knowing what's theoretically important is like being able to identify a bird species in a field guide—impressive but not useful. Help people spot important opportunities the way a master birder teaches others to spot a species in the wild, when it's in motion and out of clear view. Call out W.I.N.s in real time and help people see what's important now.

Issue permit. Give people the confidence they need to venture beyond their formal job boundaries by giving them formal permission. This permission can operate like a permit given to a hiker, who checks in with the authorities and registers their destination before venturing into dangerous backcountry alone. Agree on (1) where they are headed and (2) what parts of their core job they need to continue to do well. You can also help people step up and take a leadership role by letting them know a particular issue would benefit from their unique capabilities or perspective—that it has their name "written all over it."

Practice 2: Step Up, then Step Back

Focus on what's in their control. To help people reinforce the belief that they have the power to improve a situation, help them see what they do have control or influence over. When facing frustrating or challenging situations, ask coaching questions such as:

- What can you control in this situation?
- What is beyond your control?
- Where do you lack full control but might have influence?
- What is the best way to influence the situation?

Additionally, managers can help model this mindset during staff meetings, ensuring that team conversations focus on problem solving within the team's sphere of influence and don't devolve into blame-and-complain sessions.

Exercise choice. Encourage a spirit of volunteerism and stewardship on your team by allowing staff members to sign up to work on projects led by others, rather than being assigned to or even chosen for those projects. Exercising their ability to choose where they can contribute best will strengthen their willingness to lead and enlist the support of others.

Deputize your team. I was once a passenger on a very small aircraft flying between two remote islands in Central America. Before takeoff, the sole pilot turned to the four passengers behind him, gave the obligatory safety briefing, and then matter-of-factly announced, "If you see anything unusual or alarming during the flight, please let me know." We laughed, but when he didn't, we realized we had been deputized as copilots. We stayed alert. Likewise, you can deputize your team and let them know to watch for problems, be ready to take charge, and perhaps even make a citizen's arrest as needed.

Expand your guest list. When Alan Mulally was the CEO at Ford Motor Company and leading a massive transformation at the then-troubled automaker, he asked each senior executive to include a more junior manager or employee as a guest during key executive meetings. Having onlookers present encouraged full transparency and good leadership behavior on the executive team. It also created more leaders across the company who understood the business agenda. Try expanding your guest list by including lower-level contributors in key discussions. Though they may be silent observers during the meeting, the perspectives they gain will help them later operate like leaders, not bystanders.

Offer immunity to initiators. When people take initiative, they are bound to make mistakes, break some minor rules, or simply do things differently than you would. Responding with correction may improve their work, but it will likely reduce their initiative next time. You can prioritize progress over perfection by overlooking minor infractions for those taking charge and moving in the right direction.

Practice 3: Finish Stronger

Recall past moments of resiliency. Research has shown that having experience with obstacles (whether in childhood, personal life, or the workplace) helps an individual become more resilient in the future.[28] You can help people deal effectively with new challenges by having them remember those experiences and reflect on how their past approaches apply to their current challenges. Ask questions such as these to build mental muscle memory:

- What similar challenges have you faced in the past?
- What did you do that helped you overcome those challenges?
- Which of those strategies or tactics could help you resolve this current challenge?

Reframe obstacles as challenges. Use an exercise from the Stoics called "Turning the Obstacle Upside Down." Ask an individual to identify every "bad" aspect of a challenge. Then ask them to turn those upside down so each bad aspect can become a new source of good, specifically a source of personal growth. For example, an unreasonable client is an opportunity to learn scope control.[29]

Define the W.I.N. Instead of giving people detailed instructions for their job, make sure they know the fundamental job to be done. When you delegate, provide clarity by articulating "the three whats" of a successful operation. These are: (1) *the performance standard:* what a great job looks like; (2) *the finish line:* what a complete job looks like; and (3) *the boundaries:* what's not part of the job.

Focus on the finish line. According to Heidi Grant, "Great managers create great finishers by reminding their employees to keep their eyes on the prize and are careful to avoid giving effusive praise or rewards for hitting milestones along the way." Encouragement is important, but to keep your team motivated, save the accolades for a job well—and completely—done. Applaud milestones, but focus on what's left to be done rather than how much has already been done.

Get out of the way. When people are struggling to cross the finish line, managers tend to intervene by adding extra force to help people push past the obstacles. However, there may be an easier way. As organizational psychologist Kurt Lewin suggested, greater gains can often be made by reducing the restraining forces. And, often what most holds people back is too much management intervention—too much direction, too much input, and too much feedback. Instead of helping people drive forward, try simply getting out of their way. You might find people move faster and can go further without excessive management.

Practice 4: Ask and Adjust

Build trust. When the leader expresses trust in team members, it bolsters the their self-confidence, increases their ability to learn and adapt, and opens a pathway for reciprocal feedback. Find ways to express each of these forms of trust, not only through your words but also through the responsibilities you entrust to each individual.

- I believe you—I trust your integrity.
- I believe in you—I trust in your abilities and your capacity to learn.
- I believe you have my best interests in mind—I trust your intentions.
- I believe you can handle this—I believe you can learn and adapt.

Give feedback. Providing rich feedback is an essential part of a leader's job. To make it easier for people to receive feedback, treat it as helpful information people need to do their jobs well rather than a personal performance appraisal conveying either criticism or praise. As Kim Scott argues in her book *Radical Candor*, you may give difficult feedback if the person you're giving feedback to knows that you care personally for them. Be direct, because the best feedback is radically candid. Use these tips from *Radical Candor* to provide direct, helpful feedback:[30]

- Be clear about how you intend to help and state your intention to be helpful.
- Be precise about what is needed and what doesn't work.
- Build a trusting relationship by establishing a consistent pattern of action in good faith and by spending a little time alone with each of your direct reports on a regular basis.
- Solicit criticism and give praise before giving criticism.
- The way you ask for criticism and treat it when you get it goes a long way toward building trust—or destroying it.

Rebuild confidence. Confidence, once lost, can be difficult to regain. Several years ago my mother and I were working on a project together. At one particularly difficult point in the process, her confidence was shaken and she became reluctant to make decisions. Of course, I knew she was extraordinarily capable and could handle these challenges, so I called her to set her straight. I affirmed my belief in her and her ability to be successful. She appreciated my effort but said, "You can't give me confidence. Only I can give myself confidence." It's true; we can't gift other people confidence. However, we can create conditions that allow people to rebuild their own confidence. You can reestablish a pattern of success by rescoping the work to create a series of wins:

1. Start with smaller blocks of concrete work that provide easy wins.

2. Celebrate these victories, but don't overdo it.

3. Add a layer of more challenging blocks.

4. Keep expanding the scope and complexity of the work until the individual's confidence matches the size and complexity of the work that lies ahead.

Practice 5: Make Work Light

Invite others in. We can use our influence or relative privilege to make it easier for others to feel like they belong; in fact, it may be our very uniqueness that breaks through a stereotype and opens a pathway for others to belong as well. According to an article in *Harvard Business Review*, leaders and colleagues who serve as fair-minded allies not only increase inclusion for others but also buffer them from the exclusionary behavior of others.[31] Leaders can help each team member see that they matter to a group by discussing each person's native genius as a team. Focus on one team member at a time, inviting others to describe what they see as the person's natural brilliance.

Celebrate the assist. If you want team members to actively help one another, make heroes of the people who provide "the assist." In athletics, an assist is a contribution by a player that helps score a goal (and is recorded in the official statistics). So don't just recognize the individuals who score goals (e.g., make big sales or release new products), recognize those who set them up for success.

Don't tolerate difficult behavior. "The culture of any organization is shaped by the worst behavior the leader is willing to tolerate," wrote Steve Gruenert and Todd Whitaker.[32] As a leader, if you tolerate high-maintenance behavior, you will breed it across a team. If you want a low-maintenance team, define what it means to be easy to work with, then reject and redirect high-maintenance behavior. Instead of indulging people as they complain about their colleagues, ask them to resolve the issues directly with the other party. If someone sends you a long, rambling email, ask them to resend a brief one. If someone is making long-winded presentations, ask them to begin with their key points and then provide detail only as requested. If someone is dominating meetings, ask them to play fewer chips in order to give their colleagues an opportunity to play their chips too.

Multiplier Leadership Practices

A number of the leadership practices in *Multipliers: How the Best Leaders Make Everyone Smarter* will help you develop the Impact Player mindset on your team and create an environment where everyone contributes at their best. See appendix E in *Multipliers*, revised and updated edition, for additional guidance.

1. **Give 51 percent of the vote.** To encourage someone to take full ownership, put them in charge by giving them majority vote on a particular project or issue.

2. **Give it back.** When someone brings you a problem that they are capable of solving, play the role of coach rather than problem solver. And if someone legitimately needs help, jump in and contribute, but then make sure you clearly give the ownership back.

3. **Talk up your mistakes.** When you let people know the mistakes you have made and what you have learned from them, it makes it safer for them to acknowledge and learn from their own mistakes.

4. **Make space for mistakes.** Create a safe space where people can experiment by clarifying the areas of work where there is room to take risks versus the areas where the stakes are too high to allow failure.

5. **Identify native genius.** To get your team members' best, identify their native genius—what they do easily and freely. Discuss it with them, and identify ways it can be better utilized on the most important work.

CHAPTER 8 SUMMARY: BUILD A HIGH-IMPACT TEAM

This chapter is written for managers who want to build a team of Impact Players. It outlines how leaders can build a team where everyone is contributing at their fullest and a culture that inspires excellence long after individual Impact Players leave the team. It also includes strategies for creating an inclusive culture that sees and elevates the missing Impact Player.

RECRUITING IMPACT PLAYERS. Certain aspects of the Impact Player Mindset are less coachable, so recruit for these particular mindsets and focus your coaching efforts on the more learnable mindsets and behaviors. Behavioral-based interviewing or psychometric testing can help you identify people with these mindsets and a track record of the habits exhibited by Impact Players.

DEVELOPING IMPACT PLAYERS. The best leaders cultivate a climate that is both comfortable and intense because people perform and grow best with equal doses of safety and stretch.

BUILDING A CHAMPION TEAM. Leaders can build an entire team of all-stars by accelerating the spread of high-impact habits and slowing the spread of other, less effective behaviors.

SUSTAINING A WINNING CULTURE. Building a team with an Impact Player ethos will help build a larger organizational culture that places value on accountability, agility, collaboration, courage, customer service, inclusion, initiative, innovation, learning, and performance.

Chapter 9

PLAY ALL IN

We cannot change the cards we are dealt,
just how we play the hand.
—RANDY PAUSCH

You may recall that when Karen Kaplan (profiled in chapter 6) joined the ad agency Hill Holliday, she was looking for an easy job that would get her through law school. When she was offered a job as receptionist, the founder told her that she would be the face and voice of the company. That's when she realized that her job was important and her work made a difference. So she decided she would be the CEO of reception. Then she raised her hand and accepted each opportunity that came her way, appointing herself the CEO of those responsibilities as well. Now, thirty years later, she is the CEO of Hill Holliday, which gives her the ability to provide these types of opportunities to others.

Remember Paulo Büttenbender, the software development architect for SAP in São Leopoldo, Brazil (mentioned in chapters 1 and 7), who listens longer? His empathy allows him to design apps that fit the customer's needs like a finely tailored suit, which means he gets tapped for the most-critical assignments. Roberto, his manager, said, "Everyone says they need Paulo." Indeed, his work has taken him all over the world—from London to Sydney, India, and Saudi Arabia. Paulo admits, "One opportunity has just led to another. I've seen the world. I've worked in the amazing Canadian Rocky Mountains at Banff and had the best steak in the world in the countryside of Argentina." But, steaks aside, Paulo's reputation as someone who gets the hard jobs done means he gets to do work he finds deeply fulfilling.

If you recollect all the way back to chapter 1, you may remember Jojo Mirador, the scrub tech. Jojo's the one who doesn't just hand surgeons the instrument they ask for; he gives them the one they most need. During surgery other scrub techs simply hand the surgeon the requested instrument. But Jojo watches the surgeon's hands, anticipates their next move, and figures out what the surgeon needs before they ask for it. He offers his recommendations with such sincerity that the surgeons thank him gratefully. And because he knows his stuff so well, they seek out his opinion. He admitted, "Yes, it's flattering when the surgeons ask for my opinion and want me on their team." Jojo's manager continually fields requests from surgical teams that insist they need Jojo in their operating room. However, these conflicts get worked out because everyone acknowledges that the team doing the most complicated procedure is the one that really needs Jojo managing the instruments. Why? Because Jojo is not just present in the operating room; he's all in during the surgical procedure. And when you play all in, you play bigger and have a deeper impact.

When Philadelphia 76ers former CEO Scott O'Neil was searching for a word to describe Jake Reynolds, he said, "Passion's not the right word. There's probably some all-encompassing word that means that you're all in—'I'm with you, I'm next to you, I'm in front of you when things happen, I'm behind you when you're falling, I'm completely committed.' Whatever that one word is, that's what he has."

This is what I call a high-contribution environment—a setting where people bring their best thinking and do their best work, each person's intelligence is deeply utilized, and everyone on the team adds value. It's an environment in which people are "all in"—fully committed to or involved in an endeavor. Vincent van Gogh described that state when he said, "I am seeking, I am striving, I am in it with all my heart." Legendary footballer Kevin Greene, who recorded the third most sacks in NFL history, "played the game with every molecule in his body," according to his coach.[1] Marie Curie, Nobel laureate in both physics and chemistry, wrote in a letter to her brother, "I regret only one thing, which is that the days are so short and that they pass so quickly."[2] Toward the end of her life she lamented, "I don't know whether I could live without a laboratory."[3]

Eugene O'Kelly, former chairman and CEO of KPMG, was reflecting on his life (later cut short by cancer) when he said, "Too often, commitment was measured by how many hours you were willing to work. But commitment is best measured not by the time one is willing to give up, but by the energy one wants to put in."[4] Being all in is not the same as being exhausted—tired and depleted of energy, resources, and strength. In hard-charging organizations, people are driven hard, pushed, prodded, and often left exhausted. In high-contribution organizations, people are given an opportunity to contribute at their fullest and are in with both feet. What's the difference? Agency and choice. In one culture, management makes demands; in the other, people contribute freely. When leaders create conditions in which people can contribute fully and wholeheartedly, work is exhilarating. Work becomes more than a mere job or even a career; it becomes a joyful expression of our most complete selves.

An all-in environment, where people are neither used up nor underutilized, is attainable with contributors who play for impact and leaders who bring out the best in others. Impact Players and Multiplier leaders are a powerful combination because each person's contribution—their value add—gets multiplied. And when individuals can manage themselves, it gives their managers the opportunity to really lead. It's a proposition that makes sense in the modern workplace. Today most professionals want to make an impact, not just earn a paycheck; they want to be coached, not managed; and frankly, no one really wants to manage people anymore.

If you are an aspiring leader, the Impact Player mentality is your path to leadership. When you think and work this way, you are viewed as a leader, and when leadership opportunities arise, you will be a natural pick. For those of you who may not be interested in being a manager per se, the mindsets and practices we've explored will put you on a path to greater impact. Your ideas will get heard, and your work will have greater influence. As an Impact Player, you will be a difference maker.

Managers, building a team of Impact Players is your ticket out of management and into leadership. When you no longer need to step in and fill the gaps left by talented but under-contributing employees, it becomes easier to be a good leader. You can reclaim your equanimity and fulfill your own role with clear vision and composure. It's also how you take your organization to the next level. Furthermore, it will help you up-level your own leadership capabilities. For those aspiring to be Multiplier leaders, building a team of people with the Impact Player Mindset will supercharge your effectiveness.

While the career path for the most impactful players may lead to greater rewards, the real prize might be a better work experience: greater choice, more fun, deeper fulfillment. Indeed, the best reason for playing at your fullest may just be for the experience itself. Mike Singletary, NFL Hall of Fame linebacker, asked, "Do you know what my favorite part of the game is? The opportunity to play." Do it for the chance not just to participate but to play at your best.

In the opening scene of the movie *Forrest Gump*, a feather falls from the sky and is tossed and tumbled in the breeze. Like this feather, life is uncertain. So are most careers. Opportunities present themselves like feathers in the wind. Tom Hanks, reflecting on the messages of the movie, said, "Our destiny is only defined by how we deal with the chance elements to our life. . . . Here is this [feather] that can land anywhere and it lands at your feet."[5] What do we do with random chances? Do we see them as threats, or do we seize the opportunities they present? Forrest's mother tells him, "I happen to believe you make your own destiny." In studying the most influential players and top contributors in the workplace, I've come to agree.

Though all people have value and bring capability to their jobs, some make themselves more valuable than others. They play bigger. They find a need and fill it. They turn uncertainty and ambiguity into opportunity. Yet the way they work is anything but random. They find out what's important to those they serve, and they make it important to themselves. They take the lead and finish the job. They stay light on their feet to adapt quickly, and they make work light for others.

How big do you plan to play? As Marianne Williamson said, "Your playing small doesn't serve the world." Where can you be of greatest value? What is life summoning you to do?

If you want to make a difference, look around. Notice what needs your attention. Tap into your passion and your purpose, and find a way to contribute, to create impact, to play bigger and better. Imagine the impact of starting right now.

ACKNOWLEDGMENTS

Most authors would agree that completing a book feels like crossing the finish line after running an ultramarathon (or two or three). In reality, it's more like winning a big game; it's a team effort, made possible by teammates, coaches, boosters, and those who cheer you on.

The Team

First, I'd like to acknowledge the team behind this book, beginning with Hollis Heimbouch at Harper Business, who was not just the publisher but a cocreator and collaborator at every step of the way. After four book projects together, I remain amazed at her ability to provide guidance and sharp correction while allowing me full control over my work. Thank you, Rebecca Raskin and Wendy Wong, for managing the project and the rest of the HarperCollins team that brought the book to life.

To our team at the Wiseman Group—Alyssa Gallagher, Lauren Hancock, Judy Jung, Jayson Sevison, Shawn Vanderhoven, Karina Wilhelms, Amanda Wiseman, and Larry Wiseman—thank you for offering your insights, making my work better, and helping me carry the load in a very difficult year. Karina, thank you for getting this project off to a great start and helping us finish strong. You are a joy. Particular gratitude goes to Lauren, an invaluable thought partner, fierce editor, brilliant data scientist, and loyal critic. You made this book better in every way.

My appreciation and admiration go out to the talented artists Dillon Blue and Amy Stellhorn for giving clarity to the ideas and to Jared Perry for giving the book its cover. Thank you for jamming with us.

The Boosters

Our research partners, who opened up their organizations for our interviews and analysis and gave us access to some of their top talent, made the research possible. Much thanks go to Weston McMillan at Adobe; Lisa Gevelber, Susan Martin, and Jenni Shideler at Google; Jan Tai and Mark Turner at LinkedIn; Brandi Higgins at NASA; Lisa Marshall at Salesforce; Jeanne DeFelice at SAP; Susan Rusconi at Splunk; Jared Roberts at Stanford Health Care; and Jen Huerd at Target. And the book would be nothing without the stories from the Impact Players and their leaders, who are named throughout the book, as well as the insights we gained from the 170 managers who generously gave of their time. There are unfortunately too many to name here.

The Coaches

Several colleagues loaned me their brains throughout the process, including Michael Bungay Stanier, my favorite fountain of ideas; Dolly Chugh, who provided research guidance and coaching; Mark Fortier, who helped shape the ideas early on; Greg Pal, who shares his brilliant mind so willingly and is always up for being a test pilot of new ideas; and Ben Putterman, my dear friend and career-long thought partner, who both inspires and grounds my thinking. I am also indebted to a wonderful group of colleagues who read early copies of the book and told me what I needed to hear and fix. They include Wade Anderson, Rami Branitsky, Heidi Brandow, Fernando Carrillo, Stefan Cronje, Rob Delange, Yolanda Elliott, Charlee Garden, Mark Hecht, Hazel Jackson, Tony Mercer, Josh Miner, Len Pritchett, Mark Sato, Lisa Shiveley, Jake Tennant, A. J. Thomas, Nicola Tyler, Andrew Webb, and Melinda Wells Karlsson. Extra kudos go to these super-reviewers, who reviewed and rereviewed the manuscript: Sue Warnke, Mike Maughan, Susie McNamara, Judith Jamieson, Ryan Nichols, Lois Allen, and Andrew Wilhelms. I'm also grateful for my colleagues at Marshall Goldsmith 100 who shared their insights on coaching.

The Cheering Section

I am particularly grateful for my friends and family, who cheered me on and whose interest, love, and faith sustained me during a difficult 2020. Jan Marsh, I felt buoyed by your constant prayers on my behalf. Eric Volmar and Eric Kuhnen, our nightly devotionals kept me grounded and fed my soul. Josh Jaramillo (Dr. Josh), who epitomizes the Impact Player mindset in his own work, thank you for being interested and asking me every single day how the book, and I, were doing. Mom, thank you for being my on-demand editor for twelve years running and for your example of service. To my children, Megan, Amanda, Christian, and Josh (little Josh), and my sons-in-law, Austin and Josh (tall Josh), thank you for being interested, even on days when I knew you weren't. And Larry, thank you for your unwavering support and for giving me the gift of time to write.

APPENDIX A:
BUILDING UPWARD CREDIBILITY

We asked 170 leaders (from first-line managers to senior executives) what their team members did that most frustrated them and eroded value. These are nearly guaranteed to be credibility killers and are listed below:

CREDIBILITY KILLERS
Aka Fifteen Surefire Ways to Alienate Your Boss

1. Give your boss problems without solutions.
2. Wait for your boss to tell you what to do.
3. Make your boss chase you down and remind you what to do.
4. Don't worry about the big picture; just do your piece.
5. Ask your boss about your next promotion or raise.
6. Send long, meandering emails.
7. Bad-mouth your colleagues, create drama, and stir up conflict.
8. Surprise your boss . . . with bad news . . . at the last minute . . . when nothing can be done.
9. Ask to revisit decisions that have already been made.
10. Leave out inconvenient facts and the other side of a story.
11. Blame others for your own mistakes.
12. Agree to your boss's face but disagree behind his or her back.
13. Tell your boss that something is not your job.
14. Listen to your boss's feedback, then ignore it.
15. Show up late to meetings, multitask, interrupt others.

CREDIBILITY BUILDERS

Aka Fifteen Ways to Earn Trust

IMPACT PRACTICES	Do the Job That's Needed	Step Up, Step Back	Finish Stronger	Ask and Adjust	Make Work Light
1. Doing things without being asked		✓			
2. Anticipating problems and having a plan to solve them	✓				
3. Helping your teammates					✓
4. Doing a little extra			✓		
5. Being curious and asking good questions				✓	
6. Asking for feedback				✓	
7. Admitting your mistakes and fixing them fast				✓	
8. Bringing good energy, having fun, making others laugh					✓
9. Figuring out what to do for yourself	✓				
10. Finishing a job without having to be reminded to do so			✓		
11. Cooperating with your boss					✓
12. Being willing to change and take smart risks			✓		
13. Getting to the point and telling it to your boss straight					✓
14. Doing your homework and coming prepared					✓
15. Making your boss and the team look good					✓

APPENDIX B:
FREQUENTLY ASKED QUESTIONS (FAQS)

Q: I'd like to have more impact in my work, but this is all a little overwhelming. Where do I start?

Like any professional development effort, you should begin by knowing where you currently stand. The assessment available at ImpactPlayersQuiz.com can help you understand if you are making the impact you'd like and pinpoint where you may need to take action to increase your influence and impact. But don't stop with a self-assessment—start a conversation with your stakeholders to get their perspective and guidance. Use the Impact Player framework to discuss which mindsets and practices are your current strengths and which need purposeful strengthening.

Additionally, your efforts will likely have the greatest effect as you focus on the mindsets and behaviors that are the most learnable. According to the top coaches we surveyed, these include:

MOST LEARNABLE MINDSETS	MOST LEARNABLE BEHAVIORS
Growth: I can develop ability through effort.	**Seek feedback:** Seek feedback, correction, and contrary views
Belonging: I am an important part of a team.	**Offer help:** Offer help and support to colleagues and leaders
Proactivity: I can improve the situation.	**Influence others:** Get others involved through influence rather than authority
Resilience: I can overcome adversity.	**See the big picture:** Understand the big picture instead of just doing my piece.

Focusing on these mindsets and behaviors will help you generate quick wins and build momentum, but you will achieve the most sustained improvement by working on the master skills at the foundation of the Impact Player Mindset. You may want to revisit "Master the Underlying Beliefs and Behaviors" on page 207.

If you are still wondering where to start, try a simple two-part vision exercise. When things are most chaotic or frustrating, look for two things: (1) the other party's perspective (e.g., your manager's, your client's, your collaborator's) and (2) the opportunity to add value, which is clearer once you see your stakeholder's perspective.

Q: How many of these practices do I need to embody to be considered an Impact Player?

The high-impact contributors in our study typically had three or four of the Impact Player practices at which they really shone (on average 3.17 out of 5), according to their managers, but they lacked major deficiencies in any of the five practices. Though you do not need to follow all five of the practices, one significant problem area can quickly erode a lot of other value. Despite being strong in several of the five Impact Player practices, you can quickly descend to under-contributor status by being bad at just one. For example, consider those who are stellar leaders, finishers, and learners but are high maintenance and difficult to work with. People will likely avoid working with them, and they will soon find themselves on the periphery of the most important work. Their strengths will be underutilized and grow cold in the shadow of their weakness.

The message in the data is congruent with a principle we see in leadership skills as well: you don't need to be stellar at everything, but you can't stink at any one thing. You are more likely to earn a reputation as an Impact Player if you (1) build a strong core by getting good at three of the Impact Player practices; (2) develop one practice into a towering, visible strength—something you become known for; and (3) eliminate any signs of under-contributor behavior. Neutralizing a weakness and building just one towering strength will help you tip the scale. But before you jump in, you might want to assess your current standing using the assessment tool we've created, which you can find at ImpactPlayersQuiz.com. This assessment will help you pinpoint your strength as an Impact Player and spot the decoys that might be keeping you from contributing at your fullest.

Q: Can the Impact Player Mindset be developed, or are some people just born with it?

You've likely heard someone ask, "Are leaders born or made?" The same question could be asked of high-impact contributors. Were they born with these characteristics? Did they absorb these lessons at home as they observed their mother or father at work? Or were these practices acquired in the workplace, taught by mentors, or learned in the school of hard knocks?

Certainly, some had a head start. For example, Zack Kaplan watched his mother start as a receptionist, learn fast, step up, take responsibility, and eventually become the CEO of her company. However, Zack was shy and reserved all through high school. Being proactive and taking the lead was something he learned to do in the workplace. When Fiona Su began her career, tenacity and strength came naturally, but developing empathy and learning to see through the eyes of her colleagues came after she received some tough feedback that she was smart but "a bull in a china shop." Parth Vaishnav, the software engineer who was called in to resolve a complex, cross-product bug, began his career focused on his own work. He began really considering the broader impact of his work only after he was blasted with some harsh feedback (and choice swear words) from the product architect after he uploaded code and broke a larger code set.

Yes, some people have an early advantage. They may have had the right role models, mentors, and managers or a conducive environment, but it is never too late to start. Be sure to set yourself up for success by starting with the mindsets and behaviors that are most learnable (see the first question: "Where do I start?")

Q: Can the Impact Player Mindset lead to workaholism or burnout?

There was a strong work ethic among the high-impact contributors in our study, but it wasn't workaholism, the compulsive need to work incessantly. Each Impact Player profiled in this book has found their own work/life equilibrium. Some work much more than their peers, while others work no more hours than their colleagues. All the Impact Players we studied, however, work more *intensely* and *intently* than others. They work intensely in that, while at work, they work wholeheartedly and energetically. They work intently in that they put great thought into their approach to their work.

There is a danger that some people may interpret the Impact Player Mindset as a justification for working harder or longer or asking others to do the same, which will likely lead to burnout. However, you don't necessarily need to work harder to increase your impact. In fact, the opposite may be true: people who have impact and influence tend to want to work harder because their work is fulfilling.

If you want to contribute at your fullest, don't just work harder; rather, strive to do work that is more valuable, be more influential, and maximize your impact. If you have a strict limit on the amount of time you can spend working, work as diligently as possible during that time. When you combine these two approaches, you will avoid burning out because your work will give you energy, not sap it.

Q: What if the Impact Player Mindset isn't valued in my company or by my management?

Every organization has a unique culture and set of values. Part of being impactful is discovering what is valued inside your organization, by your stakeholders, and by the leaders to whom you are accountable. Use the Find the Double W.I.N. and Get In on the W.I.N. Smart Plays on page 59. If the practices in this book aren't valued by your manager, find out what is. Ask: What's important to you? What are the dos and don'ts of working with you? Remember that when you work on the agenda that's valued inside your organization and in the way that creates greatest value for your leaders, you earn respect and increase your influence—which affords you the latitude to bring *your* values to the equation.

If you are able to create a situation that jives with your values, stay and help shape an environment where others can thrive, too. If not—or if you have a boss with questionable values—leave if you can.

But don't just look for the right company or role; shop for a boss who values impact over activity. If you are unable to make a change, check out the strategies in chapter 8, "Dealing with Diminishers," in my book *Multipliers: How the Best Leaders Make Everyone Smarter*, revised and updated edition. Whatever you do, don't stay physically but quit mentally.

Q: I want to share the Impact Player framework with my team. How should I do it?

Most managers will want to share the ideals and insights from this book with the teams they lead. However, if you do, take an approach that favors dialogue over dissemination. Broadcasting the ideas over email en masse without inviting dialogue is a surefire way to cause resentment and rejection. For example, one CEO of a start-up company read an early copy of this book and sent an enthusiastic companywide email announcing five practices for being successful at the company. The employees didn't understand what had precipitated the email, and those who had been working the hardest felt unappreciated, not praised. Similarly, using the framework to label others will also shut down learning.

If you want to create interest and sustained impact, share the ideas rather than inflict them upon someone. Start a conversation, perhaps with a book discussion in your team. Talk about the Impact Player Mindset as a mode of thinking that we tend to move into and out of rather than as a classification of individuals. Be introspective, considering the ways in which you personally are striving to be an Impact Player but falling short. Discuss the decoys that seem productive but actually reduce impact. Talk about the framework as a set of habits that will require constant attention for people to shift, but be aware that some individuals will be frustrated because they lack the sense of agency and control needed for the ideas to feel within reach. Most important, remember that these discussions will have their greatest impact when, as leaders, you are as committed to your own self-reflection and awareness as you are to the development and improvement of your team. For suggested discussion topics and additional guidance, check out ImpactPlayersBook.com.

In addition to discussing these ideas as a team, you can use the framework to set the right expectations and give people permission to deviate from more traditional ways of working. Look for inflection points when people are getting started, for example, new-hire induction, project kickoffs, or transfers between departments. Additionally, these practices can be incorporated into hiring criteria, leadership models, talent development programs, and inclusion strategies.

Q: Are Impact Players similar to classic superstars (for example, a programmer who is considered to be a "10× developer" or a salesperson who's called an "elephant hunter")?

These distinctions refer to people who are extremely talented and whose productivity is much higher than that of their peers. Such players can be extraordinarily valuable but for different reasons than Impact Players are. These superstars can also come at a cost because, although they deliver results, they can be extremely difficult to work with, resistant to feedback, and even dysfunctional to team play. Yet organizations are often willing to deal with them because they are so good at what they do, which is often the same reason why diminishing managers are tolerated at even many of the most respected organizations.

Though this type of contributor certainly exists and provides value, it is important to note that the vast majority (if not all) of the individuals described in our interviews with managers did not fit this profile. They were not prima donnas or lone wolves. They were talented, influential contributors who also knew how to play on a team. They typically made the entire team better as well.

There is a difference between a team of all-stars and a champion team, and there is a growing body of research that shows that a team that works well together can triumph over a collection of talented individuals. For example, Dave Ulrich, a leading HR thought leader, wrote, "Our research (The RBL Group and University of Michigan) found that the capabilities of an organization have four times the impact on business results than [sic] the competence of individuals. For example, teams with individuals who work well together as a team will outperform a team of individual all-stars that don't work well together."[1]

Being a solitary superstar may be a pathway for success for the über talented and can be an effective approach in a number of settings, but the Impact Player profile builds collective strength and provides a playbook for the rest of us.

Q: Is an Impact Player the same as a high performer?

No. Our study was not a comparison of high and low performers; it was a study of people doing high-value, high-impact work as compared to equally smart, capable people who were contributing in less valuable, less impactful ways. There are many people who are performing their jobs well but may not be having a significant impact. Likewise, the concept of under-contribution is different from that of low performance. There are many reasons someone may be performing at low levels—it may be a function of low ability, low effort, or any number of extenuating circumstances (both systemic and individual) may interfere with someone's ability to work in productive ways. In summary, we were not trying to understand why people perform poorly but rather wanted to understand the reasons smart, capable people contribute below their ability level.

Q: Why did you focus only on the difference between Impact Players and Contributors? What about the under-contributors you studied?

Our study looked at three levels of contribution: (1) *high-impact contributors:* those doing work of exceptional value and impact;

(2) *typical contributors:* the vast majority of people, who are doing solid (if not great) work; and (3) *under-contributors:* smart, talented people playing below their capability level. In this book, I chose to focus on the differences between the top two categories because I believe that understanding the differences between good and truly great will provide the greatest benefit to the largest number of people. Further, the mindsets that lead to under-contribution are often complex and may call for deeper psychotherapeutic treatment.

Though this book focuses on the difference between high-impact and typical contributors, the research did show clear patterns of beliefs and behaviors for the individuals identified as under-contributing. A summary of the assumptions and practices of all three mindsets—Impact Player, Contributor, and under-contributor—can be found at ImpactPlayersBook.com.

NOTES

CHAPTER 1: THE IMPACT PLAYERS

1. Dax Shepard, "Kristen Bell," *Armchair Expert with Dax Shepard*, podcast, episode 2, February 14, 2018, https://armchairexpertpod.com/pods/kristen-bell.

2. Jen Hatmaker, "Armchair Expert-Ise with Podcast Creator and Host Monica Padman," *For the Love of Podcasts*, podcast, episode 7, November 19, 2019, https://jenhatmaker.com/podcast/series-21/armchair-expert-ise-with-podcast-creator-and-host-monica-padman/.

3. The annual Service to America Medals honor the unsung heroes of the career federal workforce for their achievements and contributions to the nation's health, safety, and prosperity. In addition to Dr. Ripley's story, you can see more stories of public service leadership at https://servicetoamerica medals.org.

4. Thegamechangersinc, "Eric Boles: Running Around the Wedge—TheGameChangersInc," YouTube, October 19, 2010, https://www.youtube.com/watch?v=uD5dDUqxbHY; Eric Boles, *Moving to Great: Unleashing Your Best in Life and Work* (New York: Stone Lounge Press, 2017).

5. This quote, and all other quotes without citation, have been taken from our interviews with Impact Players and/or their managers between 2019 and 2021 as part of the foundational research for this book.

6. The quotes have been lightly edited for brevity and clarity.

7. Neil deGrasse Tyson, "What You Know Is Not as Important as How You Think," Master Class, https://www.masterclass.com/classes/neil-de grasse-tyson-teaches-scientific-thinking-and-communication/chapters /what-you-know-is-not-as-important-as-how-you-think#.

CHAPTER 2: MAKE YOURSELF USEFUL

1. Theodore Kinni, "The Critical Difference Between Complex and Complicated," *MIT Sloan Management Review*, June 21, 2017, https://sloanreview .mit.edu/article/the-critical-difference-between-complex-and-complicated/.

2. Names have been changed to provide confidentiality.

3. "Brilliant Miller's Favorite Quotations," School for Good Living, https://goodliving.com/quotation/george-martin-the-greatest-attribute-a-producer -can-have-is-the-ability-to-see-the-whole-picture-most-artists-whe/.

4. Mohan Gopinath, Aswathi Nair, and Viswanathan Thangaraj, "Espoused and Enacted Values in an Organization: Workforce Implications," *Journal of Organizational Behavior* 43, no. 4 (October 8, 2018): 277–93, https://doi.org/10.1177/0258042X18797757.

5. Amir Goldberg, Sameer B. Srivastava, V. Govid Manian, William Monroe, and Christopher Potts, "Fitting In or Standing Out? The Tradeoffs of Struc-

tural and Cultural Embeddedness," *American Sociological Review* 81, no 6 (October 2016): 1190–1222, https://doi.org/10.1177/0003122416671873.

6. Claus Lamm, C. Daniel Batson, and Jean Decety, "The Neural Substrate of Human Empathy: Effects of Perspective-Taking and Cognitive Appraisal," *Journal of Cognitive Neuroscience* 19, no. 1 (January 2007): 42–58.

7. Adam D. Galinsky, Joe C. Magee, M. Ena Inesi, and Deborah H, Gruenfeld, "Power and Perspectives Not Taken," *Psychological Science* 17, no. 12 (2006): 1068–74, https://doi.org/10.1111/j.1467-9280.2006.01824.x.

8. Chad Storlie, "Manage Uncertainty with Commander's Intent," *Harvard Business Review*, November 3, 2010, https://hbr.org/2010/11/dont-play-golf-in-a-football-g.

9. Name has been changed to provide confidentiality.

10. Oliver Segovia, "To Find Happiness, Forget About Passion," *Harvard Business Review*, January 13, 2012, https://hbr.org/2012/01/to-find-happiness-forget-about.

11. In 2020, Ryan Smith purchased the Utah Jazz from Gail Miller.

12. Tom Peters, Twitter, November 10, 2019, 7:26 a.m., https://twitter.com/tom_peters/status/1193520200890699776.

13. Steve Jobs, "You've Got to Find What You Love," Stanford News, June 14, 2005, https://news.stanford.edu/2005/06/14/jobs-061505/.

14. Among millennial job seekers, 44 percent indicated that "being in a role you're passionate about" was the top priority, beating out "money" at 42 percent. See Jane Burnett, "Millennials Want Passion More than Money at Work," Ladders, January 10, 2018, https://www.theladders.com/career-advice/survey-millennials-want-passion-more-than-money.

15. Celia Jameson, "The 'Short Step' from Love to Hypnosis: A Reconsideration of the Stockholm Syndrome," *Journal for Cultural Research* 14, no. 4 (2010): 337–55, https://doi.org/10.1080/14797581003765309.

CHAPTER 3: STEP UP, STEP BACK

1. "The Troubles," Wikipedia, https://en.wikipedia.org/wiki/The_Troubles.

2. "Betty Williams, Winner of the Nobel Peace Prize for Her Work in Northern Ireland—Obituary," *Telegraph*, March 19, 2020, https://www.telegraph.co.uk/obituaries/2020/03/19/betty-williams-winner-nobel-peace-prize-work-northern-ireland/.

3. "Mairead Maguire," Wikipedia, https://en.wikipedia.org/wiki/Mairead_Maguire.

4. "Betty Williams (Peace Activist)," Wikipedia, https://en.wikipedia.org/wiki/Betty_Williams_(peace_activist).

5. Archival footage, used in 2006 clip: Nickelback, "If Everyone Cared," music video, Roadrunner Records, 2006, https://www.youtube.com/watch?v=-IUSZyjiYuY, accessed 2020.

6. Emily Langer, "Betty Williams, Nobel Laureate and Leader of Peace Movement in Northern Ireland, Dies at 76," *Washington Post*, March 23, 2020, https://www.washingtonpost.com/local/obituaries/betty-williams-nobel

-laureate-and-leader-of-peace-movement-in-northern-ireland-dies-at-76 /2020/03/23/d9010784-6a9d-11ea-abef-020f086a3fab_story.html.

7. Robert B. Semple, Jr., "Two Women Bring New Hope to Ulster," *New York Times*, September 6, 1976, https://www.nytimes.com/1976/09/06/archives /two-women-bring-new-hope-to-ulster-two-women-bringing-a-new-feeling .html.

8. Michael C. Mankins and Eric Garton, "An Organization's Productive Power—and How to Unleash It," in *Time, Talent, Energy: Overcome Organizational Drag and Unleash Your Team's Productive Power* (Boston: Harvard Business Review Press, 2017), 11.

9. Stephanie Vozza, "Why Employees at Apple and Google Are More Productive," *Fast Company*, March 13, 2017, https://www.fastcompany.com /3068771/how-employees-at-apple-and-google-are-more-productive.

10. The stock price on December 31, 2015, was $73.21; on December 31, 2019, it was $128.21.

11. "The World's 50 Most Innovative Companies of 2019," *Fast Company*, February 20, 2019, https://www.fastcompany.com/most-innovative-com panies/2019.

12. Bronti Baptiste, "The Relationship Between the Big Five Personality Traits and Authentic Leadership," doctoral diss., Walden University, Scholar-Works, 2018, https://scholarworks.waldenu.edu/cgi/viewcontent.cgi?article =5993&context=dissertations.

13. Tony Robbins, Twitter, April 22, 2009, 12:34 p.m., https://twitter.com /TonyRobbins/status/1586010857.

14. "Playmaker," Dictionary.com, https://www.dictionary.com/browse/play maker.

15. Kamala Harris, Twitter, June 5, 2020, 5:46 p.m., https://twitter.com/Ka malaHarris/status/1269022752914264064.

16. Barton Swaim and Jeff Nussbaum, "The Perfect Presidential Stump Speech," FiveThirtyEight, November 3, 2016, https://projects.fivethirty eight.com/perfect-stump-speech/.

17. Keith Ferrazzi with Noel Weyrich, *Leading Without Authority: How the New Power of Co-Elevation Can Break Down Silos, Transform Teams, and Reinvent Collaboration* (New York: Currency, 2020), 117–18.

18. The Wiseman Group broke down complex work into doable, bite-sized pieces: thirty-four out of fifty high-impact behaviors (3.33 versus 2.05 for a typical contributor versus 1.62 for an under-contributor).

19. "Playmaker," Wikipedia, https://en.wikipedia.org/wiki/Playmaker.

20. P. B. S. Lissaman and Carl A. Shollenberger, "Formation Flight of Birds," *Science* 168, no. 3934 (1970): 1003–05, https://doi.org/10.1126/sci ence.168.3934.1003.

21. Mary Parker Follett, *Creative Experience* (New York: Peter Smith, 1924).

22. Name has been changed to provide confidentiality.

23. "Betty Williams: Biographical," The Nobel Prize, June 2008, https://www .nobelprize.org/prizes/peace/1976/williams/biographical/.

24. Daniel Russell, "America Meets a Lot. An Analysis of Meeting Length, Frequency and Cost," Attentiv, April 20, 2015, http://attentiv.com /america-meets-a-lot/.

25. Glassdoor Team, "Employers to Retain Half of Their Employees Longer If Bosses Showed More Appreciation; Glassdoor Survey," Glassdoor, November 13, 2013, https://www.glassdoor.com/employers/blog/employers -to-retain-half-of-their-employees-longer-if-bosses-showed-more-apprecia tion-glassdoor-survey/.

26. Amy Gallo, "Act Like a Leader Before You Are One," *Harvard Business Review*, May 2, 2013, https://hbr.org/2013/05/act-like-a-leader-before-you-a.

CHAPTER 4: FINISH STRONGER
1. "The Play (American Football)," Wikipedia, https://en.wikipedia.org/wiki /The_Play_(American_football).

2. *NASA Program Management and Procurement Procedures and Practices: Hearings Before the Subcommittee on Space Science and Applications of the Committee on Science and Technology*, US House of Representatives, 97th Cong., 1st sess., June 24–25, 1981 (Washington, DC: U.S. Government Printing Office, 1981).

3. Chelsea Gohd, "50 Years Ago: NASA's Apollo 12 Was Struck by Lightning Right After Launch . . . Twice! (Video)," Space.com, November 14, 2019, https://www.space.com/apollo-12-lightning-strike-twice-launch-video.html.

4. *NASA Program Management and Procurement Procedures and Practices*, 73.

5. Steve Squyres, *Roving Mars: Spirit, Opportunity, and the Exploration of the Red Planet* (New York: Hyperion, 2006), 2–3.

6. Ibid.

7. Michael Greshko, "The Mars Rover Opportunity Is Dead. Here's What It Gave Humankind," *National Geographic*, February 13, 2019, https://www .nationalgeographic.com/science/2019/02/nasa-mars-rover-opportunity -dead-what-it-gave-humankind/.

8. William Harwood, "Opportunity Launched to Mars," Spaceflight Now, July 8, 2003, https://www.spaceflightnow.com/mars/merb/030707launch .html.

9. "NASA's Opportunity Rover Mission on Mars Comes to End," NASA, February 13, 2019, https://mars.nasa.gov/news/8413/nasas-opportunity-rover -mission-on-mars-comes-to-end/.

10. Ibid., 112.

11. "Mars Exploration Rovers," NASA, https://mars.nasa.gov/mars-explora tion/missions/mars-exploration-rovers/.

12. Greshko, "The Mars Rover Opportunity Is Dead. Here's What It Gave Humankind."

13. Ibid.

14. Rosabeth Moss Kanter, "Surprises Are the New Normal; Resilience Is the New Skill," *Harvard Business Review*, July 17, 2013, https://hbr.org/2013 /07/surprises-are-the-new-normal-r.

15. Angela Duckworth, "Why Millennials Struggle for Success," CNN, May 3, 2016, https://www.cnn.com/2016/05/03/opinions/grit-is-a-gift-of-age-duckworth.

16. Research by the Wiseman Group showed the following: 98.38 percent of high-impact contributors always or often do this, 72.09 percent of high-impact contributors always do this; 48.09 percent of typical contributors always or often do this, 10.69 percent of typical contributors always do this; 12.1 percent of under-contributors always or often do this, 2.19 percent of under-contributors always do this.

17. Heidi Grant, "How to Get the Help You Need," *Harvard Business Review*, May–June 2018, https://hbr.org/2018/05/how-to-get-the-help-you-need.

18. "2017 Las Vegas Shooting," Wikipedia, https://en.wikipedia.org/wiki/2017_Las_Vegas_shooting.

19. Kevin Menes, Judith Tintinalli, and Logan Plaster, "How One Las Vegas ED Saved Hundreds of Lives After the Worst Mass Shooting in U.S. History," Emergency Physicians Monthly, November 3, 2017, https://epmonthly.com/article/not-heroes-wear-capes-one-las-vegas-ed-saved-hundreds-lives-worst-mass-shooting-u-s-history/.

20. Ibid.

21. Ibid.

22. "2017 Las Vegas Shooting," Wikipedia.

23. Menes et al., "How One Las Vegas ED Saved Hundreds of Lives After the Worst Mass Shooting in U.S. History."

24. During a race, husky and malamute sled dogs, unlike other mammals, don't require glycogen, which burns fast but is generated slowly, enabling the sled dogs to refuel quickly on slow-burning proteins and fats.

25. Douglas Robson, "Researchers Seek to Demystify the Metabolic Magic of Sled Dogs," *New York Times*, May 6, 2008, https://www.nytimes.com/2008/05/06/science/06dogs.html.

26. MinuteEarth, "Why Don't Sled Dogs Ever Get Tired?," YouTube, May 3, 2017, https://www.youtube.com/watch?v=HDG4GSypcIE.

27. Victor Mather, "Iditarod Champion and His Dogs Finally Make It Home," *New York Times*, June 3, 2020, https://www.nytimes.com/2020/06/03/sports/iditarod-champion-US-Open.html; Victor Mather, "Two Months Later, the Iditarod Champion May Finally Get a Ride Home," *New York Times*, May 26, 2020, https://www.nytimes.com/2020/05/26/sports/iditarod-coronavirus-thomas-waerner.html.

28. Ibid.

29. Kathleen Elkins, "Kobe Bryant Lives by This Mantra from His High School English Teacher," CNBC, September 22, 2018, https://www.cnbc.com/2018/09/21/kobe-bryant-lives-by-this-mantra-from-his-high-school-english-teacher.html.

30. 2 Tim. 4:7, AV.

31. Greshko, "The Mars Rover Opportunity Is Dead. Here's What It Gave Humankind."

32. Karen Northon, ed., "NASA's Record-Setting Opportunity Rover Mission on Mars Comes to End," NASA, February 13, 2019, https://www.nasa.gov/press-release/nasas-record-setting-opportunity-rover-mission-on-mars-comes-to-end.

CHAPTER 5: ASK AND ADJUST

1. Ashley Ward, "4 Famous Directors and Their Advice to Actors," Sol Acting Studios, June 12, 2019, https://solacting.com/sol-blog/4-famous-directors-and-their-advice-to-actors.
2. Ibid.
3. Mark Rober, "Automatic Bullseye, MOVING DARTBOARD," YouTube, March 21, 2017, https://www.youtube.com/watch?v=MHTizZ_XcUM.
4. Research by the Wiseman Group showed the following: "Learns quickly and eagerly when presented with a new challenge" ranked number seven in the top behaviors that differentiate high-impact and typical contributors; "Is curious and open to new ideas" is a behavior that 96 percent of high-impact contributors do always or often compared with 30 percent for typical contributors and 14 percent for under-contributors.
5. James Morehead, "Stanford University's Carol Dweck on the Growth Mindset and Education," OneDublin.org, June 19, 2012, https://onedublin.org/2012/06/19/stanford-universitys-carol-dweck-on-the-growth-mindset-and-education/.
6. Derek Thompson, "Workism Is Making Americans Miserable," *Atlantic*, February 24, 2019, https://www.theatlantic.com/ideas/archive/2019/02/religion-workism-making-americans-miserable/583441/.
7. Kate Adams, "Why Leaders Are Easier to Coach than Followers," *Harvard Business Review*, March 5, 2015, https://hbr.org/2015/03/why-leaders-are-easier-to-coach-than-followers.
8. Ibid.
9. Danielle Kost, "6 Traits That Set Top Business Leaders Apart," Working Knowledge, Harvard Business School, January 17, 2020, https://hbswk.hbs.edu/item/6-traits-that-set-top-business-leaders-apart.
10. Sheila Heen and Douglas Stone, "Finding the Coaching in Criticism," *Harvard Business Review*, January–February 2014, https://hbr.org/2014/01/find-the-coaching-in-criticism.
11. Scott Berinato, "Negative Feedback Rarely Leads to Improvement," *Harvard Business Review*, January–February 2018, https://hbr.org/2018/01/negative-feedback-rarely-leads-to-improvement; Ronald J. Burke, William Weitzel, and Tamara Weir, "Characteristics of Effective Employee Performance Review and Development Interviews: Replication and Extension," *Personnel Psychology* 31, no. 4 (1978): 903–19, https://doi.org/10.1111/j.1744-6570.1978.tb02130.x.
12. Research by the Wiseman Group showed that "admitting mistakes and recovering quickly" is the sixth highest differentiator between high-impact contributors and under-contributors.

13. Paul Krugman, "Trump and His Infallible Advisers," *New York Times*, May 4, 2020, https://www.nytimes.com/2020/05/04/opinion/trump-coronavirus.html.

14. Morehead, "Stanford University's Carol Dweck on the Growth Mindset and Education."

15. Ellie Rose, "Kim Christensen Admits Moving the Goalposts," *Guardian*, September 25, 2009, https://www.theguardian.com/football/2009/sep/25/kim-christensen-admits-moving-goalposts.

16. Stephanie Mansfield, "Jason Robards," *Washington Post*, February 27, 1983, https://www.washingtonpost.com/archive/lifestyle/style/1983/02/27/jason-robards/2c93d725-20e4-4d67-b5fc-1c87548520d1/.

17. Michelle Obama, *Becoming* (New York: Crown, 2018), 419.

18. Hayley Blunden, Jaewon Yoon, Ariella Kristal, Ashley Whillans, "Framing Feedback Giving as Advice Giving Yields More Critical and Actionable Input," Harvard Business School Working Paper no. 20-021, August 2019, https://www.hbs.edu/ris/Publication%20Files/20-021_b907e614-e44a-4f21-bae8-e4a722babb25.pdf.

CHAPTER 6: MAKE WORK LIGHT

1. "1964 Alaska Earthquake," Wikipedia, https://en.wikipedia.org/wiki/1964_Alaska_earthquake.

2. "Genie Chance and the Great Alaska Earthquake," *The Daily*, podcast, May 22, 2020, https://www.nytimes.com/2020/05/22/podcasts/the-daily/this-is-chance-alaska-earthquake.html?showTranscript=1.

3. Ibid.

4. Ibid.

5. Jon Mooallem, *This Is Chance!: The Shaking of an All-American City, a Voice That Held It Together* (New York: Random House, 2020).

6. Ibid., 172.

7. Ibid., 175.

8. "American Time Use Survey—2019 Results," Bureau of Labor Statistics, June 25, 2020, https://www.bls.gov/news.release/pdf/atus.pdf.

9. Jennifer J. Deal, "Welcome to the 72-Hour Work Week," *Harvard Business Review*, September 12, 2013, https://hbr.org/2013/09/welcome-to-the-72-hour-work-we.

10. "Workplace Stress," The American Institute of Stress, https://www.stress.org/workplace-stress.

11. "Workplace Conflict and How Businesses Can Harness It to Thrive," CPP Global Human Capital Report, July 2008, https://img.en25.com/Web/CPP/Conflict_report.pdf.

12. Rob Cross, Reb Rebele, and Adam Grant, "Collaborative Overload," *Harvard Business Review*, January–February 2016, https://hbr.org/2016/01/collaborative-overload.

13. Jennifer J. Deal, "Always On, Never Done? Don't Blame the Smartphone," Center for Creative Leadership, 2015, https://cclinnovation.org/wp-con tent/uploads/2020/02/alwayson.pdf.
14. "Employee Burnout: Causes and Cures," Gallup, May 20, 2020, https://www.gallup.com/workplace/282659/employee-burnout-perspective-paper.aspx.
15. Name has been changed to provide confidentiality.
16. Ash Buchanan, "About," Benefit Mindset, https://benefitmindset.com/about/.
17. Ibid.
18. Research by the Wiseman Group showed the following. "Is low maintenance and low drama": 89.97 percent of high-impact contributors always or often do this, 62.6 percent of high-impact contributors always do this; 40.64 percent of typical contributors always or often do this, 14.44 percent of typical contributors always do this; 15.94 percent of under-contributors always or often do this; 3.3 percent of under-contributors always do this.
19. Hatmaker, "Armchair Expert-ise with Podcast Creator and Host Monica Padman.".
20. Ronnie Lott in conversation with Steve Young at the Bill Campbell Trophy Summit, Stanford University, August 16, 2019. I attended the summit and obtained a video recording of their talk.
21. Jennifer Aaker and Naomi Bagdonas, *Humor, Seriously: Why Humor Is a Secret Weapon in Business and Life and How Anyone Can Harness It. Even You.* (New York: Currency, 2021).
22. Ibid.
23. Adrian Gostick and Scott Christopher, *The Levity Effect: Why It Pays to Lighten Up* (Hoboken, NJ: John Wiley & Sons, 2008).
24. Adrian Gostick and Chester Elton, *Leading with Gratitude: Eight Leadership Practices for Extraordinary Business Results* (New York: Harper Business, 2020).
25. "Giving Thanks Can Make You Happier," Harvard Health, November 2011, https://www.health.harvard.edu/healthbeat/giving-thanks-can-make-you-happier.
26. Susan A. Randolph, "The Power of Gratitude," *Workplace Health & Safety* 65, no. 3 (2017): 144, https://doi.org/10.1177/2165079917697217.
27. Rebecca S. Finley, "Reflection, Resilience, Relationships, and Gratitude," *American Journal of Health-System Pharmacy* 75, no. 16 (2018): 1185–90, https://doi.org/10.2146/ajhp180249.
28. Research by the Wiseman Group showed the following. "Promotes safety and wellbeing for others": 94.04 percent of high-impact contributors always or often do this, 66.67 percent of high-impact contributors always do this; 58.82 percent of typical contributors always or often do this, 28.88 percent of typical contributors always do this; 40.66 percent of under-contributors always or often do this, 13.19 percent of under-contributors always do this.

29. Sue Warnke, "I looked at the sea of color yesterday evening, and I imagined the many hands who folded them," Facebook, March 7, 2020, https://www.facebook.com/swarnke01.

30. Mooallem, *This Is Chance!*.

31. Bourree Lam, "The Two Women Who Kicked Off Salesforce's Company-Wide Salary Review," *Atlantic*, April 12, 2016, https://www.theatlantic.com/business/archive/2016/04/salesforce-seka-robbins/477912/.

32. "The High Price of a Low Performer," Robert Half International, May 15, 2018, http://rh-us.mediaroom.com/2018-05-15-The-High-Price-Of-A-Low-Performer.

33. Steve Young in conversation with Ronnie Lott at the Bill Campbell Trophy Summit, Stanford University, August 16, 2019. I attended the summit and obtained a video recording of their talk.

CHAPTER 7: INCREASE YOUR IMPACT

1. Gary Keller, *The One Thing: The Surprisingly Simple Truth Behind Extraordinary Results* (Austin, TX: Bard Press, 2013).

2. J. Bonner Ritchie, "Who Is My Neighbor?," David M. Kennedy Center for International Studies, February 2005, https://kennedy.byu.edu/who-is-my-neighbor/.

3. Ibid.

4. "Girl Scouts Look at Social Issues," *Indianapolis Star*, January 7, 1990, https://www.newspapers.com/newspage/105886091/.

5. Richard S. Lazarus and Susan Folkman, *Stress, Appraisal, and Coping* (New York: Springer, 1984).

6. "Cognitive Reframing," Wikipedia, December 9, 2020, https://en.wikipedia.org/wiki/Cognitive_reframing.

7. Robert Kegan and Lisa Lahey, "The Real Reason People Won't Change," *Harvard Business Review*, November 2001, https://hbr.org/2001/11/the-real-reason-people-wont-change.

8. Ibid.

9. "Intel Launches a Huge Advertising Campaign: * Technology: The $250-Million Blitz Is Aimed at Cutting Down the Competition and Selling Its Next-Generation 486 Microprocessors," *Los Angeles Times*, November 2, 1991, https://www.latimes.com/archives/la-xpm-1991-11-02-fi-797-story.html.

10. "Ingredient Branding," Intel, https://www.intel.com/content/www/us/en/history/virtual-vault/articles/end-user-marketing-intel-inside.html.

11. Kevin Kruse, "5 Simple Ways to Be a Better Ally at Work," *Forbes*, October 26, 2020, https://www.forbes.com/sites/kevinkruse/2020/10/26/5-simple-ways-to-be-a-better-ally-at-work/?sh=1fcb24f7642e.

12. "Getting Ready for the Future of Work," *McKinsey Quarterly*, September 12, 2017, https://www.mckinsey.com/business-functions/organization/our-insights/getting-ready-for-the-future-of-work.

13. Taffy Brodesser-Akner, "Bradley Cooper Is Not Really into This Profile," *New York Times*, September 27, 2018, https://www.nytimes.com/2018/09/27/movies/bradley-cooper-a-star-is-born.html.

CHAPTER 8: BUILD A HIGH-IMPACT TEAM

1. Heather Baldwin, "Net Profit: How the Philadelphia 76ers Slam Dunked Their Way to Sales Success Despite on Court Losses," SellingPower, November 7, 2017, https://www.sellingpower.com/2017/11/07/13192/net-profit.
2. Ibid.
3. Jake Fischer, "Despite Tough on-Court Season, 76ers' Sales Staff Finds Success," *Sports Illustrated*, May 19, 2016, https://www.si.com/nba/2016/05/19/philadelphia-76ers-sales-tickets-nba-draft-lottery-sam-hinkie-brett-brown.
4. Ibid.
5. Ibid.
6. Ibid.
7. Ibid.
8. Amy Edmondson, *The Fearless Organization: Creating Psychological Safety in the Workplace for Learning, Innovation, and Growth* (Hoboken, NJ: Wiley, 2019), xvi.
9. Ibid., 21.
10. Dan Rose, Twitter, October 17, 2020, 7:35 p.m., https://twitter.com/DanRose999/status/1317610328046280704/.
11. Ronnie Lott in conversation with Steve Young at the Bill Campbell Trophy Summit, Stanford University, August 16, 2019. I attended the summit and obtained a video recording of their talk.
12. Albert Bandura, *Social Learning Theory* (New York: General Learning Corporation, 1971).
13. Ibid..
14. Partnership for Public Service, "Government Leadership Advisory Council on Crisis Leadership," January 13, 2021, https://vimeo.com/500210129.
15. Stephen Dimmock and William C. Gerken, "Research: How One Bad Employee Can Corrupt a Whole Team," *Harvard Business Review*, March 5, 2018, https://hbr.org/2018/03/research-how-one-bad-employee-can-corrupt-a-whole-team.
16. Michael Kraus, "Advice for a Better 2021—According to the Research," Yale Insights, December 21, 2020, https://insights.som.yale.edu/insights/advice-for-better-2021-according-to-the-research.
17. Erica Volini et al., "Belonging: From Comfort to Connection to Contribution," Deloitte Insights, May 15, 2020, https://www2.deloitte.com/us/en/insights/focus/human-capital-trends/2020/creating-a-culture-of-belonging.html.
18. Joan C. Williams and Marina Multhaup, "For Women and Minorities to Get Ahead, Managers Must Assign Work Fairly," *Harvard Business Review*,

March 5, 2018, https://hbr.org/2018/03/for-women-and-minorities-to-get -ahead-managers-must-assign-work-fairly.

19. Alyssa Croft and Toni Schmader, "The Feedback Withholding Bias: Minority Students Do Not Receive Critical Feedback from Evaluators Concerned About Appearing Racist," *Journal of Experimental Social Psychology* 48, no. 5 (2012): 1139–44.

20. Renee Morad, "Women Receive Significantly Less Feedback than Men at Work—3 Ways to Change That," NBC News, February 11, 2020, https:// www.nbcnews.com/know-your-value/feature/women-receive-significantly -less-feedback-men-work-3-ways-change-ncna1134136.

21. Shelley J. Correll and Caroline Simard, "Research: Vague Feedback Is Holding Women Back," *Harvard Business Review*, April 29, 2016, https:// hbr.org/2016/04/research-vague-feedback-is-holding-women-back.

22. Kate Blackwood, "Women Hear More White Lies in Evaluations than Men: Study," Cornell Chronicle, May 18, 2020, https://news.cornell.edu/stories /2020/05/women-hear-more-white-lies-evaluations-men-study.

23. Peyton Reed, director, *Through the Eyes of Forrest Gump: The Making of an Extraordinary Film*, Paramount, 1995.

24. Catherine Moore, "What Is Job Crafting? (Incl. 5 Examples and Exercises)," PositivePsychology.com, September 1, 2020, https://positivepsy chology.com/job-crafting/.

25. Amy Wrzesniewski and Jane E. Dutton, "What Job Crafting Looks Like," *Harvard Business Review*, March 12, 2020, https://hbr.org/2020/03/what -job-crafting-looks-like.

26. Tom Rath, "Job Crafting from the Outside In," *Harvard Business Review*, March 24, 2020, https://hbr.org/2020/03/job-crafting-from-the-out side-in.

27. Chad Storlie, "Manage Uncertainty with Commander's Intent," *Harvard Business Review*, November 3, 2010, https://hbr.org/2010/11/dont-play -golf-in-a-football-g.

28. Christopher S. Howard and Justin A. Irving, "The Impact of Obstacles Defined by Developmental Antecedents on Resilience in Leadership Formation," *Management Research Review* 20, no. 1 (February 2013): 679–87, https://doi.org/10.1108/mrr-03-2013-0072.

29. Karen Doll, "23 Resilience Building Tools and Exercises (+ Mental Toughness Test)," PositivePsychology.com, October 13, 2020, https://positivepsy chology.com/resilience-activities-exercises/.

30. Kim Scott, "The 3 Best Leadership Traits for Managing Through a Crisis," Radical Candor, https://www.radicalcandor.com/candor-criticism-during -a-crisis/.

31. Evan W. Carr, Andrew Reece, Gabriella Rosen Kellerman, and Alexi Robichaux, "The Value of Belonging at Work," *Harvard Business Review*, December 16, 2019, https://hbr.org/2019/12/the-value-of-belonging-at-work.

32. Steve Gruenert and Todd Whitaker, *School Culture Rewired* (Alexandria, VA: ASCD, 2015) 36.

CHAPTER 9: PLAY ALL IN

1. Richard Sandomir, "Kevin Greene, Master of Sacking the Quarterback, Dies at 58," *New York Times*, December 22, 2020, https://www.nytimes .com/2020/12/22/sports/football/kevin-greene-dead.html.
2. Eve Curie, *Madame Curie: A Biography*, trans. Vincent Sheean (New York: ISHI Press International, 2017).
3. Ibid.
4. Eugene O'Kelly, *Chasing Daylight: How My Forthcoming Death Transformed My Life* (New York: McGraw-Hill, 2008), 78.
5. Reed, *Through the Eyes of Forrest Gump*.

APPENDIX B: FREQUENTLY ASKED QUESTIONS (FAQS)

1. Dave Ulrich, "HR's Ever-Evolving Contribution," The RBL Group, January 18, 2021, https://www.rbl.net/insights/articles/hrs-ever-evolving-con tribution.

WANT TO TAKE THE LEAD AND MULTIPLY YOUR

IMPACT?

Start by taking the Impact Players Quiz!

≥ **ImpactPlayersQuiz.com** ≤

This quiz will help you will discover where you currently stand and pinpoint actions that can increase your influence and impact.

Find additional resources for you and your team at:

ImpactPlayersBook.com

For ongoing insights, follow Liz at:

@LizWiseman   LizWiseman   Liz.Wiseman.author   ByLizWiseman

INDEX

Coach's Playbook and, 265–67
Contributors vs. Impact Players, 166
feedback frenzy, 159–60, 165
fine-tuning, 151–52
game face, feedback barrier, 159, 165
getting while working remotely, 145
as information vs. judgment,
  146–48
performance, 246–47, 258–59
"performance intel," 144
Safety Tips, 163–64
seeking affirmation vs., 159–61
Smart Plays for, 162–63
staying in tune and, 143–44, 145
Ferrazzi, Keith, 84
finish stronger, 11–12, *13*, 99–129
building credibility, 108
the choice, 101–5, 129
Contributor vs. Impact Player, 129
decoys and distractions, 122–24,
  129
exceeding expectations, 112, 127
high-impact habits, 107–21, 129
Impact Player Pro Tip, 120
the mental game, 105–7, 129
multiplying your impact, 124–26,
  129
negotiating the necessities, 115–16,
  126–27
Performance Guarantee, 111–12
Playbook, 126–28
Playbook, Coach's, 264–65
reframing obstacles, 127
resilience and grit, 106–7, 264
Statement of Work (SOW) and, 169
what leaders say, 130
Folkman, Susan, 213
Follett, Mary Parker, 88
Ford Motor Company, 263–64
Forgey, Paul, 70–73, 75, 83–84, 87–88,
  179
Forrest Gump (film), 260–61, 274

Gable, Dan, 3
Gallo, Amy, 94
Garner, Dwight, 99–100
Goff, Bob, 229
Goldsmith, Marshall, 238
Google, xvi, 25, 113, 135–36, 155, 187
  Media Lab, 107, 179
Gostick, Adrian, 186, 187
Grant, Adam, 170
Grant, Heidi, 113, 265
gratitude, 49, 187
Great Alaskan Earthquake, 167–69
Greene, Kevin, 272
Gretzky, Wayne, 28
Groff, Marcus, 149
growth mindset, 134, 138, 153, 165
  benefit mindset and, 175–76
  fixed mindset vs., 138, 153, 158
Gruenert, Steve, 267
Guiney, Aileen, 42–43

Hancock, Braden, 155–57
Hancock, Lauren, xvi, 252–53
Harris, Kamala, 83
Hawking, Stephen, 129
Hesselbein, Frances, 213, 233
Hexcel Corporation, 259
high-impact habits
  for ask and adjust, 140–57
  for coaches, 244–49
  for do the job that's needed,
    40–54
  for finish stronger, 107–21, 129
  for make work light, 176–91
  for step up, step back, 77–89
Hill Holliday agency, 183–84, 188, 271
Hong, Evan, 42–43
House of Lies (Showtime series), 3
Howard, Ron, 131–32
Hume, David, 220
Humor, Seriously (Aaker and Bagdonas),
  185–86

MORE BY LIZ WISEMAN

A revised and updated edition of the acclaimed *Wall Street Journal* bestseller *Multipliers* that explores why some leaders drain capability and intelligence from their teams while others amplify it to produce better results.

MORE BY LIZ WISEMAN

In this essential guide, leadership expert Liz Wiseman explains how to reclaim and cultivate this curious, flexible, youthful mindset called Rookie Smarts. She argues that the most successful rookies are hunter-gatherers—alert and seeking, cautious but quick like firewalkers, and hungry and relentless like pioneers. Most importantly, she identifies a breed of leaders she refers to as "perpetual rookies." Despite years of experience, they retain their rookie smarts, thinking and operating with the mindsets and practices of these high-performing rookies.